Praise for *Barefoot to Avalon*

"This is a brave book with beautiful sentences on every page, but there's nothing showy about it. Mr. Payne writes with the intensity and urgency of a man trying to save his own life."
—Carmela Ciuraru, *New York Times*

"Burns starkly and powerfully . . . a book that is, as much as anything, a study in the power of inexhaustible candor . . . like the best memoirs, it's about something far harder to pin down, something unspecific and ineffable in the way time moves and lives fade, the moments that none of us can get back . . . Payne's writing is loose, confident and snappy, and he has a rare ability to distill enormous scope into a single sentence, sometimes a single image . . . [Payne] gives us the ambiguities of real life, a story that is sometimes hard to take, but always worth it."
—Lucas Mann, *San Francisco Chronicle*

"A searing account of Payne's complicated relationship with his father and his brother . . . What's powerful about this book is [Payne's] language."
—Charlie Rose

"Piercing . . . a tour de force."   —David L. Ulin, *Los Angeles Times*

"[A] masterpiece of nonfiction . . . From the first page, Payne's evocative, often poetic prose will put you under its spell . . . it will be the rare reader who does not see something of his or her own experiences in this perceptive, beautiful and passionate memoir."
—Linda C. Brinson, *Greensboro News & Record*

"What gives these biographical particulars their existential wallop is Payne's raw, sustained intensity. Reading Payne can feel like a near-physical experience, of being swept along by sinister forces that in different ages have gone by such names as original sin, melancholia, madness, and most recently, brain chemistry."
—John Murawski, *News & Observer*

"Intense, painful, and beautifully rendered . . . The story is built like a labyrinth. Memories and experiences are pathways leading into and out of others, deftly moving the reader forward and back in time . . . That David cuts himself no slack, and boldly, unflinchingly tells his own faulty story is remarkable."
—Patricia Ann McNair,
Washington Independent Review of Books

"A superhonest, affecting personal narrative; Payne writes about his childhood, his parents, and his career with a novelist's sensitivity to detail." —GQ.com

"A memoir as raw, intimate and courageous as a series of midnight confessions fueled by a bottle of vodka . . . [Payne's] barefoot journey, every brave and bloody step over broken glass, shows how even the darkest emotions and deepest wounds can yield to love." —Gina Webb, *Atlanta Journal-Constitution*

"David Payne goes to the bone in his deeply felt *Barefoot to Avalon*." —Elissa Schappell, *Vanity Fair*

"Payne explores his family and all its troubled relationships and history, striking universal notes that will hit you where you live . . . Not since William Styron's 1951 debut novel *Lie Down in Darkness* has there been a more eloquent, courageous depiction."
—*Winston-Salem Journal*

"Riveting family history [asks] complex questions about social prestige, mental health, and the ties that bind . . . powerful."
—*Kirkus Reviews*

"The tangled ties of adult siblings are one of the most underexplored themes in literature. In *Barefoot to Avalon*, David Payne transforms the story of a brother's death into a potent and heartbreaking meditation on love and loss and the long climb out of grief." —Jenny Offill

David Payne

Barefoot to Avalon

A Brother's Story

Grove Press
New York

Note from the author: *Though this book is a memoir, I've changed the names, residences and certain background details to preserve the privacy of characters who aren't members of my immediate family.*

Published simultaneously in Canada
Printed in the United States of America

First published by Grove Atlantic, August 2015

ISBN 978-0-8021-2517-0
eISBN 978-0-8021-9184-7

FIRST PAPERBACK EDITION, August 2016

Grove Press
an imprint of Grove Atlantic
154 West 14th Street
New York, NY 10011

Distributed by Publishers Group West

groveatlantic.com

16 17 18 19   10 9 8 7 6 5 4 3 2 1

Contents

To George A.

"In a way brothers probably know each other better than they ever know anyone else."

"How they know each other, in my experience, is as a kind of deformation of themselves."

—*The Counterlife,* Philip Roth

Prologue

In my earliest memory I'm three years old, running down the hall of our old house in Henderson, North Carolina, a small, gray-shingled one in a stand of oak trees on a hilltop overlooking Ruin Creek. I'm wearing my special cowboy outfit, black hat and vest with tinselly *Charro* trim. My mother has just come out of the bathroom, and we collide. Margaret, twenty-two, seems ageless, a film goddess from a prior era caught in close-up on the big screen at the drive-in. Her black hair is down and she wears a loose robe. As she sashes it, I note her swollen belly.

–You're fat! I cry gleefully, as though I've caught her at some trespass the way she frequently does me.

Margaret smiles as though about to share a wonderful surprise.

–You're going to have a new little brother or sister, she tells me.

I stand there, smiling vacantly. In my head, a static noise like the TV after midnight station sign-off, when the Indian Head test pattern appears after the singing of the anthem.

I take my silver six-gun, place it against her stomach and pull the trigger.

–Bang! I say and run off laughing.

I

2000

And the Lord said unto him . . . What hast thou done?
The voice of thy brother's blood crieth unto me from
the ground.

—Genesis 4:10

1

ON NOVEMBER 7, 2000, at around 8:30 in the evening, as the polls are closing in the East and the networks give the early edge to Gore, I lock the door of our house in Wells, Vermont, and place the key, by prearrangement with the realtor, in a Tupperware container under the back steps. In the dark front yard, a twenty-six-foot U-Haul truck sits low on its suspension, its lights angled toward the culvert at the top of our steep gravel drive. The high beams splash a stand of birches and lose themselves in the thick woods on Northeast Mountain, which looms over the protected meadow I bought eleven years ago and where I built the house I'm leaving.

My 1996 Ford Explorer idles nearby, and I can see George A., my brother—forty-two and heavy, his thick black hair and mustache sable-frosted—smoking in the greenish backwash from the panel. On the hitch is the twelve-foot trailer I didn't think we'd need when he flew up last week to help. Stacy, my wife, is already in North Carolina with our two-year-old daughter and our infant son. Having the children underfoot, we've agreed, would make a stressful job more difficult.

For eight days, George A.'s gone with me room by room and shelf by shelf, taking the Wells house apart, down to the wild turkey feathers and New York City restaurant matchbooks, the loose change scattered at the bottoms of the drawers.

My original plan had us leaving after lunch on Sunday, two days ago, November 5. By midnight Sunday we'd just started to attack the bookcase in the great room I drew and built with nine-foot sidewalls and a vaulted ceiling and a loft and barn sash windows in the gables. On a ladder, pulling volumes down, I handed George A. the family pictures and fragile ware, and he—crossed-legged on the plank pine floor in soiled white socks—swaddled them in Bubble Wrap, tearing ragged swaths of masking tape and fighting with the roll. It seemed to me the tremor in his hands had worsened and the smudges beneath his eyes were darker— like the eye grease he wore when he played ball beneath the lights on Friday nights in high school. The difference was worrisome.

It had been eight months, perhaps a year, since I'd seen him. The last time I visited Winston-Salem, I caught the smell of George A.'s cigarettes as soon as I walked in the front door of Margaret's town house, where I found her alone in a pool of lamplight in the small front parlor, working on a book and a glass of Pinot. She—who'd stopped smoking years before—looked up at me with a grievance in black eyes that were George A.'s eyes, too—something bemused and sad and angry and exhausted, resolved above all else to see it through—while George A. chain-smoked in the larger den in back and sipped a beer and laughed his croupy laugh at *South Park*. Once a top producer in the Winston office of Dean Witter Reynolds, married with two sons in private school, a BMW and a house in the tony district, Buena Vista, George A. had been there with Margaret for nine years. The tension was so thick a knife would not have scratched it. During the day when Margaret was at work, he smoked and watched the back crawl of the ticker tape on the financial channel. At night when she came home, Margaret cooked his supper and took it to him on a tray, and when he'd eaten, George A. left it for her on the kitchen counter and she'd tiptoe up and kiss his cheek and tuck a $10 or $20 in his pocket as he headed to the bar—no longer the one favored by the hotshot brokers with their Gordon Gecko haircuts and spiffy braces—but to Rita's, a humbler establishment in Clemmons, an exurb twelve miles distant, where Margaret had lived with Jack Furst, her second husband, after they were married.

I knew why our mother did this, why she cooked his meals and paid his medical and life insurance premiums, why she'd bought him the new Chevy Blazer and took his guns and hid them at a friend's house, including the double-barreled A. H. Fox our grandfather had left me that was reassigned to George A. in the aftermath of his first breakdown. George A. had been diagnosed with manic depression, or bipolar I disorder.

The *DSM*, the manual of the American Psychiatric Association, categorizes bipolar I by degree, as mild, moderate or severe. George A.'s was "severe, with psychotic features." Since the age of seventeen, he'd experienced periodic breakdowns—manic highs followed by protracted, crippling depressions—at three- or four-year intervals. During manic phases, George A. experienced the incandescent highs that tempt so many sufferers to go off their meds, pour out their secrets to bewildered strangers on the street, risk their savings on a hand of cards, embark on dubious business ventures and occasionally to triumph. The list of brilliant sufferers is long and includes many artists—Byron, Hemingway, van Gogh, Virginia Woolf, Graham Greene and scores of others. In George A.'s case, over weeks and months, the mania accelerated toward psychosis, when he experienced hallucinations and delusions, believed he'd been assigned "missions" by supernatural agents. Then, he'd wind up in the psych ward.

People with bipolar disorder commit suicide at a rate fifteen times that of the general population, and we know George A. had attempted it at least once. His episodes lasted a few months, three or four on average, and between them, for years at a time, he was seemingly normal and high-functioning. A gifted and successful broker, well liked and relied on by his clients, he was promoted many times at his office. From his first breakdown in 1975, until 1991, he gathered himself after each episode and went back to his life, career and family. Sixteen years after that first one, however, in a manic phase, he made unauthorized trades at work, was sued and lost his job and his wife divorced him. After the hospital that time, George A. went home to Margaret's to recover and never left. According to the *DSM*, "Many individuals with bipolar disorder return to a fully functional level between episodes." George A. had been one of them. Now he'd become part of a different group, the 30 percent who suffer "severe impairment in work role function."

Living far away, I'd failed to see the deterioration as it happened and didn't really understand it. He'd risen from the ashes so many times—why not this time? His intelligence appeared unimpaired. When he could scrape the cash together, he still made short sales, traded options and executed complex financial gambits. It seemed to me that there was too much left of George A., too much of Margaret, for them to fall into the enchantment that held them in the black woods they were lost in. As the years went by I visited North Carolina less frequently and spoke to him less often. Sometimes when I called, Margaret put him on and we spoke for a minute about the season prospects for the Tar Heels or cracked wise about Bill Payne, our long-vanished father.

Those tremors, though, those smudges had something more serious in them than I'd grasped. Against it, my certainties and resentments seemed suddenly small and brittle.

Once upon a time in that gray-shingled house on Ruin Creek in the little amber room we shared, George A. slept beneath me in the bottom bunk and we had matching cowboy quilts and college pennants thumbtacked to the wall. On summer nights we kept the windows open and could hear the creek below us in the creekbed. My oldest competitor and ally, he was the only one who knew or ever would know what that time and place had been for me, as I was the only one who knew for George A.—our much younger brother, Bennett, grew up after I left home, in Margaret's second marriage, in a different house, a different town, a different family under Margaret's second husband Jack's regime. Preoccupied with my affairs and far away, I'd failed to see what had happened to George A. and had let things shutter down till there was almost no light left between us.

Then the lightning struck me. After working four years on a novel under contract, I sent in the final pages and the editor rejected it. Instead of the installment payment I expected on completion, suddenly I owed back four years' worth of income. In the two years it took me to resolve this, Stacy and I lived on credit card advances and I burned out my thyroid gland and cracked four bottom molars, grinding them while sleeping. By the end, I could barely bring myself to walk down to the mailbox, afraid to find the letter commencing legal action. My single-jigger vodka had become a double and I was often having double doubles and, on bad days, triple doubles, and Stacy and I were either fighting about money or practicing mutual avoidance, and in Vermont it was as if we were under an enchantment like George A. and Margaret's down in Winston, and maybe that was why I could no longer call my brother.

Then Stacy, pregnant for the second time in two years, took our toddler and told me she was leaving, moving back to North Carolina with me or without me, and that if I wanted to be married to her and to be a father to our child—our children—that's where I could find her, and then she walked off down the jetway in Albany carrying

Grace, our towheaded little daughter, who looked back at me over her mother's shoulder. And as I drove home to Wells and set out into the meadow with my chain saw, I knew I was saying goodbye to the place and bringing in my firewood for the last time.

I called the realtor. I called Mayflower. The quote they gave me for the men with the big van was about as feasible by then as a summer on the Riviera. I called Margaret and told her I was moving back to try to save my marriage and that I meant to rent a truck and pack it.

–Why don't you ask George A. to help you? she asked.

–Let me sleep on that, I answered.

I didn't get to. Less than an hour after we hung up, the phone rang and it was George A., offering his help.

And here he was—by then we'd been at it since 8 A.M.— wrestling the masking tape with his unsteady hands at midnight Sunday, November 5.

And though on the first day, when I picked him up in Albany, we were careful and subdued in the beginning, by evening we were cracking jokes and playing music. I played him *OK Computer,* and he played me Tupac's "I Ain't Mad at Cha" and "Picture Me Rollin'." We picked it up where we'd dropped it somewhere long before, as if no time had passed at all. In the middle of a bad thing, I got back my brother.

–Check this one out, I said, handing him a faded 4x6 in a cheap Plexiglas frame. It was him, bare-chested, wearing Birdwell boardshorts, on the beach at Four Roses, our family summer house, a week or two before his seventeenth birthday.

−Was this the day I beat you to the pier?

−The one time, I said.

George A. stared at it like a pilgrim at a relic.

−I was pretty good-looking, wasn't I?

−*Was*, I said. Not that you're that bad now—just not, you know, good.

−I guess we've all seen better days, he answered, glancing at my ball cap, the one I'd taken to wearing as my hair thinned, while his stayed thicker than a mink's pelt.

−Touché, dickwad.

−Heh heh heh, said George A., and his old laugh had something new in it, a hint of broken crockery or gravel. I did kick your ass pretty bad, though, didn't I?

−You beat me by a small, small margin, bro. Inches.

I held a thumb and index finger up.

−I think you're measuring something else, he said.

I widened my eyes.

−*Ass*-hole!

And George A.—who was as prone to laugh at his own jokes as I am—rolled over on his side and slapped the floor, convulsing.

−Jesus. Jesus, he said, tapering off. I've got to go to bed, DP. I'm going to catch a smoke and hit it.

−Go on and fire it up in here, I told him as he started rising. Doesn't make much difference now.

All week he'd been going out to the front porch, using a Hellmann's mayo jar lid for an ashtray and tucking it into the mulch in the front bed as though to hide the evidence.

–Nah, that's okay, he said, and so I joined him outside in the Indian summer weather. The meadows had just been mowed and the air was fragrant with green hay scent with an undertone of something inorganic, perhaps diesel from my neighbor's tractor.

–You can really see the stars up here, George A. said, blowing his smoke toward them.

–The summer I was building, I used to drive up the Taconic from the city on Friday nights, and I'd camp here and build a fire when the stud walls were going up. The night the house was finished—it was right around this time, but cold—I got here after midnight and the northern lights were playing. Right up there—I pointed over Northeast Mountain. Pulsing waves. Green, like an oscilloscope. That was the only time I ever saw them. I'm going to miss this place.

–I think you're doing the right thing.

I was quiet for a bit after he said that.

–I hope so, George A. Listen. Hear that?

In the middle distance, below the culvert, the brook, a trickle over big stones.

–Sounds familiar, he said, smiling.

–Does, doesn't it? I said, smiling back.

A lefty, George A. stabbed out his Winston in his right hand and tucked the jar lid in the mulch beneath the blueberries. He put an arm around my shoulder and hugged me, and I kissed him on the hair above his ear the way I did when he was four and I was seven.

–Sleep tight, buddy.

–You too, David.

After he went in, I sat out a little longer and thought about the day I first came here in 1988. Thirty-three and living in Manhattan, I'd just sold my second book and gone from struggling to make rent to shopping for apartments. One weekend on a visit up here, I thought what the hell and called a realtor, and though land wasn't what I sought, he took me to see a fifty-acre parcel on the lower slope of Northeast Mountain outside a little town called Wells. Five miles up an enclosed and wooded gravel road, the landscape suddenly opened into a hidden valley a half-mile wide and a mile long that held the late-day sunlight like a little bowl holds water. On the right as we advanced was a pond fed by a brook that came from higher up and around the pond a meadow full of black-eyed Susans, daisies, Joe Pye weed and chickory. Over the ledge, the land stair-stepped to a second higher meadow that beetled over the town road, and above that, the mountain disappeared into a low cloud bank. As I looked up I felt the hair rise on my back and a little current arcing, and then the realtor put his Wagoneer in four-wheel and drove me up to the top meadow, and we got out on that height and as I looked out to the west, through a small gap I could see the Adirondacks in blue profile fifty miles away. Standing there with me, this garrulous Irish fellow—who'd probably seen this happen scores of times with other clients—had the good sense to keep quiet. Dusk was falling and the wind picked up and I heard it rustling in the treetops and the brook murmuring over stones as it came down Northeast Mountain, and something in me remembered summer nights in the gray-shingled house in Henderson with George A. in the bunk below me when we kept the windows open and Ruin Creek whispered in the creekbed down below us. It came to me, *This is where the house goes,* and I was lost then just that quickly.

I dreamed the house and built it and wrote the novel I called *Ruin Creek* about George A. and me, and Bill, our father, and Margaret, our mother, when we were still a family and believed that family love is stronger than time or death, except it wasn't. Love was like the sunlight on the surface of the iceberg; beneath, some dark force was operating in the underwater portion, and it was stronger than love and we were scattered by it.

And now Stacy and I had been scattered in our turn and to try to save it, I was giving up the house and land I loved and had made out of my life's work.

I think you're doing the right thing, George A. said.

I hope so.

In my mind's eye I saw Grace, her little face looking back at me over her mother's shoulder. At fifteen months she started walking and I began to take her with me out on the old logging trails where Stacy had never been much interested in going. I showed Grace the secret glade beneath the hemlocks, where we sat in silence and listened as the wind blew through the treetops. And often in the sodden leaf mold, Grace with her keen eye picked out the hidden life, the orange newts that lived there under fallen logs, creatures I'd never noticed. Grace studied them with thrilling focus, reached down and picked them up with no fear, watched them crawl over her hands and then put them back respectfully. And as I watched her something tightened in my chest, I had difficulty breathing, my heart was pierced with some new feeling, something urgent, I didn't know what to call it, regret or grief or fear, but that feeling had something to do with selling out and going, and up there with her when the wind blew through the treetops I seemed to hear its voice speaking, trying to tell me something.

And a curious thing is that not long before I picked George A. up in Albany, I was mowing the lawn in Wells on my red Wheel Horse tractor and in my mind's eye I saw two men in a room facing off at gunpoint, and one was white, one black, and the white man held a gun, and there was nothing left except for him to walk away or pull the trigger. They were from different times, I sensed, and had taken some sort of impossible journey—inward, or back in time, or both—to arrive in this room together. And somehow they were brothers, this black man and this white man, and their dispute concerned a woman. The white brother had lost her. And in the moment just before he pulls the trigger, the white man realizes that the black man is himself, that if he pulls the trigger, he, the shooter, dies too—not symbolically or metaphorically. Literally dies.

That scene is on a Zip disk in the drive bay of my computer, where I've left it for safekeeping in the rear of the Explorer. It's November 7 now, it's 9 P.M., the polls have closed, we're in the yard, the truck is packed, and George A., at the wheel, sits smoking in the greenish backwash from the panel with the trailer on the hitch I didn't think we'd need when he flew up last week and didn't even think we'd need this morning.

As he collapses into the driver's seat, reaching for the Winstons he's been smoking on the porch all week, I walk backward down the hallway with the mop, like an Indian with a swag of pine, erasing a decade's worth of tracks from the house I thought I'd grow old in. *Now this will be just another place I've left,* I think as I switch the lights off. And as I place the keys under the steps and stand, I catch the hay scent in the humid, unseasonably warm air, together with that hint of something inorganic. As I smell it, something wild and desperate stabs me, so unfamiliar I struggle for the name and finally call it grief.

Opening the Explorer's hatch to stow the mop, I see the last, most fragile items in cloudy Bubble Wrap—the Staffordshire greyhound from my great-aunt with the bloody rabbit in its teeth, my diplomas, the framed letter from my first editor—and something makes me take them out of the Explorer and place them in the truck with me. Framed posters of my books are there, along with our household electronics, including my PC with that Zip disk in the drive, the one I've left there for safekeeping and will find in the debris field on November 8. Tomorrow.

Tonight, I close the hatch and tap the driver's-side window, and George A., surprised, drops the Winston to his lap reflexively, as though to hide what I already see. I motion him to roll down the window, and when he does, I lean in on an elbow.

–Ready?

–Whenever you are, he says.

Looking at the Winston glowing on his thigh, I almost say something about my pristine ashtray.

–Thanks, George A., I choose instead.

–It's no big deal.

–No, seriously, man, I say. I couldn't have done this without you. You're a good brother.

These are words he hasn't heard from me in quite some time. He contemplates them for a beat and then he raises the Winston to his lips.

–It's okay, David, he says.

As the Winston brightens near his face, his features press into the darkness in the cab—the high cheekbones and strong chin, the black, pelt-thick hair already threaded, at forty-two, with silver. The dim light conceals the two black eyes—like a fighter who's staggered on the ropes night after night—the tremor in his hands. He was so good-looking once, and splendid physically, with his broad shoulders and warm, dark eyes. He reminded me of a young Clark Gable, only the confidence in Gable that flirted with conceit and smugness was in George A. nuanced, sly and sweet. For a moment in the cab's deceptive light, he resembles that other person, the boy and young man in that picture on the beach, the photo I think of as Before, as in before his illness, and have carried with me and put out in every house I've ever lived in.

"It's okay, David."

The truth is, I don't make that much of it at the time. It's hours later than we meant to start, and I'm dirty, stressed, and tired, on the verge of leaving everything I've taken as my life. I simply squeeze his shoulder, turn away, and whistle up Leon, my brindled hound, who gains the high seat of the truck with one lithe spring, and we set off, riding the groaning brakes of our unfamiliar, overloaded rigs downhill.

Only later does it nag me that George A. didn't say, "You're a good brother, too," or "You've helped me in the past, so I help you," or any of the countless other things he might have said. What he says is, "It's okay, David," not resentfully, but like someone at the end of a long contest, who's been on the receiving end of something and is ready to forgive it.

And I knew George A. was sick, but, looking back, it strikes me that the fundamental image of him I still carried in my heart was of the boy who'd run beside me barefoot to the pier and could have beat me on any given outing. If he was no longer that person, I wanted it to be his fault for giving up too early or Margaret's for enabling him to do it. I wanted him to try a little harder, for there to be another angle, another way to run the numbers and not have to accept that my little brother had run as long and hard and far as he was able and was going to and the race was over, there was never going to be another, better chapter. If I'd looked more closely at those tremors and those smudges, I might have seen that the black gods had touched and marked him with a finger, and I'd have said, *What's one more day? It's late, we're tired, let's go in and look at it again tomorrow when we're clearer.*

But I didn't.

We speak later on that night at a rest stop in New York State, where George A. tells me he's tired and needs to turn in, and at the motel in Binghamton where we spend the night, and the next morning in the common room of the same Super 8, pouring milk over stale Froot Loops from a cloudy bin. I recall a television blaring overhead—the tide by then has turned his way, for Bush. We gas up once that afternoon and would have spoken there, and again, and finally, at the Taco Bell where we stop for lunch a little after 1 P.M., somewhere off that little stretch of 81 that zips so quickly through Maryland and the West Virginia panhandle before it crosses into the Shenandoah and travels down the flank of the Blue Ridge through endless, high Virginia. We speak in all those places, but I can't remember what we said. And so those words—"It's okay, David"—spoken in the dark yard in Wells before we leave must count for me as the last ones my brother ever said.

As I turn the big truck south on the dirt town road, I check the sideviews for him for the first of many times. Windshield, left mirror, right mirror, windshield, left, right, straight ahead . . . That becomes the rhythm of the drive, and I estimate I checked those mirrors every ten or fifteen seconds for the whole of our five-hour drive that night, and for seven hours the following day, November 8. Four times a minute for twelve hours—almost three thousand times—I look for George A. in the mirror, and he's there, okay, each time except the last.

II
2006

The way it works is this:
we devote ourselves to an image
we can't live with and try to kill
anything that suggests it could be otherwise.

—"It All Comes Together Outside
the Restroom in Hogansville,"
James Seay

2

SEPTEMBER 10, 2006. GEORGE A. would be forty-eight today. I'm standing at the kitchen window of our North Carolina house, hungover, at 8:15 A.M., thinking that in a bit I'm going to have to call Margaret to mark the anniversary.

Stacy and the kids pulled out a little while ago. From the porch, I waved, and Grace and Will, eight and six, returned their somber goodbyes. Stacy, in dark glasses, merely held my stare, ducked into the Odyssey and drove away without a word.

I'm staring at a set of footprints—I count six—dark green, in the dew-silvered grass outside the window. These proceed from our back steps to the trellis on the shed wall, where a dark stain spreads at the base of the rosebush I planted shortly after George A. died. The sun is warming up, and as the dew evaporates, it looks as if some infernal thing has passed there, leaving smoking footprints.

After Stacy pulled off, I walked out in the yard and poured my vodka on the rosebush. I left the tracks, apparently, without knowing that I made them. Eliot is playing in my head, the passage from "Burnt Norton" I read Stacy the night we first sat up exchanging thirty-minute kisses and filling ashtrays till the sky grayed in the window.

> *Footfalls echo in the memory*
> *Down the passage which we did not take*
> *Towards the door we never opened*

And where does the door open? Into the rose garden. And there are my footprints leading to the rosebush.

I'm superstitious, I admit it. I don't want to back away from this, though, for it's as though if I close one eye and regard those footprints through the other, everything is normal. If I reverse and look again, I know I'm in trouble. I am, personally, and we are in our marriage. I don't know when it even started. Once upon a time I knew it in Vermont, and then George A. died and I fell asleep and have been asleep for six years, and a part of me wants to go on sleeping and another part is bidding, *Wake up, David*. And perhaps that's why as soon as Stacy pulled off, I poured my Burnett's around the rosebush, a brand-new 1.75-liter bottle minus thirteen and a half ounces. That's how much I polished off yesterday. And, yes, I know the precise figure because some time ago, in the hope of curtailing my consumption, I began to use a jigger, a strategy that hasn't actually worked, but has made me more informed about my drinking.

How many times have I dumped my bottle since George A. died up there on that Virginia highway? Five times? Ten? Fifteen's probably closer. Till today, though, till this moment, it's never occurred to me to wonder why the rosebush. Why not pour the vodka on that mulberry, those peonies, the cedars nearby in the lane, why not simply down the drain? Like a somnambulist, I've been drawn time and again to that specific place by some mysterious gravity. And I suddenly remember Sundays as a boy in Henderson—was it on Easter? On our way to morning service at the Episcopal church, we stopped at the Pine State Creamery on Granite Street. While Bill left the engine running, Margaret—they were Daddy and Mama then—clipped four red roses from the hedge that rioted along the chain-link fence, pinning them to our lapels with straight pins beaded with dark green. Everyone at Holy Innocents wore boutonnieres that day—a red one if your mother was still living, a white one if she wasn't.

Not Easter. Mother's Day.

And now the phone rings, and it's Margaret.

−I was about to call. How are you?

−Not good, she answers, tearful. How are you?

−I've had better days, but I'm okay. Why are you not good?

−Why do you think? I miss him. I want him back.

−I'm sorry, I say.

−Why should you be sorry? Don't be sorry, David. You were a good brother to him.

Was I? I don't know.

−Wasn't it right around now? I say. It seems to me he always got sick around his birthday.

This is the cue for Margaret to chime in, for the duet to begin. So many of the family stories came down to me this way. But today there's resistance on the storyteller's end.

—What's the matter? I finally ask. You're being quiet.

—I don't want you writing about this.

—What do you mean? I'm already writing about it. I told you I was doing this last summer.

—I know you did, I'm sorry. But I've changed my mind. I think it's exploitative.

Suddenly I can't think what "exploitative" means. In my head, that static sound like midnight station sign-off in the old days, one that years of therapy have taught me to call dissociation.

—It's disrespectful to your dead brother's memory, she continues. He's not here to defend himself. Write something else, something that belongs to you.

—Wait, I say. This doesn't belong to me? George A. died in my car, sitting in my seat. I was on that highway with him, no one else. Who does that belong to if not me?

—I think it belongs to him.

This stops me.

—Just him? Not me?

—That's what I think.

I stare out the window. The lawn seems darkened, as though a cloud has passed across the sun. The dew has started to evaporate. I can still make out the footprints, but the path is disappearing.

And now, unprompted, Margaret fills the silence.

—I don't know what you thought I was supposed to do, David. Kick him out on the street? Let him become a homeless person? George A. fought the illness for a long time, as long as he could, and then it defeated him, it just did, and all I knew to do was try to make him comfortable.

—I know. You think I don't understand the sacrifice you made? You kept him here for nine years longer than he would have had without you. But it's more complicated. The story's not just about George A. and you. It's about me and Stacy and our children.

—Then leave your brother out.

—I can't.

—I don't want you writing about this. I think it's wrong.

—Look, I'm feeling ambushed here, I say. I need to hang up now and think this over before one of us says something we'll regret.

—I hope you will. I'm sure you'll make the right decision.

—I think you mean you think I've made the wrong one and you're sure I'll come around to yours.

—I'll talk to you soon, she says curtly and hangs up.

In my head, on its constant loop, the old voice is chanting *Bad! Wrong! Selfish!*

In my office, I look the word up in my online dictionary.

Exploitative . . . Exploit . . . To make use of selfishly or unethically.

I throw the handset across the room into the sofa cushions.

Suddenly, I'm regretting my Burnett's, the blue-capped soldier I poured out on the roses. Maybe George A.'s birthday wasn't the best time to stop drinking . . . like those ten or fifteen other times weren't either.

But how can I not write it? Two months ago—not even two: on July 22, my son's sixth birthday—I came back from a book event on Pawleys Island and called Will from the Hampton Inn, where I was staying, and wished him happy birthday. And I then unzipped my little suitcase, where— together with a toothbrush and T-shirt and change of boxers for the drive home—I had my big Burnett's and the green Martini & Rossi for the needful quarter-capful and my jar of fancy olives, and I poured myself a triple and as I raised it to my lips, something in me said, *It's time to write about George A.*, spoke it right aloud there, bell-clear. And the hair rose on my forearms, and I leaped up as well as my bad knees will leap now and wrote it down on a half sheet of foolscap and knew I'd been assigned my next book, and I dated it because I was afraid I might forget it if I didn't. And then Atlanta, the memory, came back and I wrote a note about that also, about Margaret's phone call to me in New York in 1980 when I was twenty-five and first lived there. George A., twenty-two, had been hired by Merrill Lynch straight out of Carolina, the youngest broker in their Buckhead office. And one morning after three or four months on the job, he went into the bathroom, took off his tie and jacket, unbuttoned and removed his shirt, took out his wallet, and shredded his credit cards and license and flushed them down the toilet. Having stripped and removed all trace of personal identity, he announced that he'd been tapped to undertake a mission to go to Tehran to rescue the

American hostages at the embassy. My recollection is that police and paramedics were called in and wrestled George A. into submission, though whether this is memory or assumption I can't be certain at this distance. I do know he ended in the psych ward through the agency of strangers.

I flew home to Winston and drove down to Atlanta with a U-Haul and collected his belongings. George A.'s apartment read like a bleak and terrifying novel—weeks of dirty laundry, pizza boxes, fast food wrappers, overflowing ashtrays, unsleeved albums, notes scrawled in his shaky, disordered hand like hieroglyphics. In the kitchen, the Formica countertops were pocked with cigarette burns; so, too, the carpets, and the fridge, a petri dish with old take-out boxes sprouting multicolored strains of mold.

I stayed two weeks in Winston, and after George A. stabilized we took long walks in Buena Vista, where Jack and Margaret lived then, on Georgia Avenue and Runnymede and in Hanes Park around the tennis courts and ball fields, and as we went we talked about the hostages. I asked George A. who he thought they were, where they came from and what mission his unconscious might be proposing for him.

A psychiatrist will later tell me that psychotic fantasy often deals with national security issues and that George A.'s images might have been generic, generated by the headlines, and whether that was so or not, I never forgot it, and fifteen years later at Margaret's town house in the '90s, when I walked in and caught the smell of George A.'s Winstons from the back room and Margaret looked up from her pool of lamplight with that look of grievance, she seemed like a hostage in her own home. It was as if they were under a spell and the reason I stayed away was because I feared it.

That's what I remembered and wrote down at the Hampton Inn in Pawleys when I knew a book had been assigned me, and my first thought was that it might be something wistful, elegiac, something like *A River Runs Through It*, and I could pose George A. the way Norman Maclean posed Paul on a big rock in the Little Blackfoot River, shadow-casting with the sun dazzle all around him, and leave him there young and beautiful forever.

But this morning, September 10, on what would be George A.'s forty-eighth birthday, I know that whatever this is, it isn't *A River Runs Through It*. And Margaret, whom I called when I came back from Pawleys in July, must have known before I knew, and that's why she doesn't want me to write it. And I not only love my mother, I respect and like her also, but I already know I'm going to write it. I have to. And why? Because the same spell that fell over George A. and Margaret once upon a time in Winston has fallen over us and over me now. I tried to keep it at a distance but it's here, right here in the kitchen of our North Carolina house, where I come to after my brief fugue state to find the kids' cereal bowls on the table side by side with last night's dishes, and on the range the pots and pans I used for supper. On the counter, eight or ten days' worth of mail, and now the dryer buzzes, another load to add to the three or four already on the sofa, waiting to be folded and carried upstairs to the various dressers in the various bedrooms. I'll attack this as I write and prep tomorrow's class—a three-hour seminar sandwiched between two three-and-a-half-hour drives, to and back from South Carolina. And there's tonight's dinner to contrive and put together, and then I'll need to fetch the kids at after-school. By the time we finish homework, supper, bath, Stacy should be home.

This is how our days go since she started work a year ago. During the week, she leaves with the kids at 8 A.M. and shows up most nights between 6:30 and 7. After ten years at home, she's putting in long hours at her job and learning what she's doing as she does it. In the meantime, all the cooking and cleaning and laundry and the lion's share of child care—all the things Stacy used to do, which I took for granted—has fallen in my lap, while I write five days a week and sometimes six and on the seventh do my round-trip drive to teach in South Carolina. Even on the rare occasion when I catch up with basics, the porches go unswept and the garden Stacy planted with the kids in May has gone to seed, the little fruit it did produce unpicked and blackened.

And most days this seems normal, our particular version of quotidian reality. That's how it appears with one eye open. Today, though, as I scrape a greasy clot of black beans from a place mat, I notice Stacy's supper dishes on the table with the children's where she left them, I see the stack of mail she put atop the previous eight or ten days' worth she left for me to sort whenever I should find or make the time to sort it. I think about the nights I pad upstairs to find her sleeping with her back turned, and it strikes me that Stacy's mad like I am, and what we're mad at is each other, only we aren't fighting, the conflict isn't in the open, we don't even know the subject. Something's wrong only it's so old and deep we've both been afraid to look at it or speak of it, afraid even to allow ourselves to know it exists for fear that if we did, we would not survive it, our marriage wouldn't.

Our conflict has to do with who does what, who owes, who pays, with getting our needs met and each meeting the other's. It has to do with money, labor, time, attention, affection, sex, and energy—what the Taoists call *qi,* or lifeforce. It's a *qi*-exchange equation. How much of mine do I owe her, how much of hers does she owe me, how much into our common operation?

Stacy and I have never had a clear understanding on these issues. We fell in love as children in our twenties and thought love should be enough and *amor vincit omnia.* We entered the relationship carrying assumptions from each of our first families that to us seemed reasonable, universal and self-evident, only to discover quickly that the other found them suspect if not appalling. Rather than bring our differences into sunlight and negotiate toward the middle, we've each spent twenty years trying to convert, educate, persuade and finally coerce the other to the proper viewpoint. We've failed and ended in a state of warfare with the person we know best and love or once loved deeply, and I don't know how this happened or how we got here.

We each secretly suspect the other of malingering, forcing us to shoulder more than our share of the burden, taking too much *qi* and giving back too little, though when we look hard and close and fairly—the way I'm trying to—I can see that Stacy works just as hard as I do, and has no more rest or luxury or ease than I have. The most ready explanation for the hell we're in is that the other must have caused it. Why assume this? Because we both remember a time before hell opened, a time when we were single and lived in clean, bright spaces we maintained with modest effort, a time when we woke up with a cheerful outlook and went about our business with a sunny spirit and succeeded at it mostly. We weren't in hell then, hell came after we joined forces and *post hoc, ergo propter hoc* would be the obvious assumption—after this, therefore because of this: a classic fallacy in logic. Hell came after the other did—*post hoc*—ergo the other must have brought it with her—him, if you are Stacy—from the forest of his or her first family along with the stone arrowheads, the nosebone and organic poisons. And the specific hell we're in is one we colluded to create and have perpetuated, and neither one of us is innocent, and of the two of us I may be the guiltier. I know Stacy thinks so, and I fear it.

And standing here staring at her dishes, the message I receive is: You wanted me to work outside the home and earn? Well, now I am, see how you like it. And in my Sent email queue right now is one I shot to her at work last week—*Drinking, pls get kids.* I sent that at 5 in the afternoon, thirty minutes before I was due to be in the car line for pickup. On that particular day, I'd miscalculated my afternoon consumption and by the time it came to leave I was in no condition to drive to get them. Stacy received this, she told me later, in the middle of a meeting, and the people around her said, What's the matter? Is everything okay? Has David had an accident? And this morning, with one eye open—the one that enables me to read the message Stacy left me—I can see that mine to her was: This is too much, come home and pitch in, I need help, I'm drowning.

And where I'm drowning is in a bottle, and the reason why I poured my vodka on the rosebush and have done so ten or fifteen times before this is because I don't want to do this, it's not okay, I know it isn't, and I'm not okay either and haven't been in quite some time, and because I'm not, I'm making it not okay for those around me.

A one-drink night now constitutes a victory. And "one" now means three jiggers—four and a half ounces—of 80-proof Burnett's on cubes in a double old-fashioned glass, a quarter-capful of dry vermouth, two olives, maybe three. There was a time when one single-jigger drink gave me just the kick I wanted, the little "click" that Brick awaits in *Cat on a Hot Tin Roof.*

More often than not in the last year, one triple doesn't do it. And when I have the second—yesterday, for instance—I succumb to a suspect form of Big Picture Thinking, according to which the idea of restraint seems rather paltry. And once I've crossed that line, you see, there's no compelling reason not to continue and have three. Two drinks constitute a kind of *nec plus ultra,* and once I sail past that rocky outcrop into the wide and windswept wine-dark sea, once I hear the taut snap of my sails and feel the sting of salt spray in my face, turning back holds no further interest and is virtually impossible for me. Beyond lie my three-drink nights, which are bad, and my four-drink nights, which are catastrophes. On four-drink nights, after downing eighteen ounces, I shut myself away behind closed doors and let my family's night unfold upstairs without me.

Last night was a three-drink night, or rather afternoon, for my MO is to write up to exhaustion, and then, as my concentration frays, to start to sauce it. Passing the Pillars yesterday, between Drinks 2 and 3, I had my little private party, the one that makes life seem—for thirty minutes, maybe forty-five—what it might or should have been. But even as the crowd roared and the ticker tape rained down, I heard the whistling in my ears, the sound of the not-too-smart bomb homing in, and when it hit me yesterday at 3, after I'd knocked back those thirteen and a half ounces in sixty minutes, I was no longer capable of typing. In that condition, I make two or three mistakes for every key I strike correctly, so writing's out. Instead, I staggered to the couch, smutch-faced and hair on end, like a cartoon character with tweety birds circling my head and revolving pinwheels where my eyes had been. There, I fell into the delicious sleep, long dreamt of and long denied, that I rarely—that is, never—get at night. After ten minutes, though—fifteen, tops—my eyelids popped up like window shades, and that was it, all I got, and all I ever get.

And that, for the last nine months or a year, counts as an average afternoon.

When I woke from my nap, I was no longer quite so drunk, no longer stumbling. Though still impaired and groggy, when an hour had passed—by four—I could type normally again. By 5:30, when it was time to get the kids, I'd passed from drunkenness itself, the Big City, across the bridge into the depressing suburbs. Putting on dark glasses, I set out to pick them up at after-school.

Around the time I poured Drink 1, I'd put on Cuban black bean soup to simmer, a recipe my old flame Nell taught me in New Haven that's easy and since the kids were small, a favorite.

On the way home, we stopped for sour cream, and I was halfway down the dairy aisle when I realized Will wasn't with us. I found him in the foyer, eyeing the glass bubble of the jawbreaker machine.

—Daddy . . . ?

—Don't even think about it. Dinner's in twenty minutes. We're having black bean soup and rice.

—Beans and rice! he said with dramatic, six-year-old unhappiness. I hate beans and rice!

—Since when?

—I hate them.

Bemused, I looked at his big sister.

—Maybe we could have something else tonight? Grace suggested with cautious diplomacy.

—Look, guys, I said, I'm sorry, but beans and rice is what I made, and it's what we're having—and sourdough, the good kind you like from Whole Foods.

—I hate sourdough, Will said. Can I have a gumball for after supper?

—No, I answered, at the simmer now. They're a waste of money, plus they rot your teeth.

–Can we have ice cream then? Will's grimace, by this point, was reminiscent of the mask of tragedy.

–No ice cream. Come on. Now.

–Fine! Will said, and stamped his foot. With the cashier and the people in the checkout line fixing disapproving stares, I choked my anger down and shopped.

At home, I put the rice on and sent them up to take their baths. While I was checking email, Will peeked in.

–I thought I told you to take a bath.

–Grace is going first. Can I play Danny Phantom on nick.com?

–I'm using the computer.

–Can I watch the Cartoon Network then?

–You know we don't watch TV on school nights.

–Please, Daddy, please . . . just for a few minutes, just till Grace gets out?

–I let you watch last week, Will—remember what happened? When it was time to turn it off, you stomped and fumed and slammed your door and made everybody tense, and that was why we made the rule.

–But I won't, Daddy, please, just this once.

–Damnit, Will, no. N-O. Why do we have to do this every night? We don't watch on school nights. Period. Now go upstairs and find something to do for twenty minutes.

–Will you play with me?

For a moment, the anger in his face lifts like a dark curtain, and I see him as he was before it dropped its heavy folds around him—a little boy with a sunny temperament and a big, energetic personality, seeking a connection and asking me directly. Only I'm too wiped out to make it—the flash is too brief, the momentum of battle too established—and I fail him.

—Maybe after supper, I hedge guiltily. Right now, I have to answer this email.

—I don't have anything to do.

—You have a whole closetful of toys to play with.

—No *good* ones.

Now the anger's back, and his sparks mine. I flash to the shelves of books, the action figures—superheroes, monsters, villains, bots, droids, transformers, pirates—the ceaseless torrent of cheap Chinese plastic pouring out of bins that we bundle up in trash bags quarterly and cart off to Goodwill. "No *good* ones," Will says, and this is when I start to feel the malignant spirit in the mine shaft, rattling its chains.

—Will, go upstairs, I say. Now. I'm getting mad. I need you to get out of my face.

—*Fine!* he says, and as he turns away, he mumbles, not quite sotto voce, I need you to get out of *my* face.

—What did you say?

—*Nothing!* And he stomps off through the living room so heavily he makes the crystal in the corner cupboard ring the same way Bill, my father, once did.

Ten minutes later, when I serve the meal, he pushes the bowl to arm's length.

—Yuck! I'm not eating this.

—Take one bite, I say.

Will glares and locks his arms across his chest.

I walk toward him.

−Try those beans, I say, in a low, warning tone. One bite. If you don't like them . . .

He doesn't budge.

Grace, at her place, watches with brooding, dour eyes.

−Goddamnit it, Will, I've had it with your—

Suddenly, the key jangles in the lock.

−Mommy! Mommy! they both cry, making for the door like whale ship conscripts for a white beach.

−Mommy, I'm starving, Will cries.

−Me too! Me too! says Grace.

−Are you? Stacy says. I think there are some mini-pizzas in the freezer.

Exuding a perfume of fresh air, she comes in with a smile, glancing at the mail, which she then puts down on the stack for me.

−Hold on a minute, I say. I made black bean soup and rice.

−We don't like beans and rice! they cry accusingly.

−Why don't we microwave those little pizzas? Stacy suggests.

−Look, I'm responsible for dinner, right? I say, already feeling like the bad guy. The last time I made this they scarfed it down and asked for seconds—remember? And don't we have a rule they have to try one bite? This isn't a restaurant. I'm tired of making two and three dinners every night till we hit on the mystery combo they're going to like. This is what there is for dinner. As far as I'm concerned, they can either eat it or go without.

Stacy's expression drops incrementally through this. To me, it reads: *Here we go again, another of David's mystery moods*

that blow in like the weather, who knows when or where? Why are
you like this? What's wrong with you? Who are you?

—Look, I'm tired, let's not fight, okay? she says. Why make
this heart surgery? Let's just find something everyone will
eat and get on with our evening.

Will now, behind her back, smiles at me victoriously. He
raises his hands and puts his index fingers in the air, shrug-
ging his shoulders up and down, a Travolta disco move, an
"I'm too sexy for my shirt" routine.

The malignant spirit bursts into the light.

—Get your ass upstairs! I shout. Goddamnit, you disrespectful little shit, do you hear me, get upstairs this minute!

—David, Stacy says, alarmed and stepping between, you
need to back off—do you hear me? Now. Right now.

—You do this every time, Stacy, every fucking time, I say,
turning on her then. You blow out of here at 8 A.M., leave
the house a wreck for me to clean, ask me to take responsibility for dinner, and when I do, you waltz in here at
what—I glance at the clock—7:15, and erase everything I've
done. They take their cue from you and don't take a word
I say seriously, and then, guess what, I explode on cue. I'm
the bad guy; you're Wonder Mom with mini-pizzas. Do you
see how you set me up? This is because of you.

—Me? That's such a crock. You make yourself the bad guy,
David. You don't need any setup.

Behind her, on the stairs, Will does "I'm too sexy for my
shirt" again, but his eyes are smoky, on the verge of tears.

As I blow past, Stacy grabs my arm, but I wrench away
and put my finger in his face.

–Goddamnit, don't you do that. Don't you mock me. I won't be mocked by you, you hear me?

Will frowns, making no response.

–ANSWER ME, GODDAMNIT!

–Yes, in that same grudging, resentful tone.

–SAY, "YES, SIR!"

He glowers. His bottom lip is trembling.

–SAY, "YES, SIR!" I shout, beside myself.

–Yes, sir.

–Get upstairs right now, you hear me? Right fucking now! And when you're hungry, you can have the rice and beans I made, or you can wait till breakfast.

Tears are running down his face by now. Hiccuping sobs, Will turns away, head bowed, shoulders hunched, and goes. I've conquered his resistance. I've wiped him out.

–Nice, says Stacy, taking Grace's hand and going after him, and the look she gives me is the old one: *Who are you? What's wrong with you? What happened to you in your childhood?*

I stalk off the other way, toward my office, where I check email again, looking for what I don't know, the mysterious message that will come in from the blue and somehow change this. I sit there, sick to my stomach with regret, replaying what I've thought and said and done, and justifying everything.

The thing I thought could never happen has: I've become my father, annihilating Will the way Bill once upon a time annihilated George A. and me. And though some puny voice inside whines, *It's different! It's different!,* it really isn't different. I want to say that a malignant spirit rises from the deep, that alcohol erodes the chains that hold it in the ancient mine shaft, that it possesses me, that I don't will it, that "I" am not even really there, so how exactly can I intervene to stop it? I want to say that I don't know the spirit's name, that it's as alien and repugnant to me as it is to Stacy and the children, but all of this is bullshit. However it infected me, the spirit lives in me now, the way it once lived in my father, who didn't create it either. And the only difference there can ever be between me and him is in the future, if I change it the way he didn't.

And there's a part of me that's scared, but underneath fear, it's as if something I've longed for and despaired would never happen is finally going to, I'm going to tell the truth.

And you see, I've fancied myself a truth-teller all along, fancied I'd been telling it for twenty-five years in fiction, speaking about myself, my life, my loves, my family relationships, wearing various masks and straining it through various filters. But suddenly today I realize I wasn't. I've kept who I really am a secret, not just from the world, but from myself. And now I think I have to tell it, whether or not anybody else is listening.

And could it be that the story of George A. is the doorway that opens into something bigger that includes me also, some kind of building, perhaps a church or even a cathedral that it's time for me to build my little piece of as others before us built their pieces, those whose names are chiseled on the headstones outside in the graveyard?

Or is the door that opens through George A. not to a church or a cathedral after all, but to a charnel house or an asylum. If the unfiltered truth is such a good idea, why does it seem dangerous, revolutionary, maybe even crazy, and why am I so nervous? What if the footprints in the yard are leading toward a precipice like the one that George A. fell from? The one thing that's clear is that I'm going. *Today's the day, there is no other day but this.* And here I sign my name in blood upon this contract with my children and the future.

Will I succeed? I guess by six o'clock the verdict will be in.

III
1975

All of a sudden he discovered, not what he wanted to do but what he just had to do, had to do whether he wanted to or not, because if he did not do it he knew that he could never live with himself for the rest of this life, never live with what all the men and women that had died to make him had left inside of him for him to pass on, with all the dead ones waiting and watching to see if he was going to do it right, fix things right so that he would be able to look in the face not only the old dead ones but all the living ones that would come after him when he would be one of the dead.

—*Absalom, Absalom!*, William Faulkner

3

A MONTH SHY OF TURNING SEVENTEEN, George A. stands alone on the beach after a swim. Slicked back from a widow's peak, that thick, mink-black hair I envied adds, even wet, a good two inches to his height, and is long enough in back to show a curl escaping under his right ear. George A.'s smiling, squinting in a glare no longer evident, head tilted slightly. His sense of humor would be hard to miss, even for a casual observer. That he's sticking it to the cameraman may be less obvious. If George A.'s cheerful here and full of beans, it's because we've just come from a run—down to the pier at Avalon and back—and today for the first time he's beaten me. *Here's looking at you, big bruh,* he's saying with that grin and little squint, *This one's for you, DP.* My reply, delivered wordlessly, in kind: *Enjoy it while it lasts* . . . The camera clicks.

We've spent the summer at Four Roses, our family summerhouse in Kill Devil Hills, North Carolina, and are leaving in a week, George A. to start early football in Virginia, me for my junior year at UNC. The month before he's asked if he might run with me.

We're downstairs at Four Roses at the time. Our base-ment room is called "the lair." George A. and I have shared the place since he was three and got promoted to the big boys' quarters, where our cousins sometimes join us. At the back of the garage, the lair features a rat slab floor and exposed joists overhead, where Margaret, in a short-lived decorating fit, stapled the old seine we used to catch our morning's bait when we went bottom-fishing in the Albemarle with Pa Rose—her dad, the first George A.—who built this place. The walls are planks of inch-thick juniper in random widths, and there are surfboards leaning in a corner and board games in a spavined cupboard inher-ited from some old aunt.

Our books go back to *One Fish Two Fish,* George A.'s early favorite, which his kids will pass to mine in a distant future. When Colleen, his ex-wife, sends the book, I'm intrigued to find the text bedizened, starred and underlined in many colors, something I write off to a delinquent impulse in the nursery. On my college-era shelf, Jung and Eliot rest alongside books on Taoism and astrophysics. In one of the latter, I first read about the Twin Paradox and Brother A, who boards a rocket traveling at light speed only to return to Earth years later to find Brother B, his twin, an old man, prematurely aged from time dilation. After four years up north in boarding school, I feel as if I've come south not to a future world but to a past one represented by this summerhouse where Margaret and her older sister, Genevieve, grew up much as George A. and I and our much younger brother Bennett have, a world where girls aspired to marry well and mother children, to carry the social water for their families, and boys went into business and dealt in timber, farms and profits. I've come back from Exeter as someone different, on a space trip and unsure where my spaceship's headed.

With the surfboards and guitars, the overflowing ashtrays and trails of puddled, dirty underpants, the place looks like the Lost Boys' Adirondack summer camp, one from which the counselors absconded long ago. As I pan across the scene, a ghostly cameraman, I note, too, the bottles, amber, green and clear, some empty, others half full of room-temp beer. We're drinking now, in fact, a little after breakfast, and George A.'s puffing on a joint.

—When I get back, I have to run a mile in under six, he tells me, worry burrowing between his brows. If we're going to do this, I need you to really kick my ass.

—Do I have to pay, or is this privilege free? I ask in my overelaborate English-major sort of way.

He turns a droll deadpan on me.

—I'm serious, David.

—Yeah, sure, okay. No problem.

Running since fourteen, I'm putting in thirty-five or forty miles a week this summer, sometimes twelve or fifteen on a Saturday or Sunday. George A.'s out of shape as we begin, but I don't mind, I'm pleased he asked me. I get to help and also beat him on a daily basis.

George A. is flipping through his blues LPs, a new obsession brought back from boarding school the previous semester, along with that new Gibson lying on his unmade bed, a J-45, a sweet instrument that really bugs me. Why? Because I know George A. simply asked and he received it, and I could never ask, you see. I assign myself, on this account, a secret brotherly superiority—I'm "self-sufficient," "pure," "not into material things," whereas George A. is "needy," "superficial," "selfish." But the true basis, as I now perceive it, is fear: mine, not his. If I asked for a guitar and got it—and the giver, whose name I'm strangely hesitant to speak, is Margaret—if I asked Margaret for a guitar and got it, something bad would happen.

At twenty, I have no idea what this is. The response goes back so far and deep I can't see to the bottom. What comes to mind, though, is when I was four and had my tonsils out in Mariah Parham Hospital and Margaret brought me an ice-cream soda from the drugstore. I still see the white lump of vanilla bobbing in the cola and feel the pleasant tickle of effervescing bubbles. Margaret stroked my hair and said, *Poor thing, poor darling,* and her expression—tender, jocular, warm, available—shocked me with electric happiness.

When I came home, though, she greeted me with a prim smile and her gaze caromed off me to Infant George A. in the cradle, who couldn't walk or talk or mind his manners or control his bowels, and got, for nothing, what my independent efforts failed to win me. I expect I fudged it on occasion, exaggerating a stubbed toe or putting a frog into my voice to gain back the electric something. But I didn't like the feeling that came afterward. Though I got something, I had to give up something for it—what, I couldn't put my finger on, but I sensed the bargain was not a good one. You had to be sick or hurt or on your back and in her power to receive it, and when you were well, it vanished and you—that is, I—became invisible. And if this wasn't good for me, it wasn't good for George A. either. So much of our relationship, or mine as older brother, has consisted in trying to teach him not to take what isn't good for us even if we can't help wanting. My Older Brother lessons have never been more than intermittently successful. George A. listens, but it's more as if he's humoring me than convinced by my position. Somehow it's not the same for us, and I suspect this has to do with why, so early, I've turned my ambitions toward the immaterial realm of psychology and poetry. George A., by contrast, is firmly launched on the trajectory that will make him the youngest broker in Merrill's Buckhead office. Though at twenty I don't pretend to understand it, I've begun to ask the question—how, coming from the same family, did George A. become George A. and I become me?

Facedown beside the Gibson on George A.'s bed lies his summer reading, *Guitar Styles of Brownie McGhee* by McGhee and Happy Traum. George A.'s been teaching himself the rudiments of the Piedmont style, the alternating thumb bass with the melody picked on the treble strings. His ambition for the summer—to play the "Cocaine Blues" like the Reverend Gary Davis—has proved out of reach, but George A.'s made it farther up the hill than you might think and has even spent an hour here and there walking his big brother through some simple turnarounds in E.

He has on scuffed work boots, a filthy T and paint-spattered khakis sagging at the knees. It's 9:30 in the morning and he's just off his shift with the town sanitation crew, a job I had some summers back. Every night at midnight, the big truck rolls up at the bottom of our drive, the brake lights flash, and George A., with his coffee in a thermos and a ham and cheese in his back pocket, swings aboard to hoist the heavy cans till daybreak. You can smell him coming at twenty yards, a whiff of marine sewage—turned shrimp peels and blue crabs boiled in Old Bay.

This summer I'm at the other end of the social spectrum working at the Nags Header Hotel, one of the last of the old oceanfront grande dames. It's been taken over by two thirtysomething guys from upstate, one of whom walks through each morning dispensing designer stardust with a backhand papal wave, the other limping close behind, bent over under large but leaking bags of family money. They've filled the dining room with palms and potted plants and hired an artist to reprise Botticelli's *Birth of Venus* on the kitchen screen, where the naked goddess rises on a half shell from the ocean. There are starched pink linens on the tables and fresh-cut flowers by the armload. Guests are comped a glass of good champagne. And when it rains, the water pours through the roof in solid streams. Two nights out of three, there isn't any fish.

—No fish? the sunburned patrons say, smiles dying over flutes of Veuve Clicquot.

—No, sir. I'm sorry.

—Shrimp?

I shake my head.

—Oysters? Crab?

—The chicken Kiev is very good, I say, often to their backs.

It is, too, if the chef isn't drinking—and even when he is, only then it takes an hour and a half to make it to the table. The good news is, the waitstaff, after hours, gets to go down to the bar and drink all night for free. Sometimes I hook up with a summer girl and read her passages from "Burnt Norton" or "The Dry Salvages" while we're still in wait-and-see mode, getting tanked and screwing up our courage. As seduction techniques go, this has a marginal success rate.

The truth is, with my long hair and cutoffs, my bare feet calloused from going shoeless from April till Thanksgiving, I don't entirely fit in at the Nags Header. The other waiters are kids about my age from eastern North Carolina backgrounds not dissimilar from mine and George A.'s. Their dads are lawyers and doctors, own small businesses or farms. They grew up playing Midget Football and rooting for the Heels as we did, reciting the Apostles' Creed at the Episcopal church on Sunday, with no more notion than we had of what "the communion of the saints" might mean, thinking, if anything, of the buffet being laid out at the Club and a long afternoon knocking a white ball around a court or links. They've gone on to pledge DKE or Chi O at Chapel Hill like their dads and moms, and to enroll in premed or business, where George A. will wind up. I've washed ashore at UNC also, but by now my path and theirs have long diverged. I've been away four years up north while Bennett and George A. stayed home with Margaret. She and Bill divorced apocalyptically and left Henderson in full retreat,

him first, her not long after. Margaret's remarried to a handsome sales rep named Jack Furst, who has a firm handshake,
a good head of auburn hair, shoots a scratch game of golf
and has a winning smile with excellent white teeth from
which I half expect a starburst to wink off at me. At night
at the dinner table, when the sauce is flowing and the conversation starts to roll and thunder the way it did so often
with Bill Payne, Jack smiles ever brighter and sinks ever
lower in his chair until he falls asleep. Fifteen years from
now, he'll leave Margaret for a woman who looks uncannily
like Margaret now.

And Bill? When last seen, our old man was driving an
aging two-toned F-250 with a camper top and a pilfered
U-Haul on the hitch behind it, up and down the
Shenandoah Valley, seeking curios to sell, through
Lexington, Front Royal, Dayton, up there where his
father's people come from whom we know so little of,
taking back roads, following his hunch, stopping at the
little stores to talk to the old men whittling on the porches,
working them the way he works George A. and me, with
such good humor, such shrewd and large self-parody, that
they no longer care they're being worked and start to open
up and tell him what he wants to know: where the good
quilts and their makers are, up what washed-out road you
go to find the Double Wedding Rings and Broken Wheels,
the Card Tricks, Eyes of God, the Flying Geese and Hearts
and Gizzards. He collects the dolls with mountain faces
made from shriveled apples, and vintage signs—
Burma-Shave and Esso—and those with messages like,

"Mom's Not Here but the Pop's on Ice." The former English major knows a double entendre. When George A. and I speak of him we're like Ike McCaslin with the older men around the fire and Bill is our Old Ben, the spirit bear you only get to see after you leave behind your gun and hang your watch and compass on the tree branch. Since the divorce, we've both been to see him—in a trailer park on Colington Island, and an unplumbed cabin in the mountains up near Murphy, and a ranch house in Phenix City, Alabama, where Bill, so he told us, was in business with men who squared accounts with 2x4s and not in double-entry ledgers. And after every disappointment, each sad or shattering rebuff, George A. and I tell each other, and ourselves, that this time was the last, the fucking last, yet back we always go again to see him, Bill, who once upon a time was Daddy.

George A. is telling me about their most recent meeting now, as he passes me the joint and unsleeves an album and puts it on the platter of the AR.

—So when was this?

—Last spring, he says. He came up to school to take me out to dinner.

As the music starts to play, George A. grabs his sweet new Gibson and sits down in the little cane-bottomed rocker, knees almost at his shoulders, takes a toke and paints the scene for me. He's dressed for dinner—hair wet-combed, blue blazer, striped rep tie, spit-shined size 16 loafers. He knocks on the motel door at the appointed hour to find Bill on the floor with his toolbox open, shop rags, greasy pliers and wrenches spread around him. When George A. asks what he's doing, Bill gives him a portentous look and nods to the vanity mirror above the sink, where the hot and cold water handles are reflected.

–Do you see what they are?

Under pressure, George A. fails the test.

–They're inverted crosses, Bill says, giving him the crib, and for the next thirty minutes, as the reservation hour comes and goes, George A. waits, one knee jigging—as it's jigging now—as Bill removes and replaces them, reversed.

I come by my superstitious leanings honestly. We've christened Bill "Ahasuerus," after the Wandering Jew, in honor of his new career in peddling. George A. and I reserve a savage ridicule for Bill similar to that we turn on Jack, yet different, too, for Ahasuerus, to us, was once a king, and when we speak of him we drop our voices to a tone that flirts with religious awe. And our religion, the kind that can still make us quake and fall down on our knees, is of an angry Old Testament God who stalked our childhoods, often drunk, pulling doors off hinges, whose roar shook the house foundation and the stones beneath it.

> *Some are sad.*
> *And some are glad.*
> *And some are very, very bad.*
> *Why are they*
> *sad and glad and bad?*
> *I do not know.*
> *Go ask your dad.*

This is among the passages most floridly defaced in that *One Fish Two Fish* Colleen will one day send, less a child's doing, more as if the text has been parsed—closely and repeatedly—by a mad exegete with an unsteady hand. Did George A. do it when he was manic?

Perhaps I'm wrong, perhaps my path—which is George A.'s, too, for now, at least—diverged from our eastern North Carolina peers' before I went away to Exeter, before we left Henderson in full retreat, and the gray-shingled house on the hill above Ruin Creek, where George A. and I shared twin bunks with matching cowboy quilts in that little amber room with college pennants thumbtacked to the wall, model airplanes hanging from the ceiling on clear monofilament and silver trophies on the chest of drawers.

Sometimes at the Nags Header this summer, and in Chapel Hill the previous year, walking past frat row on Saturday nights, I stop and gaze into a courtyard where a band of men—black men—is playing beach music to kids—white kids—who are shagging, cutting up, and it's as if I'm looking back into a prior world, seeing who my grandparents and parents were and who I might have been and won't be now. On the outside looking in, I'm like a ghost that can't come home again and can't quite leave. Why don't I cross the road and join them?

The answer goes back six years earlier, to an afternoon in Henderson in 1968, when Bill, in his solemn baritone, calls down to my bedroom.

–David, come upstairs, your mother and I would like to speak to you.

I find them waiting in the formal living room we rarely use, seated side by side and gravely posed. I'm thirteen in this scene, which makes them thirty-one and -three. Margaret, by the look of things, has just come back from an engagement—luncheon at the Club perhaps, or Altar Guild. She's wearing a tweed suit in an autumnal plaid, black and tan, with round, black fabric–covered buttons, like something you might see Jackie O. wear. Her long black hair is in a beehive like Audrey Hepburn's in *Breakfast at Tiffany's*. She's a noted beauty in our hometown. Her black-brown eyes are solemn windows into something deep and old I can't see to the bottom of, though the grievance in them is familiar to me, like a shadowed grove in an ancient sun-drenched country.

Yet even as I write, I recall her saying how she would come home from school in the middle of the afternoon in her saddle oxfords and her turned-down bobby socks and see Pa's car in the driveway where it wasn't supposed to be till supper, would enter the back door to find the whiskey bottle—Seagram's 7—open on the sideboard, and a sinking feeling would come over her. And I remember when I was in my thirties surprising fiftysomething Margaret on the sofa once, with her legs curled under her, watching *Beauty and the Beast* on tape, the TV series with Linda Hamilton, weeping into Kleenex after Kleenex, and as I watched, surprised and touched, she would tell me this was her all-time favorite story, her all-time favorite one.

Her father, George A. Rose, whom we called Pa, was king of our first world. He built the big brick house on Woodland

Road in Henderson and Four Roses, where we summered, and in the depths of the Depression started Rose Oil Company, the family business, and on the side dealt in farms and real estate and timber. For fifty weeks a year, Pa pulled the plow for everybody else, and then once or so a season he locked himself away in the big house like Bête in the enchanted castle and drank apocalyptically for five or six days running. And if his sober labors—like mine when I was four and came home from Mariah Parham Hospital—went unnoticed, when he drank the family paid attention. His wife, Mary, threw up her hands or collapsed with vapors. Genevieve, Margaret's older sister, cleared out and slammed the door behind her. And Margaret? I expect Margaret ministered and stroked his head and said, *Poor Daddy*, and perhaps that was the time they were closest, when Pa took to bed and drank the ice-cream soda. And when he'd got his quota and received the rest he could no longer give himself in any other fashion, Pa rose, slapped Aqua Velva on his cheeks, put on a Hickey Freeman suit, and went to work with a blood-dotted scrap of tissue pasted to his Adam's apple and bought another farm or built another service station.

And Margaret, who—just as I did—loved Pa above all others, married Bill Payne, a man as unlike George A. Rose as possible, one from a teetotaling family who, in the upshot, couldn't hold his liquor either. And she drinks, too, Margaret—she's not so solemn when she's had a couple—as George A. and I are drinking in the lair at 9:30 in the morning, as I now, writing this, am thinking of the vodka

in the freezer, glancing at the clock on my computer—1:30
P.M., September 9, 2006, a little early, but I've been at it
since 5 A.M. and didn't sleep so well last night and haven't,
if the truth be known, in fifteen years or longer. Life consists
of so much struggle after all, and I look forward to my brief
reprieve, the little private party that begins each day at an
uncertain hour, that makes me feel, for the first thirty minutes, maybe forty-five, as though life is what it should have
been, what I still thought it would be when George A. and
I were together in this scene.

To pour the thick iced vodka on the cubes, to hear the
viscous *glug glug glug,* to drop the olive in and see that little
liquid starburst wink at me. When I resist, I feel it as a pressure in my chest and lungs, as though an invisible cinch is
being tightened, restricting my ability to breathe. Or it's as
if I'm sinking in deep water, watching the silver shimmer
on the surface recede, recede, recede. I'm panicking; I have
to breathe, but there's no oxygen, so I breathe alcohol.
Drowning's a release, and maybe now I'll get my fifteen
minutes on the sofa and when I'm once more capable of
typing I can write my wife the email in the middle of her
meeting and she can get the children and come home and
stroke my head and whisper, *Poor David, poor, poor David,*
and finally pay attention.

—What's the matter? Did I do something wrong? I, thirteen,
ask Bill and Margaret as I come up from my basement
bedroom.

—Have you made up your mind about school? Bill says.

–No, sir. Not yet, I answer, relieved that this is all it is.

Woodberry Forest or Exeter—we've long since winnowed down the list to these, one Southern and familiar, the other Northern, enticing, but above the family pay grade.

–You need to make a decision, son.

–Yes, sir, I know.

–Which do you think is the better school?

–Well, Exeter, I guess, but . . .

–But?

I gaze back and forth between them, but their faces, still more solemn, give no clue.

–Sit down, David, he says. I want to read you something.

Belatedly, I note the book in Bill's lap, his finger at the place. I can't tell what it is, some old edition from his college English days, I think. When he opens it, I see his class notes in the margins, written in block letters like a child's, as large and lax as mine are small and tight. He begins to read now:

> *Let us go then, you and I,*
> *When the evening is spread out against the sky . . .*

If this were a chess game—and, of course, it is—this gambit is one I could never have anticipated. Like the point man in a platoon, walking into certain ambush, I gaze at the ground for the thin gleam of the trip wire.

The idea of going off to boarding school has arrived a year before like a mysterious package on the doorstep. There's a knock, and when I open, there it is, wrapped in silver paper stamped with gold crests. I hold it to my ear and shake. Eventually I can't help opening it. Inside is a ship's manifest. Aladdin's cave, Annette Scherer's drawing room in *War and Peace,* Gatsby's West Egg mansion—as a port of call, "Exeter" seems as glamorous and no more real than these are. Yet, strangely, when I scan the columns, I find my name already set down. When I ask, my parents answer, *But, David, don't you know? It's always been there; your name was written there before the world was made. Even when you were a little boy, we knew that you would go.* And as they tell me this—and by "tell" and "ask," you understand, I mean the deeper sort that passes without words—I fall into a trance, the same one I'm in now as my father reads in his beautiful, hypnotic baritone, and it's as if I, too, have always known, as if the idea doesn't come from outside, but is my own.

> *Streets that follow like a tedious argument*
> *of insidious intent*
> *To lead you to an overwhelming question . . .*
> *Oh, do not ask, "What is it?"*

As he reads, Margaret sits composed and silent on the sofa, swept along, like me, on the flood tide of my father's energy.

Here's the thing, though—Bill Payne is the child of two public school teachers who scrimped to make ends meet. His father came down from the Shenandoah during the Depression, penniless, to teach high school math and coach the football team. He rose to become the principal at Henderson High, the school I'll be leaving whether I choose Exeter or Woodberry, and either amounts to a rejection of his lifework and his values. And does my father—whose paternal refrain, in later years, when asked for help, will always be, "No one ever did it for me"—did he, then, at thirty-three, come up with the extravagant generosity of Exeter? No, though the power seems to flow from him, on revisiting this scene, I see now what I didn't then.

It's my mother, who sits—hands clasped in her lap, ankles crossed just so—and never speaks a word, who goes to her family, the Roses, for the money. It's she who grew up with boarding school as a social possibility. In high school, she went away herself—to St. Mary's in Raleigh, a finishing school for affluent North Carolina girls, where her sister, Genevieve, went before her, and their mother, Mary, and Mary's sister, Polly. Margaret put on white gloves that buttoned at the wrist and a fashionable hat for chapel every morning, and at night she snuck out through a hole in the back fence, where Bill Payne with his duckbill haircut and his purple stovepipe corduroys waited in his father's hand-me-down jalopy.

They drove to Chapel Hill and hit the parties on frat row, where bands of black men played for white children, who were dancing, cutting up, and they danced and cut up, too, and drank. If alcohol brought Margaret out, it shot Bill from a cannon. Two months, not even two, after big sister Genevieve's white wedding—when the hosts assembled and the house filled up with presents—Margaret was pregnant.

Her father, the first George A., offered her the chance to go up north to have it fixed in Philadelphia, but she said no. Years later, after everything has crumbled, she'll tell me: *When I married Bill Payne, I didn't know if he was going to be a scientist and discover the cure for cancer or become the president of the New York Stock Exchange.* Something high, though, whatever it would be, and I think Margaret wanted to sit behind him on the dais in a killer outfit, Bill a way out of her family through the back fence. *We were just so much in love we couldn't stand to wait,* Margaret told me later, but if you look at twenty-year-old Bill in their wedding photos—six-foot-six and 180, in a pale summer suit too big for him, hands clasped in a formal posture—he looks like someone being escorted to his execution and trying to summon some dignity. And beside him, Margaret, eighteen, looks desperately happy.

Four months after Genevieve's white wedding, then, Margaret's black one, and she, too, through crisis, gets her needs met: autonomy, adulthood, a husband, a way out. With their parents following behind in a reluctant caravan, they drive down to Bennettsville, South Carolina, where proof of age is not required, and say their vows before a justice of the peace.

Married in September 1954, they have the baby—me—the following April and we live in a small garage apartment on Vance Street in Chapel Hill while Bill finishes his last two years of college and enrolls in med school. Before he can discover the cure for cancer, he has to get through the first-year curriculum, only it turns out Bill doesn't really want to be a doctor and doesn't make it. It was his mother's ambition for him and Margaret gets aboard with Letty though the two agree on little else and can't stand each other, frankly. So he puts down his scalpel and heads off to the KA House to shoot hoops and knock back some cold ones with his former brothers. Meanwhile, eighteen-year-old Margaret is alone with me in the apartment, trying to breast-feed with a condition called inverted nipples. Hers turn inward and it hurts to feed me and there's "blood in the breast milk," as she tells me later, and maybe that's where dependency and need turn dangerous and I become a Taoist and try to give up material sustenance and subsist on air and sunlight. And one day the Dean calls Bill in and says, *Son, it's clear you're bright and will do well at something. Not this, though—your heart's not in it.*

So what next and how now? Pa Rose, the first George A., offers Bill a stopgap job at Rose Oil Company. Margaret wants no part—Richmond, Atlanta, New York City, anywhere but Henderson. She'd rather Bill enlist, she tells him, rather be an Army wife and live on base, serving tea and cakes to other young lieutenants' wives than go back home defeated. To Bill, though, Henderson makes sense. Henderson is what Bill wants.

Why not? With a word, they—he—can have a house without a mortgage, a new car without a coupon booklet or a monthly payment, a maid to cook their meals and raise their children, a membership at the Country Club, a pew at Holy Innocents, a job at Rose Oil Company with the implication that Bill will one day run the business. As Bill was Margaret's ticket out to something brighter bigger better, so Margaret is Bill's ticket back into the fenced world that her family came from and his family didn't. As Margaret trapped him, so Bill traps her, pari passu, each taking what the other doesn't wish to give up. So sickness, injury, collapse, and crisis bring rewards that independence doesn't. You get something, but you have to give up something for it. Perhaps Bill doesn't know this; Margaret does, though, and I expect that's why she doesn't want to return to Henderson and place herself, and them, back where she started, in the power of her parents, beholden to them for the ice-cream soda.

Yet as she got her way on the marriage, Bill gets his now. So for the next fourteen years Bill will work at Rose Oil Company and take a Rose Oil paycheck and live in the gray-shingled house they build with Margaret's money and drive the car George A. and Mary Rose give them as a wedding present and sit in the Roses' pew at Holy Innocents at the 11 o'clock service, not at First Methodist where his parents sit at the same hour. And he'll eat Sunday luncheon at the Country Club where the Roses pay the dues for the young couple, and after the buffet, Bill will ride to Woodland Road with Margaret and trade repartee with Margaret's mother, whom Bill calls "Sherry Mary," as Mary calls Bill "a long tall drink of water." And on Monday morning, Bill puts on khakis, brogans, and a white T—the same uniform George A. wears in the lair when he comes off the sanitation truck—and when the dew is on the grass, Bill heads out to the Rose Oil Plant and fills the tank truck with No. 2 barn oil. For $45 a week, he drives out deep into the country, to the old pole tobacco barns in Vance and Warren Counties, where mules are hauling the drags of primed leaves to the barn and the women in bandannas tie the hands and pass them to the boys who hang them in the rooms inside. George A. comes three and a half years after me, and if I spend my first year and a half on Vance Street struggling with Margaret, George A. spends his with Eva Brame, the black woman Margaret hires on our return to Henderson, and perhaps when he wants things Eva provides them simply, without drama, and so he becomes a Dowist and later has no issue asking for the Gibson I could never ask for.

When I'm four or five and George A.'s still a toddler, I start to ride with Bill in that rattling tin can of a delivery truck, and we roll the windows down and sing "The Big Rock Candy Mountain" and "The Wabash Cannonball," and when we reach the farms, Bill unspools the hose and fills the tanks while I run with the children in the yard. Sometimes they ask us to dinner, which is to say the noon-day meal, and if it's the last stop, Daddy sits with the men, and the moonshine comes out in quart Mason jars with a pickled peach suspended like a shrunken head in each. Even at five and six, I note the way my father's accent changes when he talks to them, how he works these men with such good humor that they no longer care they're being worked and send us home with grocery bags filled with okra, squash, tomatoes and string beans. People like him. He seems happy. I'm happy being with him. *He's my Dad, there's no one like him.* So I remember thinking.

And on Thursday nights in summer, he and Pa Rose leave the Plant at 5 P.M. and pull into Four Roses at 8:30. They start the fire and throw on the steaks they brought from the Henderson Winn-Dixie where Pa is on close terms with the butcher, and we sit down to eat at 10 P.M. and Pa, who's had a couple, says, *Good bread, good meat, goddamn let's eat!*, the same grace every Thursday, and we laugh every time he says it, and Bill laughs, too. I remember that he laughed, back when he was Daddy, he seemed happy on those nights like we were, like I was, and we were a family and believed that family love was stronger than time or death, except it wasn't.

Because Bill often stays out gambling and drinking, and Margaret, at 1 and 2 A.M., will sometimes call his father—so she tells me later. And the Principal, Bill Sr., drives downtown to seek his son and namesake in whatever smoky joint young Bill is holed up in in whatever darkened alley. And one night at the Moose Lodge Bill loses $30,000 and is in the parking lot of the First Citizens Bank at 9 A.M. when the doors open the next morning. He goes in and takes out a mortgage on our house as we're waking up and eating breakfast. Someone at the bank calls George A. Rose, who's a director, and Pa goes down and pays the note, and later, Margaret tells me, Pa drives out to Ruin Creek and tells her, *I don't know what's going to happen to you when I die, Margaret, I just don't know what's going to happen to you and the children,* and he's crying when he says it.

And by 1968, my eighth-grade year, as Bill sits reading "Prufrock," Margaret has started coming down to breakfast with black eyes saying she slipped in the shower or ran into the car door. And some nights now when Bill's been out and Margaret locks the door against him, I lie downstairs flinching as he puts his shoulder to the front door and it starts to shatter in the door frame and I imagine George A. and Bennett, our new brother, not yet two, upstairs awake and frightened just like I am. And in this phase, too, Bill— the president of Rose Oil now, who hires and fires, controls the checkbook—sells a stand of Mary Rose's timber on the q.t. and puts the money in his pocket, thinking he's too slick for anyone to catch him. When this comes out in the divorce, he'll have to forfeit his Rose Oil pension and retirement and leave town with nothing in order to avoid the possibility of prison.

I believe Bill loved me, and long after they're divorced, he'll say that Margaret was the great love of his life and that he loved the first George A. and considered him a gentleman, but somewhere deep inside through all those fourteen years, I think Bill regards Margaret and the Roses as his enemies, and by day he works for Vichy and salutes and by night builds bombs for the Resistance, and ultimately in order to escape the trap he'll blow the whole thing up. In a hotel room in Boston in September 1969, the night before I enter Exeter, Bill blows up our family, his marriage, himself, and me into the bargain. And by this route, he ends up up there on those back roads in the Shenandoah, searching in his father's and his father's father's country for Who He Was and whatever he lost or left or had taken from him by Margaret and the Roses and probably someplace long

before he knew them. And I don't think Bill ever found the
answer, because after forty years of wandering, one morning
in 2008 in his house in Florida, he sits down on the toilet
and puts a pistol to his head and pulls the trigger.

> And would it have been worth it, after all . . .
> To have squeezed the universe into a ball
> To roll it towards some overwhelming question,
> To say: "I am Lazarus, come from the dead,
> Come back to tell you all, I shall tell you all"—
> If one, settling a pillow by her head,
> Should say: "That is not what I meant at all.
> That is not it, at all."

And the dark force is already working this afternoon in
1968 while Bill sits reading me "The Love Song of J. Alfred
Prufrock." As he reads, Margaret sits beside him on the sofa
like the woman in the poem, and the explosion is one year
off now, one year in the future. And there's danger in this
room, I sense it, as does Margaret; that's why her posture is
erect and formal. Looking back, I doubt she knows what
he's up to with "Prufrock" any more than I do, but she
knows the ship is sinking and that whatever Bill's agenda
with the poem, under it is hers to get out and get us out
with her—and me first, the oldest, and Exeter's the lifeboat.
And that, I think, is how the package showed up on my
doorstep wrapped in silver paper stamped with gold crests.

One day while scanning *Vogue* or *The New Yorker*—I
imagine this is how it happens—Margaret stumbles on the

name: "Exeter," the Phillips Exeter Academy. Someone famous went there and went on to do great things. The first George A. is dead now, so Margaret gets the money from her mother, Mary, and enlists Bill in the project. And I suspect one reason he agrees is because their marriage is in trouble, and this is something Margaret wants, and he can help her get it and maybe thereby salvage something.

So he puts me in the Country Squire and drives me up, we make our visits, and we both know Exeter's the one the moment we first see it. The stately Georgian buildings on the lawn, the elms and maples red and gold with autumn. The new library designed by Louis Kahn has a quarter-million-volume shelf capacity. The new Love Gym has 220,000 square feet—two ice hockey rinks, three b-ball courts. There are thirty acres of playing fields, a domed observatory with a motor-driven telescope.

All this in the silver package stamped with gold crests. And here we are in the living room. He and Margaret both regard me with solemn expectation. It's time to decide, time to go down to the wharf and climb aboard the ship, time to smell the North Atlantic brine and listen to the seagulls' cries and give three heavyhearted cheers and plunge like fate into the dark Atlantic. And what if I say, *Yes, I want it?* What if I reach out and take something neither of them had, something no one in our family has had before me?

> *And indeed there will be time.*
> *To wonder, "Do I dare?" and, "Do I dare?"*

I feel like the point man walking into ambush. I'm excited, but I'm also frightened, because I can't shake the feeling that if you want nice things and ask, bad things happen. And Exeter is something very nice, much nicer than a Gibson, and there's danger in this room, years and years of danger, and Bill doesn't say, *Exeter or Woodberry—what's it going to be, son?* He reads a poem, and the poem makes it a riddle, and only Bill knows the answer and if I get it wrong, I don't know what's going to happen, and if I get it right, I don't know what's going to happen either.

I have seen the moment of my greatness flicker

Bill's stopped. His voice is hitched.

—What's the matter, Daddy?

He turns a fierce, wet look at me. His eyes are red. He shakes his head and goes on. The poem is all the answer I receive.

And now he reads on to the end and there's a heavy beat of silence. He looks up.

—Do you know why I read you this?

—No, sir.

I stand there with the pressure in my lungs and chest— the cinch—knowing to a dead certainty I'm going to fail the test.

—What do you think it means, David, to measure out your life with coffee spoons?

A moment passes now, a second, and suddenly it's as if a draft wafts through, blowing all the doors and windows open.

Bill sees me get it, and his eyes burn.

I'm Prufrock, don't you be, David. Measure out your life in gallons, bushels, hogsheads, don't be dissuaded by the woman or the women on the sofas, even if she's your pregnant girlfriend or your wife or mother and you love her, ask your overwhelming question and don't let anybody stop you, go, Godspeed, goddamn you, go, and may you have the victory I thought I'd have but stepped aside to give you. This is your fate, written in the manifest, not in ink but in the blood of our parental sacrifice.

An afternoon in Henderson, North Carolina, in 1968, and my future is decided by the reading of a poem. Go, he says, and I do. Four years later, at Exeter on graduation day, I declare to all my teachers that I'm going to be a poet. They look at me, these men in their bowties and rumpled tweeds, who seem so mild and old at thirty-three and thirty-five, they regard me with amused, defeated eyes, and say, *Ah, Mr. Payne, ah, well good luck to you, it may not be so easy.* I already know there's nothing else for me, and looking back, I wonder whether it was freedom and a shot at larger life that called or if I went to Exeter to win my parents' love and their approval and thereby lost what George A. won by staying.

And here he is, my smart, good-looking brother, drinking and getting high with me at 9:30 in the morning. Just off his job on the Kill Devil Hills sanitation truck, in a week he's heading back to school to try out for the varsity. Woodberry Forest, the place our parents once upon a time suggested wasn't good enough for me, is good enough for

him, apparently, because that's where he'll be playing football if he makes it. Strange, though, isn't it, I get Exeter, and
there he sits with the Gibson I could never ask for, and on
his finger, Pa's gold signet, which Margaret gave him though
I was the oldest. And two years beyond this summer, he'll
pledge DKE at UNC—the first George A.'s fraternity—and
become a business major, and the traditional values passed
down in our family become my brother's values. So when
I, aspiring poet, Taoist, stand in the shadows on S Columbia
Street, gazing into Big Frat Court as into a diorama, I'm
seeing not just who our grandparents and parents were and
who I might have been, but who George A. will be and is
already on his way to becoming. The children dancing there
look happier than I am.

How were these lots assigned and these decisions made?
By whom? And why? Who I Am is all bound up with
Who We Were. It's part of you, George A., and part of me,
and how our parents saw us and apportioned their love
between us.

It is impossible to say just what I mean!
But as if a magic lantern threw the nerves in patterns on a screen

So I, the child of Bill and Margaret's failed escape from
Henderson, will be about divestiture and leaving, George
A., the child of their return, about staying and accumulation,
and who Bill and Margaret were when they conceived us
is who we'll be and each of us will walk that path forever
after. How explain it?

Not one of them is like another.
Don't ask us why.
Go ask your mother.

In his old *One Fish Two Fish,* this passage, too, has stars
and exclamations.

The music's come up now.

–Who's this?

–Blind Boy Fuller, George A. tells me.

I don't recognize the name, or his real one either, Fulton
Allen, which George A. offers with the joint he passes, and
we're quiet and I listen as I've listened to the other blues
LPs he brought back from Woodberry last semester, his new
obsession. All summer, as I've whipped him into shape out
on the beach, George A.'s played me bits and pieces of this
music. It has a strange familiarity and I'm curious and can't
decide completely if I like it. It sounds tinny, small, arcane
and lonely, not like the blues I've come to know. It's not like
"The Lemon Song" with Jimmy Page or Keith and Mick
on "Gimme Shelter" or Clapton covering Big Bill Broonzy.
The way those English white boys play it, the blues lifts you
up and takes you someplace it feels good to be in, but this
other blues that George A.'s brought home isn't like that,
and it's not Robert Johnson and the Mississippi Delta players either. The stuff he's listening to is from the same place
we are, the Eastern Piedmont—Brownie McGhee and
Sonny Terry from up the road in Durham, and back before
them, Bull City Red and the Reverend Gary Davis. This
music is like being in a bus station late at night, and some

old fellow with a cardboard suitcase offers you a swig of something and you don't want to insult him so you drink, and then he tells you how his child got sick and died because he didn't have the money for the medicine because he drank it and his woman left him and here he is at midnight, no longer young, with a cardboard suitcase, and he's telling you the truth and offering no relief because he has none, and the worst part is, as he speaks, it dawns on you it's midnight and you're in the same bus station he's in. And there isn't the same uplift in this music, no rocking out the way there is with Jimmy Page and Keith and Clapton and the other English white boys, and I don't know that I want to hear this old man's story or drink with him or sit beside him in the station, and how exactly did my little brother find his way here, and why exactly did he bring me?

As the song concludes, George A. lifts the needle and starts the whole thing over and, settling the Gibson, plays through the turnaround into the resolving I chord in the first beat of the twelfth bar, and as he picks this old black music that issued out of poverty and deprivation, Pa's gold signet flashes on his finger. He tries it twice and can't quite get it, though the second time is better.

—Close, I tell him.

—No cigar, though.

—Maybe a cigarillo?

With a fatalistic shrug, he puts the guitar facedown on the bed he slept in and turns up the volume.

—Guess how old he is, he says.

—How old?

–Guess.

–Sixty, sixty–five?

He shakes his head.

–He died when he was thirty-three. He was twenty-eight when he made this.

He puts the roach into a clip and offers me the last toke. Silenced, I listen more closely now to the antique hiss and crackle on the tape, and George A. leans back in the rocker as Fulton Allen sings, in this scratchy old recording from the '30s, "Stealing Bo-Hog," "Boots and Shoes," "If You See My Pigmeat," and "Funny Feeling Blues."

My brother's eyes are closed, his chin lifted slightly toward the ceiling. Though it may be only concentration, there's a pained quality to George A.'s expression, and as I listen with him, it's as if the downstairs room we've shared since we were boys has become a kind of church, and we're here together at a funeral for someone important, someone to whom we're both indebted, and at the time I don't know who, but now I think about a photo of him as a toddler. Standing close behind George A., her index fingers clutched in his small fists, is Eva Brame, who raised us, raised me from the time that I was one and George A. from the cradle.

While Bill and I were out in Warren County playing hooky with the farmers and Margaret was at Altar Guild, George A. was home in the gray-shingled house with Eva listening to the radio, to the station Eva would have chosen, and as George A. lay on the floor playing with his cars or coloring, Eva hummed and did her ironing, and when the cardinal flashed past the window, it was Eva who said "bird," and George A. will first say bird the same way Eva says it, which is subtly different from the way our mother says it, though when Margaret's had a couple and gets into that certain mood and wants to put on music, her accent changes, the rhythms of her speech relax, for she, too, was raised by a black woman, Otelia Franklin. And when Nanny, Margaret's mother, speaks, her speech is filled with Black English idioms and rhythms more pronounced than either Eva's or Otelia's.

On and on and back and back it goes, this mixing, black on white and white on black, I heard it in Keith and Jimmy Page and Clapton, and back before them, Elvis, and it's on frat row in Chapel Hill where those white kids are dancing to beach music and as I stand in the shadows on S Columbia it's part of my attraction, part of what I'm seeing in the diorama and why I sometimes long to cross the street and join them. And it's here now in the lair with us in George A.'s music, his new obsession which isn't really new, and I don't know my brother's heart, I barely know my own, but I wonder if the reason why my brother looks as if he's grieving goes back to Eva, who cared for me, too, but was with him from the cradle, long before he knew that she was black and that he wasn't or that Eva was in a subordinate position and that to be with us she wasn't there with her own children who had to miss her so that we could have her. And maybe George A. once believed, as I did, that Eva belonged to him and he to Eva, but she really didn't and he didn't really either, he had Eva—we did—because once upon a time our people took from hers what they didn't

78

wish to give us, as once upon a time Margaret took from Bill what he didn't wish to give her, as Bill later took from Margaret and the Roses what they didn't wish to give him, and now Eva's gone, too, we've lost her just like we lost Bill and Margaret, and George A. and I are all alone here. And I see now what this scene is, it's the last one of our childhood, once we leave we're never going to be together here in the same way, and we're all that's left to each other who once believed that family love was stronger than time or death, except it wasn't, and I'm going to lose him, too, and George A.'s going to lose me, and maybe that's the funeral, and here we are in the station and the old man's telling us his story, which is our story also, the differences are minor, and it doesn't lift you up and take you anywhere you want to be in, the only consolation is that the story's true and we're here together as we listen.

—You know he's buried up in Durham, George A. tells me as he lifts the needle.

—Blind Boy Fuller?

He nods.

—I'd like to go up there someday and see the place.

I don't know if George A. ever went. I did, though. One day a month or two after the accident, on the way to Henderson I detoured into Durham following a set of Internet directions and found my way to Beamon Street, where Allen lived with his wife, Cora Mae, and later looked for Grove Hill Cemetery, getting progressively more lost as I went deeper and deeper into Durham. In the place where Blind Boy Fuller aka Fulton Allen is supposed to lie, I found a vacant grassy lot, unmarked, and at the edge of it, a playground with children laughing on a swing set.

George A. re-sleeves the album now and turns off the stereo, and when he looks at me I can tell he's thinking the same thing I am.

–So, man, what now? I say. Avalon awaits. You want to go?

–Not really.

–Me neither.

He smiles and I smile back.

–Let's do it then.

–Let's go.

So he slips off his khakis and the filthy T and dons the Birdwell jams he's wearing in the beach photo I later hand him in Vermont the night before we leave there. I had a pair myself, but their color has long since drifted through the sieve. George A.'s, though, are still right here: dark green with a double white stripe down the right side. They cover just the top third of his thigh and look like shrink-wrap applied with heat, as dated now as hot pants or the shorties we high school b-ball players wore back in the day.

So down to Avalon we go, a four-mile out and back, through troves of shells that ring like easy money when the waves sheet through them over our bare feet. My practice for this month has been to pace him to the pier and halfway back, and then I fly, leaving him to follow my footprints as the waves erase them. Today, though, in the final mile, when I start to pull away, he picks up his pace. I glance over— *Feeling feisty, are we?*—and pick it up again; again, he matches me. Far too early, with a half mile left, I kick it into a full sprint. I can see George A.'s determination. He's suffering now, but he keeps up. It's getting serious. I'm suffering, too, and when I push, I find that I don't have another gear. In the last hundred yards, he walks away, ending fifteen yards beyond me. I've given it my all, and George A.'s flat-out beaten me. We stand there panting in the wash, hands on knees, not speaking, as waves sheet in around us. When I look up, trying not to let my anger show, I find him trying not to grin at me.

–Asshole! I say.

I shoot him a bird, and George A. laughs and shoots one back at me.

–Come on, he says, and we both dive into the ocean.

By the time we emerge, Margaret and Jack are setting up their chairs and staking the umbrella.

–*Cheese,* I say to George A., borrowing the camera.

So, you see, he's happy when I snap him and sticking it to the cameraman a little. I can take it, though. The truth is, when it comes to us, I want to crush him in the dust, but when it comes to anybody else, to the whole outside, other world, I want George A. to win. I want that for us both. And on this day I still feel no less sure of him than of myself.

In the photo you can tell the boy's an athlete of some kind. Six-foot-seven and 210 or 215, he's lean-waisted, broad across the shoulders and the chest, more man than boy, though there's still a spindly coltish something in his legs that marks him at the tremble point. From hoisting those heavy cans all summer, he has thick, good arms as "good" was then, in a more casual time, and I recall him sneaking discreet squeezes of his biceps when he thought no one was looking, or making a fist to see the vein stand in his forearm, a vanity I knew to watch for because I did the same thing. George A.'s proud of the body he's achieved. In the way his arms fall at his sides, there's a tad of the gunslinger pose. He's like someone with a new suit he paid a lot of money for and doesn't want to wrinkle in the wearing, or a cherry car he parks at the far edge of the lot to ward off dings.

I thought my brother was the best-looking boy I ever knew, among the best-looking I ever saw. As I study this old photo, though, I think perhaps it isn't Gable that I'm searching for, but those clean-cut all-American boys on lawns and beaches, posing for the camera with their girls and paste-waxed cars, before they went away to World War II. George A.'s smile extends a friendly confidence like theirs, but a little further back, I see something that's prepared for disappointment, and it strikes me that George A., too, this day in 1975, is going off to war, an inward war no less real. It will last twenty-five long years and the rest of his short life, and George A. won't return from it. This picture is the last glimpse I'll ever have of him, which I guess is why I kept it and put it out in every place I ever lived in. *Here's looking at you, DP,* he's saying with that grin and little squint. *This one's for you.* My reply in kind: *Enjoy it while it lasts . . .* Oh, do.

Click, and over thirty years go by. Though George A.'s image in the foreground remains clear, time has faded the Atlantic at his back to a dull spectral pinkish bronze. The background looks less washed out than dematerialized or dematerializing, which makes it seem as if George A. is standing on the border of a world that isn't this world anymore, and the moment after this he'll have to raise his hand and go, and there's a part of me that wants to reach out and hold him by main force the way our mother did for years, and is it love; I loved him, but there's that other part, you see, that wished to beat him and was angry at the genius flank maneuver by which he threw the race and won by losing, and then he came to help me in Vermont and died and, see, I won by George A.'s dying.

4

So GEORGE A. RETURNS TO Woodberry, to concussion
drills and double sessions in the August heat, I to
Carolina, where I train to be a Poet, a not entirely
literary undertaking. Early this semester, I dream of one of
the black-water sloughs that line the highway in eastern
North Carolina, the roads we always take to reach Four
Roses in the summer. Police cruisers with flashing lights are
parked helter-skelter on the bank as a wrecker winches a
submerged car from the water. In the backseat is a body
whose condition suggests the accident's an old one. There
with the law enforcement team, I watch the operation with
a troubled feeling. I know something about this crime or
am implicated in some fashion, only I don't know how and
don't want to look into it too closely. As I wake, the dream
feels as real as a recovered memory. I begin to write a poem
I'll work on for months and can never seem to finish.

Two years ago, one of my professors gave me *Memories,
Dreams, Reflections,* and Jung's autobiography has become a
kind of bible for me in this era, particularly his account of
the events of 1912, after he broke with Freud and had a
brush with what was probably psychosis.

I lived as if under constant inner pressure. At times this became so strong that I suspected there was some psychic disturbance in myself . . . I stood helpless before an alien world; everything in it seemed difficult and incomprehensible. I was living in a constant state of tension; often I felt as if gigantic blocks of stone were tumbling down upon me . . . I said to myself, "Since I know nothing at all, I shall simply do whatever occurs to me." Thus I consciously submitted myself to the impulses of the unconscious.

And when the stone blocks came tumbling, what Jung's unconscious led him to do was to start playing. On the lakeshore near his home in Küsnacht, he built a toy city out of stones and when he finished and placed the altar in the church at village center, a crucial dream came back to him from childhood. Everything he accomplished in his life, he later wrote, came out of the dreams and fantasies of this time and his decision to "consciously submit . . . to the impulses of the unconscious." Somewhere he calls this *letting the libido follow its own gradient,* and, at twenty, this has become the first and greatest commandment of my personal religion. And what Jung did beside Lake Zurich, I'm attempting in my poems, using words instead of stones to build with. I see myself as on a treasure hunt that I don't have the map to, and the treasure that I seek is my True Self, what Whitman calls "the precious idiocrasy." Pursuing that is what it means to me to be a Poet.

So while George A.'s running wind sprints in Virginia, you can find me in the stacks at Wilson Library, poring over

Symbols of Transformation and working out my stanzas. Often at 3 or 4 P.M., I emerge with bleary eyes and tousled hair in the disordered ponytail I'm wearing, and I change and set out running west of Chapel Hill, out Calvander, past mown fields where lightning bugs blink over summer's hay bales. I do six miles, sometimes eight at night, and twelve or fifteen on a Saturday or Sunday. I'm up to forty, forty-five miles a week now, and occasionally someone remarks upon my "discipline," and I take the compliment with pleasure, but if discipline is doing something you don't want to do because you're supposed to do it, the truth is I have little or no discipline whatever. I'm doing what I want to do because I want to do it, which is something different, letting my libido follow its own gradient, and increasingly I'm doing little else besides that, opting out on calculus and poli-sci and macroeconomics. "I would prefer not to" becomes my catchphrase for a season, cadged from Melville's "Bartleby, the Scrivener."

As regularly as I run or read, on Friday nights, I close my books and head downtown to Town Hall or He's Not Here, some bar on Franklin Street, where I unwind with a few beers. And this is usually when I see her, the girl, across the bar, the one who interests me, she's almost always Blonde and Insubordinate, a type as unlike my dark-haired, well-bred mother as conceivable—though Margaret, on consideration, when she snuck out through the hole in the back fence at St. Mary's to join the Wolfman in his purple stovepipe corduroys, wasn't exactly playing from the Miss Manners playbook, and, as noted, is not so solemn when she's had a couple. So perhaps the insubordination in these girls is not entirely unfamiliar, something I might see if I ever actually looked at Margaret.

As regards the girl, though, after six beers, maybe eight, I can allow myself to meet her eye and seek the signal and risk I may not get it. Sometimes I do, though. She smiles or holds my gaze for a few beats and I cross the room to join her, my feet bare in the sawdust and the floor beneath the sawdust tacky. We strike up a conversation, or attempt to. I speak to her, she smiles and shakes her head; she speaks to me, her lips move, I smile and point to my ear. Eventually we make our way outside to Franklin, where suddenly we can hear the cars whoosh by and there's fresh air on our faces. Sometimes we go to her place, and once I wake up in a strange apartment with no recollection of the woman in bed beside me. I walk outside and shelf my hand over my eyes and do a slow 360, unable to identify a single land-mark, uncertain whether I'm still in Chapel Hill or possibly in Europe.

More often, though, she comes with me, we make the twenty-minute trek cross-campus, past Big Frat Court where the bands of black men are playing in the diorama. Along the route we sometimes rest on a bench or make out in a doorway. When we get back to Avery, my dorm, we climb the stairs to the room I share with Sal, a curly-haired Italian kid from Maple Shade, New Jersey, a schol-arship wrestler who's five-foot-three or -four and whose upper bod and chest are like a nest of pythons twitching underneath a flesh-toned tarp—his biceps have their own biceps. Once there, I might read her something from "Burnt Norton," a shallow ploy that often fails and even turns off some girls who come here willing. But as one thing can be two things, a high one and a low one, I also read to show them what I'm up to, to see if among their number there might be a Spacegirl who's on a space trip of her own or might like to take one with me to that different, better Earth I'm seeking without the poison in the wheat or in the water. I don't want to go alone there, I want someone to love me the way no one ever has, the way I fear my mother didn't, and I suspect that may be why I never look at Margaret in this era, because I don't want to know this, that something went wrong between us somewhere so far back it's like a shadowed grove in an ancient sun-drenched country. What happened I don't know; the ring of trees conceals it. The idiocrasy I was was strange to her, not precious, and perhaps no one held hers precious either. I sense she sent me off to Exeter to become someone different, I'm not sure who, perhaps someone who dealt in timber, farms and profits like her father, only more so. And I came back this bright-eyed, long-haired boy whose feet are black and calloused from going barefoot from April till Thanksgiving, who spends his weeks in a carrel, writing poems and poring over *Symbols of Transformation*. And these girls I bring back to the dorm don't get me either, some flee at high speed when I take down my books and others wait impatiently for me to finish reading so we can get on to the business we've contracted and contract it. And the truth is I don't get me either, I don't know Who I Am, and maybe that's what's in the backseat of the sunken car in my dream, my True Self, which I've been sent back to recover. How did it come to be there? The question seems to me the only one that's worth pursuing.

And one morning this September I wake up and look around and for a beat, perhaps two beats—*one thousand one, one thousand two*—I can't nail my location. The place looks familiar and generic—a generic boys' room, generic desks and bunk beds, generic albums in a fruit crate. It's like the lair, like my old dorm at Exeter. The idea of a hotel floats up, but it's not a hotel either. There's a rectangle of daylight at the window and the blueness in the sky is not the blue of morning. Now I hear whistles and the snare drums, *one thousand three,* I get it. Avery, my dorm, just down from Kenan Stadium. It's Saturday, game day. Uphill, the marching band has launched into the Tar Heel Fight Song, "Rah, rah, Car'lina-lina . . ."

–Bullshit, I mutter, and I sit up, nauseated, in the top bunk, noting that I still have my clothes on.

What happened? I don't remember going to bed, don't remember coming back here. I must have blacked out. Obviously I blacked out. As I look around, I have a bad feeling. The room suggests an oh-so-familiar crime scene, and I'm the detective who's implicated in some way I don't want to look into too closely. The clues are all around— bottles, amber, green and clear ones, and a half-full beer cup in which floats a cigarette butt with a lipstick stain the same red the cup is. And my Eliot is out and open. Seeing it, I flash to the girl—not her name or face, but just the fact that there was one.

And here I am, hungover, with my clothes on, and it's afternoon, the band is playing up the hill at Kenan. The girl? Was she a high-speed fleer? Maybe. Only I don't think so. The platter of my AR's turning and the album jacket standing in the cubby shows a youthful Springsteen fingering that scruffy 'stash he wears on *The Wild, The Innocent & the E-Street Shuffle*. The Springsteen belongs to Sal, who calls me "Hillbilly" or "Hillbilly Dave" and likes to accompany my entrances and exits with banjo music or the squeal Ned Beatty makes in *Deliverance*.

And speaking of the devil, here is Sal now.

—You got a phone call.

—Me?

—No, the other guy named Dave who looks exactly like you and is standing where you are listening to me as I'm talking.

—Who is it?

—One of your hillbilly relatives.

—Were there fiddles playing in the background, or did you deduce his montane origins by other means?

—He had one of those double names—Billy Bob, Ray Don. Something.

—George A.?

—That's it.

There's something odd in Sal's demeanor. He's grinning like a Bad Wolf if not a very Big one.

—What's up, Sal? Why are you grinning like that?

—What? Is there a law against it? I had a good night.

—You had a good night . . .

I leave a beat, inviting him to fill it.

He doesn't.

—Was there a girl here when you got back last night?

—Uh-huh. There was.

—You saw her?

—I "saw" her, he confirms, putting quotes around the verb that I, Detective, don't want to look into too closely.

—Go take your phone call, he says. I gotta take a shower. I feel a little gamy.

And Sal—having had a good night and now having a good morning . . . make that afternoon—walks down the hallway, chortling a little.

A riddle wrapped in a mystery inside an enigma!

I pick up the pay phone in the corridor.

—George A.?

—Guess what?

—What?

—I made eleven tackles.

—*What?*

—Eleven, he says.

—Fuck me! When?

—Last night in the game. I'm starting!

—Bullshit! You're starting?

—Hell, yes.

—Eleven?

–Eleven.

–Well, fuck you, asshole! Fuck you, and congratulations.

–Heh heh heh.

He's buoyant as he says it, and I'm happy for him and the roar comes down the hill from Kenan, and I can hear the shower running and suddenly I'm queasy. What is it? I have the clearest image of my old coach at Exeter, the one who tapped me for the JV team in my first year—I was the only freshman in the school who made it. That's not it, though— the flash is from my senior year, when he took me aside to say, *What happened to your heart, Payne?*

–Thanks for helping me, George A. says on the phone now.

–What?

–Thanks for helping me get in shape this summer.

It takes a beat.

–You're welcome, man. You did it, though. I'm proud of you, George A.

–Thanks, DP.

For the big game against Episcopal, he tells me now, Margaret and Jack are driving up from Winston-Salem, and Bill from Phenix City, Alabama, and from Henderson the Paynes, our grandparents, Letty and Bill Sr., the Principal, and even Uncle Allen all the way from Philly.

–I was kind of hoping you might come, too, he says.

–I'll try, okay?

–Okay.

–I gotta run.

–Me, too.

The September sky outside my window is the same blue I remember over Boston.

It's 1969. I'm fourteen, in the backseat of the Country Squire with Bill driving and Margaret riding shotgun.

We've spent two days heading north up 81, so Bill, who's planned the trip with fanfare, can "smell the mountains" up there in the Shenandoah, where his father and his father's people come from. Somewhere near Lexington one morning, where the clouds hang on the road, he stops the Country Squire, gets out and affects to wash his face and hands in them. He climbs back in, beaming. His mood suggests a victory march, a Second Honeymoon, a new beginning. Margaret—in dark glasses in the shotgun seat—studies him like a riddle she invested years in solving but that holds no further interest.

She's done, only here to see me in the lifeboat. As I look back, her silence hangs over that trip like a kind of doom as we cross the Susquehanna, where Lee passed with his troops in July of 1863, proceeding north through rich Pennsylvania farmland, past stone barns the Amish built to last forever. And this is the same route George A. and I will take thirty-one years later in the opposite direction.

We arrive in Boston Saturday afternoon and throw our bags into the single room we've booked. Tired and later than we've planned, we set out on the walking tour, following the redbrick path along the Freedom Trail, through the Common to the State House, past the Old North Church, and finally across the river to the *Constitution* at her mooring, with her tarry rigging and her piles of antique cannonballs like black grapes. We're somewhere in north Boston, lost, as dusk is falling. It's time to start back to the hotel, and Margaret, still in her dark glasses, is walking half a block behind. When Bill calls, she won't respond. He looks like he may scream or weep, that look that makes me want to comfort him, or else retreat into a bunker.

Back at the hotel, Margaret heads into the bath and locks the door. Bill tears the water glass out of its wrap and fills it to the brim with J&B. We're late for our dinner reservation, he tells her, knocking. No answer. Tossing his Scotch down with a wince, he refills the glass and regards me somberly, his eyes a charged void like the sky before a lightning storm.

–Talk to her, okay?

I wonder what it must have cost him to have to ask me and, when I knock, to hear her answer.

At Anthony's Pier 4, where Bill's research has led us, Bill drinks harder till he's slurring words and fumbling the Lucky Strikes he's lighting. He's making toasts, grand, purple ones—to us, to me, to my future—working us the way he worked those men around the tobacco barns in Vance and Warren Counties, confident his charms will win us. At adjoining tables, people have begun to stare, and I'm both mortified and angry at these strangers for regarding him with such expressions.

Across from him, Margaret sits up straighter in her chair. She's like an envoy at a parley who, before settling at the table, has carefully scoped out the location of the exits. Bill has planned this with such fanfare, though; he's found the restaurant and ordered the expensive wine the sommelier's suggested. All he wants is for us to join him in the artificial Happy Land he's made, the one he's generating on magician's fingertips right now—see it like a snow globe, like a hologram, dancing amid crackles of cobalt-blue lightning. Because we can't, the celebration's turning dangerous, and Bill, who's creating all the danger, wants our gratitude— expects it—and is starting to feel victimized when we withhold it. I know you so well, don't I, Daddy, because I, who loved you more than anyone or anything in childhood, who took a blood oath never to be like you, became so anyway. Under the toasts, I hear the old theme: *Go, Godspeed, goddamn you, go and have the victory that eluded me, the victory I thought I'd have but stepped aside to give you. And may your labors bring you the same happy fruits that mine brought me, the very same, my boy, tooth for tooth and eye for eye.*

When we return to the hotel, he steers Margaret through the lobby toward the bar and sends me upstairs to the room. There, I shine my loafers—they're black with tassels—and lay out the new blazer Margaret bought for me last week in Raleigh. We took a special trip to Nowell's and had lunch in Cameron Village the way that she did once upon a time with her father, the first George A., before she went off to St. Mary's. She encouraged me to buy a winter coat as well, and I picked the most beautiful one they had there, a knee-length herringbone with a tapered waist and a black velvet half collar. Thinking of it now, that coat strikes me as the sort you'd buy if you imagined New England winters as Currier and Ives affairs of horse-drawn sleighs with tinkling harness bells and Exonians as little investment bankers disporting on the Upper East Side or East Egg. What I find curious now is how much I loved it, the careless and un-self-critical entitlement with which I picked it out, the same way I picked Exeter. I wanted both with unreserved longing and asked straight-out, the way George A. asked for and got the Gibson and so many things before and after, and look what happened to me, little bro, which is how I know.

Asleep on the rollaway, I wake up to the sound of breaking glass. Margaret's crying in the bathroom. When I knock, Bill roars, *Go away!* in that voice that rang the crystal in the cupboard. When I don't, he opens the door in nothing but a towel that does little to conceal the state he's in.

—Get back in bed or else I'm going to kill you, he says, and it's as if our life together is a swath of decorative wallpaper that suddenly tears and shows the black depths of outer space.

One of Bill's eyes is bright, avid, fixed, a bird of prey's, the other has a drooping lid. I sense that he's been awaiting this encounter for some time. *Let us go then, you and I . . .*

—Bill? *Bill!*

Margaret's cry breaks his fixed attention. Eventually they emerge and climb into the big bed. For a moment, things grow quiet. On the rollaway, I turn my back and lie there with a pounding heart, wondering if it's over, and if it isn't, what then? The bedsprings start to creak now. When I turn, Margaret's up and running toward the window, and Bill, staggering after her with arms extended like Frankenstein's monster, corners her against the bank of windows that looks out from a high floor north and east across the Harbor. There's a bed lamp on the table. Am I going to have to pick it up and hit him? I'm paralyzed, and just before he reaches her, Bill trips and crashes facedown like a tree felled in the forest. Margaret's hands are at her mouth. We wait for him to stir. He doesn't.

The next thing I remember, the lights are on, and Margaret's pacing up and down the room, shaking her hands as though to force blood into them. As she dresses and swabs away her makeup, she sends me off to find his wallet, which I retrieve from his pants pocket, strewn in the entry. When I hand it to her, she takes my cheeks between her hands and stares at me.

—I'm sorry, baby, she says, I'm so sorry, I have to go, I have to.

—I know. Go, Mama.

And go she does, downstairs to a taxi to the airport.

Left alone with him, I sit there all night in a chair posted like a guard. What do I feel? Looking back, that seems the all-important important question, but this sector of the drive is hopelessly corrupt now. Applying such forensics as I can, through the noise and static, I think I hear the fourteen-year-old I was then saying, *What about those summer mornings in the oil truck, Daddy? What about when we rolled the windows down and sang "The Wabash Cannonball" and "The Big Rock Candy Mountain"? What about Holy Innocents on Sundays, when we stood and sat and knelt on cue and pledged ourselves to the communion of saints, the forgiveness of sins and the resurrection of the body? Was all of it a dream, a bullshit dream, an artificial Happy Land you generated like a snow globe on magician's fingertips? And if this isn't so, if I'll feel better in the morning or next year, then tell me how we got here.*

It's Bill I charge, not Margaret. It's as if her leaving happens in accordance with an old agreement we're both party to and understand our parts in. Where did we solemnize that contract?

That night after her departure, I stare north toward the Mystic River Bridge in the distance, and off the other way, east, across the black sweep of the Harbor, toward the runway lights at Logan, where occasionally a plane takes off, one of them carrying Margaret. As the shock recedes, I feel like Brother A gazing through the porthole of my spaceship at the blue orb growing small beneath me, floating amidst pinprick stars and twinkling galaxies, and around me the room is like a crime scene—this is the hotel room I flash to at Avery five years later when I wake up in my clothes with Springsteen turning on the platter.

As the light comes up over East Boston, Bill, lying facedown on the carpet, stirs and sees me at my post there. His first impulse is to smile, and then, as he notes his nakedness, his position in the room, the calculations chalk themselves across the blank slate of his expression. *One thousand one, one thousand two . . .* And maybe to him now the room is like a crime scene.

—Where's your mom? he asks me, covering up.

He remembers nothing, so I have to tell him. My tone, as I set out, is furious and petulant. Before long, I'm sobbing.

He listens with a vacant look, his mouth open slightly. Then he calls his mother. He puts me on the phone with Letty down in Henderson.

—He raped her, I say as Bill sits listening.

—No, no, your daddy would never do that, Letty says. You must never say or even think such a thing. Things go on between men and women in a marriage that you can't understand and won't until you're older. You misunderstood.

She's right, isn't she? "Rape" is a primitive word. Whatever happened, Bill didn't consummate his action, and maybe he blacked out because he didn't really want to, or perhaps that's only wishful thinking. In any case, Letty's right, he didn't rape her, but at the time I can't let Letty have this. Because whatever Bill did or didn't do to Margaret, I feel violated by his action. At the time, my underlying sense is, If I let her, let them take this from me, if I let Letty attribute the injury I feel to a failure in my maturity and understanding, I'm lost, I won't survive it.

When Letty tries, when she pits her formidable will against my will, I feel it as a pressure in my chest and lungs. It's like a burning coal I've swallowed somewhere long ago, and Letty's message is, *You must never spit it out. To spit it out is a betrayal of your father, your people. This is what it means to be a member of a family.*

And I recall a Sunday afternoon at her house on Oxford Road when Letty told the story of her father, Edwin Finch, owning the first car in Henderson. As she reminisced, she went into a brightness, an artificial Happy Land. Letty, too, wanted—expected—us, her audience, to share the happiness this story gave her, whose point boiled down to her family's priority over all the other families in the town. And one day Margaret said, *I thought that belonged to Mr. E. G. Davis.* Margaret said this with disingenuous innocence, and Letty's smile flashed.

—No, dear, you're mistaken.

Margaret has the burning coal inside her now, and Letty's flashing smile says, *Go ahead, I dare you.*

—I always heard that it was Mr. E. G. Davis, Margaret repeats, with less conviction.

—No, dear, you're incorrect. Whoever told you that was misinformed or telling you a fib.

Letty is too much for Margaret finally. When I turn to Bill, wondering whether he'll weigh in and how, he's beside the window. I recall him sitting straighter in his chair, I recall the way his Adam's apple bobs, I see the expression of concern and hypervigilance on his handsome, expressive face, before he turns away and gazes out across the lawn, where a shadow falls as though there is a rheostat behind the sun and only Letty Payne controls it.

And would it have been worth it, after all . . .?

Somewhere Bill apparently decided that it wasn't, and when he puts me on the phone with Letty I think it's to refresh the lesson Letty taught him, that to be a member of a family means to keep the coal inside and live with it and call the damage loyalty. And because I can't bring myself to challenge him, I challenge Letty.

—Don't tell me what I understand! I was there, you weren't. I didn't misunderstand, you did. You.

And I'm screaming as I say it.

That afternoon, bleary-eyed and suffering, Bill drops me at Main Street, my dorm at Exeter, and pulls away up Water Street in the old Country Squire, and in a way that's my last glimpse of him, my father—ours—whose next stop will be Atlanta, where in order to avoid the possibility of prison for the theft of Mary Rose's timber, he goes without his pension and retirement, with no job, no money and a *lis pendens* on his property, and after that those washouts in the Shenandoah, where he disappears like Eric Robert Rudolph after the bombing in Atlanta, vanishing into the mists along the ridgelines and river bottoms up there in his father's father's country.

That night Margaret calls the dorm and the housemaster comes to get me. The moment I see the black receiver on his desk, I start to sob, and he looks at me with the expression people wear at funerals and shuts the door behind him.

—I want to come home.

—I know, baby, I know how upset you are, and I'm so sorry about what happened, David. But you'll feel better in a day or two. Believe me.

—I won't.

—This is the start of a wonderful opportunity for you. I have every confidence in you. We all do. Every confidence.

—I want to come home, Mama. Please.

—I'm sorry, baby, there's no home left to come back to.

And there's the beginning of an answer to the coach's question . . .

What happened to your heart, Payne?

I guess my family broke it.

Boo hoo, son, whose family didn't?

You're right, Coach, I know you are. Put me back in the game, okay?

Thataboy . . .

So I get up in the morning and put on my blazer and a new shirt; I have eight—four white, four blue, one for each day of the week, plus an extra for Phillips Church on Sundays. I knot my tie the way Bill taught me, smiling at me in the bathroom mirror, his hand on my shoulder as I wrapped it.

On my way to class I pass the substantial Georgian buildings. Two hundred years of New England weather have washed the brick to a soft patina. The old elms and maples on the path cast pools of black and ample shadow that contrast with the slant gold of northern sun on the lawn of the Academy Building. Above the entry door is chiseled: *Huc Venite, Pueri, Ut Viri Sitis.* Enter Here, Boys . . . something . . . something . . . In the dorm at night, I cry for hours.

In the early going what most disturbs me are the older boys with their long hair and wire-rims. They look disreputable and sallow, like Bolsheviks plotting the over-throw of something. And their clothes resemble sackcloth sewn by prison labor—not the sort you'd find at Nowell's. And while we're at it, what's this music?

In Henderson, at my farewell party, we listened to the Supremes and the Temptations, the boys in khakis, tassel loafers, V-necks, the girls in pleated skirts and soft angora sweaters, wearing strings of junior pearls they borrowed from their sisters. Now, blasting from an upper floor of Dunbar Hall, I hear

God said to Abraham kill me a son . . .

And . . .

. . . talking 'bout my guh-guh-generation . . .

A third-floor window rattles up and a flag unfurls—blood-red with a yellow star: the flag of the People's Democratic Republic of North Vietnam.

I appear to have touched down on another planet.

It's the fall of 1969, the Days of Rage. As the Weathermen plot to take down the Drake Hotel in Chicago, the dean speaks to us in assembly about Exeter's "institutional policies." An older boy stands up in back.

–That's right, he shouts through cupped hands, Mother Exeter's an institution, and when they screw you here, they screw you institutionally.

Half the room erupts in cheers, the other half in hisses. I gaze around the elegant hall—with its chandeliers and columns, its portraits of old headmasters in regalia—uncertain

whether I want to join these boys and burn down something or beat the disrespectful fuckers senseless.

My first night in Main Street, mad guitar licks boom
from the floor below me and I go out to listen in the stairwell. Descending to the landing, I take three big running
strides, launch myself into the air and slap the header,
stretching for the highest line of cinder blocks and landing
on the offender's threshold in a backward cat crouch. Over
and over, I hurl myself, making my presence as difficult to
ignore as his is. Subtext: *Whoever you are, get out here and let's
settle this.*

And sure enough, the door cracks and a fellow looks out
with dark, slightly widened eyes whose depth reminds me
of George A.'s and my mother's. A handsome Jewish kid
with a head full of loose, dark curls—a "Jew-fro," he calls it
presently—Eric Rosen has a city pallor that strikes me as
both glamorous and sickly. I invite him out to have a jumping contest; he invites me in to have a *schnecken* and listen
to Led Zeppelin.

—What's a *snecken*?

—*Schnecken*, he corrects me.

—*Snecken?*

Eric's laugh is like a whinny, high and nasal, so inconti-
nent that it infects me, too, and I crack up with him. What
intrigues me in the early going is the way Eric lobs non
sequiturs into conversation, whoopee cushions of wit that
either stop discussion cold or wrench it in some new direction. *Fruit flies like a banana . . . Time wounds all heels . . .* Eric
has an endless stock, he's like a scholar, and he also mints

his own and sometimes his mintings are so good—or bad—
that I can't tell what's original, what facsimile. Something
about this reminds me of my father. For the way Bill
charmed those tobacco farmers around the barns was with
verbal brio, too. Bill, for instance, would never simply tell
them it was cold, he'd say it was so cold the squirrels were
stacking cordwood and putting bounties on their relatives
to procure additional fur coats. And when I say such things
to Eric, he laughs that whinnying laugh, and whether he's
laughing with me or at me I can never be quite certain. In
lieu of jumping, words become our contest and collabora-
tion. It begins that first night as I sit on his bed eating
schnecken and *hamantaschen* Eric's mother has sent up from
a bakery on lower Fifth Avenue. I'm not sure I've ever seen
a pastry box before—the paper doily's fancy! As I eat, I
study the album jacket Eric hands me—white, with the
ominous silhouette of an airship, the *Hindenburg* aflame and
passing over. This is a new band, Eric tells me, the guitarist
is Jimmy Page from the Yardbirds, and though I've never
heard of Jimmy Page or the Yardbirds, after the music's initial shock-and-awe assault, I begin to note the strangeness
of Robert Plant's voice, like a mad crone shrieking proph-
esies in the stone tower of a medieval castle that isn't even
medieval, and as "Good Times, Bad Times" segues into
"Babe I'm Gonna Leave You," I begin to get what's happening among the Bolsheviks in wire-rims.

And when the music's over, Eric sends me upstairs with
the pastries, the whole box—I can't believe his generosity!
In my room, I remember what I've forgotten for an

hour—Boston—and I lie there crying and eating till there's nothing left but crumbs and that little paper doily. I can't quite bring myself to throw it out, so I put it in my drawer and leave it there most of the semester.

And when I wake up in the morning, I put on my blazer and my tie and go to Latin with Mr. Coffin, whose manner —like his name—suggests an old Nantucket whaling captain. I fear and admire him, and from the start apply my strongest effort. Every Sunday, I review the whole semester. So while the other boys are doing cannonballs off the bridge, enjoying the last warm weather, or smoking dope and venturing into the woods beyond the stadium, I'm chanting conjugations and declensions in my room at Main Street. By mid-semester, these sessions last from breakfast till lunch and are paying dividends.

My success in Latin extends to basketball: I try out for the JV team and am the only freshman in the school to make it. In an early game, I post up in the lane and when the pass comes in I nab it, feint left, then pivot right off my right foot and throw up a left-handed Lew Alcindor sky hook that hits the box and splashes through the net like easy money. And the coach runs down the sidelines shaking his fist and shouting in the gym where everyone can hear him, "Way to go, Payne, you're a quick study!" The hair rises on my forearms, and *bullshit*? No trace of that response lives anywhere inside me. I only wish someone might set the court on fire so I could run barefoot through it for him, and as I sprint back on D it never dawns on me that this will be the summit of my sports career at Exeter.

And when the first snowflakes fall, I put on my new herringbone with the black half collar and wear it proudly on the footpaths. But no one at Exeter has a coat like mine—not even the boys from Park Avenue and those with Kennebunkport compounds. So after class I fold it up into the smallest package possible and carry it like a shameful secret underneath my elbow back to Main Street and go coatless through the winter. My Nowell's blazer follows. At a church rummage sale one night on Front Street, I buy an old tweed coat for fifty cents. Grayish black with little nubbly twists of fabric, it resembles an industrial airport carpet from the 1950s and I fall for it with deep love and wear it every day to class for four years. And, after the blazer, my new oxford shirts, my tassel loafers, stiff and new, still carrying the shine I put on them in Boston, all the beautiful things my mother bought me, into the black steamer trunk, which I wrestle into the deep recesses of my closet.

And I'm spending more and more time with Eric. In his room I hear *Blonde on Blonde* and *Let It Bleed* and *Live at Leeds* and Jethro Tull and Clapton and the Velvet Underground and Zappa. And I, a Southerner, first hear the Allmans and Levon Helm singing "The Weight" on *Big Pink* by way of Manhattan and my new friend Eric. We go on to jazz, to Bird and Monk and Coltrane and Rahsaan Roland Kirk—the nose flute! One Saturday, we get high and listen to *Bitches Brew* straight through, all four sides, with a concentration I rarely give my classwork. Following Eric's lead, I begin to grasp that there are tropes in Davis's trumpet work and Shorter's sax, exploding genius nuggets filled with

107

pathos, comedy, wisdom, rage, disdain, and when these burst overhead like fireworks, Eric and I slap five in admiring recognition and when they fizzle we're merciless and brutal critics.

–I charge him with conformity!

–Sentence?

–Freedom!

–Ten years' hard liberty!

–A member of the unchained gang!

–A *life* sentence!

In Eric's wordplay there's a suggestion of what Coltrane does with *raindrops on roses,* the way he takes the phrase and splits it like an atom to see what hidden energies he can discover, and even if I can outjump him on the landing, here Eric always beats me, and when he laughs I can't tell if he's laughing with or at me, and I love him almost like a brother, and sometimes I want to crush him in the dust the way I want to crush George A., and I wish I had one thing, one thing to give Eric because the flow is so unequal, always Eric-David, never David-Eric.

And in a way that I don't grasp yet, the time I spend with Eric, the stoned, ebullient nonsense we engage in, has started to become as important to me as what happens in the gym or classroom. As I once shot baskets in the drive till dark and after dark fell, so here in Eric's room we're building another sort of reflex, sinew, timing for another sort of contest. In English class, I'm starting to turn confident and fierce in my opinions and though I'm still crying over Boston in my dorm, the periods are shorter. And as the b-ball season winds down, the coach I would have run through fire or broken glass to please at first has begun to seem rigid and tyrannical, and what wins me points in English class on the court subtracts them massively, and whole games go by in which he never looks in my direction and I don't unsnap my warm-ups.

And one day in my PO box there's a letter. I recognize Bill's writing and take it back to Main Street and open it with trepidation. I'm expecting some accounting over Boston, but, no, it's an invitation to go duck hunting with him at Christmas, just the two of us, with a private guide at the Mattamuskeet Lodge in the lowlands of Hyde County.

I know this trip will be expensive and that he's trying to square it with me. I put the letter under my desk lamp and reread it several times over the ensuing days, and finally it's clear to me that what I need to be there—*I hurt you, David, and I shouldn't have, I'm sorry*—isn't. So I write back and say no thank you, that the idea of going somewhere and "shooting and killing things" doesn't sound appealing, and in fact, I'm thinking of becoming a vegetarian. My reply is filled with wounded fourteen-year-old petulance, and the rebellion I first encountered among the Bolsheviks in assembly has begun to work its way into my feelings toward him and our family. There's a part of me that wants to go with him, but it's late November by this time and I've lain crying on my bed too many nights. Duck hunting and the Mattamuskeet Lodge—the tweeds and hand-sewn boots, the guns with sterling trigger guards, the flasks, the pedigreed retrievers, all the beautiful impedimenta—what does any of it have to do with Bill or me or with our family? It's bullshit, like Letty's story of her father owning the first car in Henderson. And if I go, I know what will happen. The lodge will be like church and the shotgun blasts and gun smoke will be the bells and incense and the silver flask will be the chalice and when Bill passes it and I take my little sip, I'll go into a trance the way I did the day he read me "Prufrock," and we'll commune and be one again in substance and my love will burn with its old unclouded brightness, and my injuries will be voided by the power of this magic and it will be as if Boston never happened. Only I don't go, I refuse him.

So Bill asks George A., and of course George A.'s going— why shouldn't he? And how can I be jealous, since Bill asked and I declined him? I am, though, and to me this feels like a chess move, Bill's way of punishing me for rejecting him because he hurt me, and so he sets George A. and me against each other. I learn about this on the dormitory pay phone, the same call in which Margaret says she's sorry but she can't afford to fly me home to North Carolina for Thanksgiving. So I eat turkey in the empty dining hall and practice Latin. My reviews now last from after breakfast till 3 and 4 P.M., when dark falls in New England, and I've pulled ahead of all my classmates.

On Christmas, though—our last in Henderson—I do go home. Though Nanny, her mother, is in the hospital dying, Margaret makes the eggnog in the sterling punchbowl the same as always and drapes evergreen along the mantel and swags the mirrors and the portraits of the Manns, her great-great-grandparents, and puts new candles in the sconces and lights and snuffs the wicks because it's done this way and it would be bad luck not to do it.

Bill is coming from Atlanta to take us out to Christmas luncheon with the Paynes, his parents, Letty and Bill Sr. He'll be here at 1 P.M., and after lunch he'll drop Bennett and me off and continue eastward with George A. to go hunting.

I recall us waiting for him outside on the porch. George A., with comb streaks in his hair, is popping wheelies in the drive on his new skateboard. I'm playing basketball with Bennett, teaching him to dribble, though he's three and doesn't show much interest. He has a red-and-blue wool scarf, three or four feet long, and he puts it on his head and Margaret bobby-pins it for him. He refers to it as "girl hair" and calls himself "Canelope," and one day Margaret observes him watching *Penelope Pitstop* and puts the two together. He's acting out the cartoon damsel-in-distress, who's threatened by her nemesis, the Hooded Claw, and must be rescued by her posse every Saturday.

I'm teaching him to dribble, only it's not taking, and 1 o'clock has turned to 2 now and is moving toward 2:30.

And now it's 3. I've had it.

—This is bullshit, *bullshit!* I say to Margaret, who's shocked at the new mouth I've brought back from the dorm at Exeter.

—I'm sure he'll call.

—Fuck this, I'm not doing this again. I'm not, I say, almost daring her to contradict me.

—Come here, she says, offering to hug me, but I don't want that.

And eventually Bill does call, at 8 or 9 o'clock, from some phone booth miles and maybe states away, to explain about the flat tire, the alternator, whatever it was.

—I'm asleep! I shout down the hall to Margaret's summons, making sure it's loud enough for Bill to hear me.

One day Bennett will call me "Mac," as in John McEnroe, for my explosive temper, so like Bill's, the person I so don't want to be like.

—This is bullshit, fucking bullshit, I mutter to my pillow.

And as I lie there, I hear George A. down the hall saying, It's okay, Daddy, we'll see you in the morning, we'll see you when you get here.

And Bill does come and George A. does go with him. He'll be a hunter all his life, and in years to come, he'll invite me and I'll sit beside him in the blind, watching through binoculars, and never fire a shotgun, and I wonder if George A. knew deep down that I'd wanted to say yes to Bill and couldn't, and if that was why he would invite me on his hunting excursions. And so perhaps Bill's move, meant to turn the two of us against each other, only worked with me, for George A., getting the special trip and Bill, had no reason to be anything but happy.

And spring brings the U.S. invasion of Cambodia, and, after it, barely a week later, Kent State, where National Guardsmen open fire on protesters. *Four dead in Ohio.* In assembly that day, the older Bolsheviks in black armbands shout down the dean and call for a strike and I put on a black armband and strike with them and skip all my classes except Latin. I'm all in with Mr. Coffin.

By spring, my Sunday reviews go on till 6, 7, even 8 P.M., and we've been through the vast tracts of regularities and rules and are beginning to push into the complex subtleties of the subjunctive—*Ut Viri Sitis:* in order that you may become men—and still each Sunday I go back to lesson one, Week One, the present indicative active of the first conjugation, *amo amas amat,* and by 8 P.M., when I'm dog-tired and have done none of my other work, I don't have the same energy to give tomorrow's lesson as the miscreants who goofed off in the woods all day doing cannonballs into the river. Now, when I turn my head, I see a couple of them gaining, and I know in some deep place that I'm hampering myself with these reviews, but I can't bring myself to stop them. In order that I might feel virtuous, my praxis requires me to go back to lesson one, Week One, and redo the whole semester every Sunday, and two weeks before Kent State I have my fifteenth birthday and have no one to tell me that this ritual is all about control, that my effort in Mr. Coffin's class is proportional to the lack I feel inside me.

By May, the homestretch, I'm staggering under the weight of these reviews. I've started out so far ahead, however, that I still manage to pass first across the finish. Handing back my blue book last, Mr. Coffin smiles and says, Congratulations, Mr. Payne, perhaps you'll share with us how long you studied to achieve this?

He must expect me to say an hour and a half, two hours, maybe three, some substantial but not impossible sum that will reprove without discouraging the others. When I answer, Twelve, beaming as I let the cat out, Mr. Coffin's expression slackens, and he stares at me as though he's never seen me till that moment. And in the next class meeting, our last, he says that though I've earned the right to go into Latin 21A, the accelerated class, some boys of a certain bent, despite their excellence, choose to go into normal Latin 21, and thrive there, and I may wish to consider this route, and I smile and thank him, insulted by his offer.

So I fly back to North Carolina, touching down in Greensboro, where Margaret picks me up and drives me to our new home off Cone Boulevard, the Sans Souci Apartments. A three-bedroom with popcorn ceilings that you enter from the stairwell, the apartment's dominated by the Charleston sideboard with its bellflower inlay and the portraits of Pa and of the Manns, Joseph and Martha, and the facing mirrors in which our images are probably still receding.

At the beach that summer, I take a job with the town sanitation crew, blazing the trail George A. will later follow. Every night at midnight, when the big truck rolls up at the bottom of our drive, I swing aboard with my sandwich in my pocket, and occasionally I do *Omnia Gallia in tres partes* for Earl, who works the left side of the truck and gets a kick from my shenanigans. When I get off my shift, I throw on my Birdwells and down to Avalon I go. Distance running, the solitude and repetitiveness of it, has started to appeal to me, a new *qigong* as Latin's fading. On our bookshelf in the lair rests my first-year Latin primer, Kirkland & Rogers, its green cloth binding worn white with hard use. I take it out a lot that June and go back dutifully to lesson one, *amo amas amat*. I rarely get beyond that, though. Somehow the thrill is gone. Instead, I put an album on—Eric has loaned me a sheaf of twenty or twenty-five canonical works—and I devote whole afternoons to *The White Album* and *John Barleycorn Must Die* and *Trout Mask Replica*. By the end of that summer, I know every word of every song and every note of every instrumental riff. And when I return to Exeter in September 1970 for my sophomore year—we're called Lowers there—I'm one of the sallow, disreputable-looking types. My Levi's have white-stringed tears, and my jacket looks like sackcloth sewn by prison labor.

In Latin 21A, I nod to my competitors from the previous year, those who, when they stumbled, saw my eager hand shoot up. I run with them for a few weeks, still with the front pack though no longer at the head of it. In the dorm at night, I find it hard to concentrate and close my book and head down to the Butt Room in the basement, where the boys with permission to smoke play scoreless bridge and shoot the shit till lights-out. And soon I'm not with the front pack anymore, or any pack, I'm all alone in back, not even running, but strolling through the woods alone, noting the moss on the north sides of trees, and the way the breeze sways the treetops and the sun winks through the leaves, telling myself that competition doesn't matter, that winning's an illusion, a Taoist in training before I know what Taoism is.

Still, with Eric the game goes on, year after year, semester after semester. I visit his family at their home on lower Fifth Avenue, where Mr. Hsi, their cook, makes *boeuf bourguignon* to celebrate Eric's homecoming. Wanting to repay their hospitality, I make a spinach casserole, calling Margaret for the recipe that lives on a yellowed index card in the tin box in her kitchen. This consists of canned Del Monte spinach and Campbell's cream of mushroom soup with melted cheddar and, on top, canned French's French Fried Onions. I go shopping at Gristedes, and when it comes bubbling from the oven, Eric's parents look at it and then at me with the same alarmed, good-natured stares that Eric turned on me when I thumped down on his threshold in a backward cat crouch. And not long afterward they include me in a family birthday outing to Le Périgord, where Eric's father orders the dessert soufflé in French before we sit down in the banquette. Soon, I take the train with Eric to his grandfather's estate on the North Shore of Long Island, where the library is as large as the gray-shingled house that I grew up in and on the wall there are framed letters from Tolstoy, among others.

There are darker expeditions, too ... In Washington Square Park, Eric introduces me to his friends and heroes, the street Odysseuses and Aphrodites, the dealers, hustlers and musicians, the skinny teenage runaways with Dead Sea stares and runny noses. Some streak of dark, romantic tenderness draws Eric to these wounded, sometimes dangerous children, whom we follow on dubious, generally drug-related adventures through snipped chain-link fences, across litter-strewn lots to abandoned buildings on the Hudson, or uptown to Harlem tenements at 2 and 3 A.M., leaping over drunks passed out in the stairwells in dark puddles of who knows what.

And one day near Thanksgiving I recall walking stoned with him through Central Park, where an expectant group of children has gathered near the entry to the zoo with their mothers and au pairs to hear the Delacorte Clock strike the hour. A few snowflakes are falling and Eric, smiling, holds a finger up as atop the brick pavilion the bronze monkey clangs the bell and, below, the carousel of animals begins to turn to the tune of a carillon. The elephant, the bear, the goat, the hippopotamus, the kangaroo, the penguin drummer—the delighted children point out their favorites, but one little boy no more than three or four stands crying in a blue coat, displeased or frightened by the spectacle, his eyes like rain-streaked city streets at midnight, as though he knows bronze animals aren't supposed to do this, to spring to life this way and do this joyless dance with fixed postures and expressions. When the clock stops, though, he stops and looks at his Person with relief and satisfaction as though his cries have stopped it. Eric and I trade looks at this the way we do when Miles or Shorter release a genius nugget or fire a Roman candle, not sure what we've witnessed but sure we've witnessed something and sure the other gets it, our friendship like a room that you could go to knowing the other would be waiting when you got there. And looking back, I'm not sure where, if anywhere, I'd ever felt this, perhaps with Pa, the first

George A., bottom-fishing in the Albemarle before our little kingdom sank beneath the ocean.

With Eric at the time, this seems no more than hanging with a cool friend from an exotic background. Looking back, though, it seems to me that I was at a master class in Eric's room, the greatest one I took anywhere. I slip from the shaken shell of my identity and into his, like Jacob into Esau's skins, and for a spell of years, I fancy myself a smart Jewish kid from Manhattan, and I not only absorb Eric's cultural influences, I ape his tics and affectations, the way he laughs, the rhythms of his speech. When Eric thinks Grace Slick is the sexiest woman alive, I affect to think it, and I throw non sequiturs and puns into my conversation, too, to blow up like whoopee cushions. And so before I've read *Absalom, Absalom!* and *Delta Wedding,* I've read *Portnoy's Complaint* and *Henderson the Rain King,* and Eric's room is less a class, it strikes me now, than an operating room in which I'm the patient, and what I receive from him are blood transfusions, pint after saving pint, and by the time I emerge years later, there's been some fundamental alteration in my DNA. And so Who I Am is as tied up with Eric as with Bill and Margaret and Eva Brame, as with Mary Rose and Letty Payne and George A. Rose and George A. Payne, my brother. In Eric's room I'm seized by some thalassic current that carries me and turns me into someone my parents seem bemused by, and the truth is I don't know who I'm becoming either, and I'm experiencing massive failure in the subject I was best at.

After Latin 21A, I end up back in Mr. Coffin's class for Latin 41, fourth-year Latin, and by this point, as we embark on the *Aeneid,* I can no longer really translate from the text or follow the discussion. Mr. Coffin greets my first failure with a look of hurt surprise, the second with his feared acerbity, meant to reawaken excellence in a former star. With advancing repetition, though, he begins to hold his tongue and simply stares at me the way the housemaster did the night when Margaret called the dorm, the way people do at funerals. Now as we go around the table, boy by boy, each translating his ten lines of Virgil, there's a tense, embarrassed silence when it comes to me that even the boys I formerly exulted over seem to take no pleasure in. And though Mother Exeter is an institution and screws you institutionally, and though she should have screwed me, too, according to the same clear, equitable policies she used to send home almost two-thirds of the boys in our prep class who didn't make it through to graduation, Mr. Coffin, the severest master there, lets me slide. And for years—years, literally—I'll dream I'm back in class with him, and when it comes to my ten lines of Virgil, I look down at the book and can no longer even recognize the language.

And by this time, I've given up on all my other subjects except English. I've begun to shoplift little items from the stores downtown, and I steal a dictionary, too, from Eric, a big expensive Random House unabridged, and Eric knows the score and when he asks, I lie to him. It's as if his words, the tradition of scholarship he comes from, are things that I can never earn by honest means, and though I love him like a brother the contest has been too unequal for too long and I'm tired of losing, tired of not quite knowing if he's laughing with or at me.

Crossing campus in the snow one night, I start to chase him and throw snowballs. Eric runs and falls, and I stand over him, laughing and pushing snow into his face, pretending it's a big joke. He can't breathe, there's a stricken look, a panic in his black, good-natured eyes that are so like my mother's and my brother's. And years later, after we're both grown men with families, when I finally apologize for this, he'll say he knew I was just goofing, but I wasn't. The dark force that erupted in my father in the hotel room in Boston has begun to erupt in me now, too, and between Eric and me it's never the same after this night. And I wonder now how different I really was from the wounded, dangerous children in Washington Square Park, and if the same tenderness that drew him to the hustlers and runaways drew him to me also. And this metamorphosis that's occurring, which began with puns and black armbands, has become quite worrisome by this point.

And the malaise has spread to basketball, where I make varsity as a junior and as a senior have a chance to start. Early in the season, the coach makes some remark about my hair, which falls below my shoulders now.

–I know you're going to want to get that cut before Monday's practice, Payne, he says, joking, but not really.

–Well, I would, Coach, if you'd explain its relevance to my performance, I reply, not really joking either.

When he looks at me, his eyes blaze with coldness now, and the distance between us widens. Season by season, my attitude's become an issue he can't overlook, or won't, and since the other boys are giving it their all, why should he overlook it?

What happened to your heart, Payne?

I guess my family broke it.

Boo hoo, son, whose family didn't? You think there's a boy out here who doesn't have a sob story just as sad as yours or sadder?

I guess not.

Take the bench, son.

Okay, Coach, okay. I turn and start to walk away, but something stops me. At the last minute I turn back, it's too much like swallowing the burning coal, and I can't do it . . .

But you know what, Coach?

He presses his lips and shakes his head and stares down at the floor as though he knows what's coming.

Goddamn basketball, I say. *Goddamn basketball and the team and you . . . And while we're at it, goddamn Exeter and non sibi and the Academy Building and Phillips Church on Sundays. Goddamn the Apostles and their creed and the forgiveness of sins and the resurrection of the body and Holy Innocents where I learned to chant these spells and Henderson, North Carolina, and New Hampshire and New England and the United States of America. And, first and foremost, goddamn my people and family love which is supposed to be stronger than time or death except it isn't. And if my sob story's no sadder than anybody else's, maybe that's why there are cities burning all across this country.*

But, no, this conversation never happens . . . In the real world of outward fact, I cut my hair, though minimally, and lose the starting job and ride out the season, moving farther and farther down the bench, taking such consolation as I can in lettering while telling myself that competition doesn't matter and winning's an illusion. And yet in another way, it does happen, I have this conversation with myself, with the boy whose parents told him, not in words, *You must redeem in blood for us the sacrifice we made in blood for you,* who came to Exeter to do that, to try to win their love and their approval. I'm not him anymore. This is where I turn my back and toss the match across my shoulder as I go.

And in the tradition of my forebears, an Eric Robert Rudolph type myself, I head off into the wilderness, and the wilderness for me lies out beyond the playing fields at Exeter, beyond the stadium. That's where you can find me now on Sundays, doing cannonballs off the bridge and getting high with the other miscreants, *mes frères, mes semblables.* I like to sit on the riverbank beneath the trees, relishing the rawness of sun through scarce-created leaves. And sometimes out there, as the breeze sways the canopies, I lift my face and almost fancy I can metabolize sunlight like a green plant.

And after the *goddamning,* what's left? After the bomb's exploded and the banks have failed, when the Statue of Liberty's torch lies gleaming dully underwater, what remains, the one true thing?

> *Let us go then, you and I,*
> *When the evening is spread out against the sky . . .*

What I felt the day Bill read me that, when it was as if a breeze wafted through, blowing all the doors and windows open.

And one day not long after this, I walk out to class one morning in my sackcloth coat and my bolo tie that observes the letter of the dress code as it parodies the spirit. There's something different in the air. I stop and look around. And then I realize: The trees have buds on them, the air is soft, the spring sun on my face feels good . . . What is this curious sensation? Happiness! It's been years since I've felt truly happy, years since I've remembered spring. Noticing again, some nameless impulse wells up from inside me; I start to trot and then I break into a run. On the path beneath the elms and maples, I jump the way I did on Eric's landing long ago, I shout and pump my fist and do 360s in the air, landing in a backward cat crouch on the lawn. What is this upwelling? I only know I've left behind the road my parents set me on and am free to find my own now. I'm going to write, I'm going to be a poet.

And two years later here I am this blue September afternoon at Avery as the marching band plays up the hill at Kenan, and the room is like a crime scene and I'm implicated in some way that I don't want to look at, and poetry which I've followed like religion hasn't saved me.

Maybe I'll go running. Twelve or fifteen miles may change the way I'm feeling, stop the rumbling in the underwater portion of the iceberg. And Sal comes from the shower wrapped only in a towel, and as he dries himself the pythons of the pythons slither.

–So what time did she leave? I ask him.

–She didn't.

–She slept here?

–She stayed. I can't say she did much sleeping ...

Sal grins and takes a beat. *Drumroll ... Top hat ...*

–Or me either for that matter.

–Bullshit! You're telling me you screwed her? With me here?

–What's the big deal? It's not like you were going to.

Badda boom, badda bing!

I don't know what hits me in this moment—something does, though, like one of Jung's stone blocks tumbling from the heavens. I stagger downstairs and set out. Meaning to run twelve or fifteen miles, I make it maybe twelve or fifteen steps and sit down. A great fatigue steals over me; I'm shivery and faint as though I've suddenly contracted dengue. There's pressure building in my head like steam behind a closed valve. Sitting makes it worse, I need to move, I need to get up, so that's me wandering downhill, a tall, skinny, shirtless kid in flats and running shorts like hot pants, my dark hair loose around my shoulders, reeling though the Rams Head parking lot at halftime.

Well-heeled alums with season tickets are eating fried chicken and potato salad on their tailgates—dads in sweater vests or blazers in tropic wool or broadcloth, dyed Carolina blue or subtle shades of grass or apple, splashing bourbon into Cokes from silver flasks with monograms, the signets winking on their fingers. Their good-looking wives are dressed in tasteful styles that occultly shave away ten years, autumnal plaids with round, black fabric-covered buttons, and I can smell their perfume, overheavy, and when they smile, I see the lipstick on their teeth, reapplied out here without the benefit of mirrors. I know them so well and regret the impasse that we've come to, for on game days once upon a time I ate fried chicken off the tailgate with them or, more often, rare roast beef sandwiches from the Rathskeller downtown with thin-sliced Bermuda onion served on dented pewter platters by black men in vests and bowties with the mien and dignity of privy counselors. And later at the stadium or Woollen Gym when they sang the Fight Song, I sang *Rah, rah, Car'lina-lina* with them, and when the Tar Heels lost, sometimes George A. cried and I put my arm around his shoulder and said, *It's okay, buddy, we'll get 'em next time,* but what I wouldn't do is mutter *Bullshit,* ever. And now these people who were once my people regard me like a lunatic escaped from an asylum, and I want to ask them, Don't you get it, I'm yours, I'm one of you, I know you, why don't you know me? Your daughter with the ribbon in her hair? I slow-danced with her in a basement playroom the night before I went away to Exeter. Your son—I once had his haircut and his manners and tassel loafers just like he has. I shined them for the last time in 1969 in a hotel room in Boston. I was him and my brother George A. still is, he still has the haircut and the blazer and made eleven tackles and he's starting, the thing you came here today to cheer for he did last night at Woodberry, and

I helped him—he called me on the phone to say so—and our parents are going to see him play in his big game against Episcopal, Jack and Margaret are driving up from Winston, and Bill, who didn't make it to my graduation, all the way from Alabama, and from Henderson, the Paynes, our grandparents, Letty and the Principal, Bill Sr.

And, see, I went away to Exeter to win their love and their approval, *Don't measure out your life in coffee spoons,* they told me, and when I came home this is who I was, and they looked at me like you do, only Margaret's look was worse, it said or seemed to me to say, I still love you, David, no matter what, whatever you've turned into, *despite who you are,* though you seem so angry and can't let bygones be bygones the way in this world we all have to, sweetheart, and you say you want to be a poet and I don't know what poets are or how they make a living or what their service is to others, I only know that in our family the men have always dealt in timber, farms and profits and found in that their duty and in duty honor, and you say you want to be a Taoist and escape the material world and metabolize sunlight like a green plant and that frightens me, I don't know how to understand or help you.

You see, they get George A. and know who he is, but they don't get or know who I am, and I don't know who I am either, I only know the answer isn't in the Rams Head parking lot this afternoon or up there in the stadium or in Big Frat Court where the dancers seem happier than I am, but that was like a dream I had to wake from, I didn't ask to wake, the glass broke and I heard my mother crying in the bathroom and I knocked and Bill said *Get back in bed or else I'm going to kill you,* I couldn't just go back to sleep, could I? I had to wake and George A. didn't, he's still on the path that leads to Big Frat Court and maybe one day he'll be here in a blazer in a subtle shade of grass or apple and have a pretty wife like these and pour bourbon from a silver flask and when he pours Pa's signet will flash on his finger, but I won't, my path leads elsewhere, I don't know where though, maybe to a precipice, perhaps I've fallen off already and that's what's happening, maybe I'm in free fall and any minute now I'm going to hit the bottom. I only know the pressure's building in my head, and I don't know what to do, so I make my way uphill into the pinewood on the east side of the stadium.

There's dappled sunlight on the paths, which are bronze and needle-strewn. Kenan Stadium, which I pass each day and barely glance at, today seems massive, elemental, frightening. It's like a rock formation, a volcanic caldera from which energy rises as it does from Steamboat or Old Faithful. The snare drums and the whistle are puffs of CO_2 and methane, and then the roar comes, and the roar's the geyser, the roar is energy, pure energy, shooting miles into the atmosphere, and it isn't sentiment that makes the hair rise on my forearms, the energy's a subtle wind that lifts it physically.

Both teams are competing for that energy, the crowd's approval; that energy is lifeforce—*qi*, the Taoists call it. The winners are uplifted by it and leave the field with shining eyes, while the losers walk away depleted. Last night Sal and

127

I were like the teams competing for the girl and sex was her approval, the form of energy she bestowed upon the winner, and because Sal won he woke up glowing, and because I lost, I've skulked away into the pinewood, and this feels familiar, so familiar.

Damnit, though, my head is splitting, I've reached my limit and can go no farther, so I lie down in the straw just off the path under the old pine trees, where stragglers steer a wide berth around me. I sling an arm across my brow and gaze up at the old sun winking through the young green needles. When the breeze moves through them, they whisper in a way that seems intelligent and purposeful. *Beauty's nothing but the beginning of terror we're still just able to bear.* So says Rilke, but I'm not at the beginning, the pressure's moving past the point where I can bear it. I close my eyes.

Against the screen of my closed lids, I see the redbrick campus path we crossed last night, the girl and I, how we stopped to make out in a doorway and set out again, only suddenly the path's become the Freedom Trail in Boston, the scene goes double and the path to Avery becomes the path to the hotel and in the hotel are Bill and Margaret and David and in the dorm are David and the girl from He's Not Here and Sal, and as Bill woke up and remembered nothing and I had to tell him, so in Avery five years later I wake up, remembering nothing, and Sal tells me. And Sal is Bill now and I'm still David, or am I Bill and is Sal David? The whole thing's mixed up, scrambled somehow, and the faceless, nameless girl is Margaret, who said I have to go and went and she's gone again now, and everything's repeating, everything is playing out the way it did the first time, Stories A and B are the same story, and my competition's not with Bill now. Is it with Sal? Or is it with George A., who made eleven tackles and is going to get the roar, the family *qi,* and be lifted up like Abel? Abel got the *qi* and was lifted up and Cain went without and was wroth and slew his brother, and how did I become Cain and end up in the pinewoods east of Kenan or of Eden? I don't know, I only know the competition is an old one, and out beyond the bridge, beyond the stadium at Exeter, as I sat beneath the trees, I conceived a wish to escape the contest altogether, to be a Poet and to find another Earth where there's no casting down of one so one can be uplifted. And I've followed poetry like a religious practice and spent hour after hour in my carrel reading Jung and Eliot and Whitman to seek a path out of the fracas, to prove that the dark force that was in my father isn't in me also.

It is, though. It's in me. The engine that once whirred in my father whirs in me now. How did it come to be there? It seems unfair that, being hurt, the hurtful thing should come to be inside me. There it is, though. And what do you do then? What next and how now?

Overhead, the sunlight coming through the pines is so intense it's turned the needles into blackened crisps, and the contrail of a jet might be a meteorite burning up in the primordial atmosphere of Earth or whatever planet this is.

The marching band is playing in the stadium; I hear the snare drums and the whistle and think of Central Park: the clock, the animals, the carillon. As the monkey strikes the bell, the elephant, the bear, the goat are visible, and then the carousel begins to turn and the hippopotamus, the kangaroo, the penguin come forward as the others disappear around the pavilion—two triangles, one in sunlight, one in shadow, one visible, one hidden, one past, one present, one advancing, one retreating; as the platter turns the present becomes the past, the past becomes the future. The animals are us, now David, Sal, the girl . . . .now David, Bill, and Margaret . . . now David, George A., Margaret . . . Their joyless dance is our dance, the fixed postures and expressions ours, the order of their presentation, the intervals between them, all us, all me, we play the roles in turn, winner, loser, giver, taker, pursued, pursuer, Abel, Cain, victim, criminal, detective.

The surface iterations are all different but underneath the one great wheel turns unseen in the pavilion, and what is the machine that drives the axle, what is its purpose, its principle of operation and of perpetuity, what is the energy it runs on? What is it that made me in the initial revolution of the carousel my father's victim, and in the second turning made me be my father?

Poetry—my project of personal reinvention—has failed me. I've become like the very thing I set out not to be like. *I am like him . . . I am like my father . . .*

So I lie there thinking, and suddenly something's different. The pressure I felt mounting like steam behind a closed valve . . . where is that now? Vanished. The valve has opened, vented, I'm no longer suffering. I stand up and brush off, I feel relaxed, at peace, a sense of wonder, even awe steals over

me and overhead the wind is rising and the pines are sway-
ing and the hair has risen on my forearms—not from the
roar; the stadium is quiet—and all around me from the
treetops is a sound like laughter, the leaves are trembling
and it's as if there are children hidden in them, laughing.

And now I write my poem, in which I'm the detective
and the victim in the backseat of the sunken car and finally
the murderer. It takes me weeks, and there's a golden light
over this time in memory. I run and put in my hours in the
carrel, parsing out my stanzas, and I'm happy as I write them
and I finish.

Seeing that I'm like my father has stopped the clock and
released me from the mechanism's whirring. The penguin
with his drum has stepped down off the platter. So I think
then. Looking back, I'm like the child in Central Park who
cried and saw the clock stop and assumed his crying stopped
it. But the clock has merely told the hour and returned to
stillness.

And one day I come back to Avery and find a note from
the RA: Call home.

From the pay phone in the corridor, I dial and Margaret
picks up.

—David, honey, your brother's sick.

—What do you mean, sick? What's the matter with him?

—He's had some kind of breakdown. We need you to
come home. We need you here as soon as possible.

5

I'M ON 40 NOW, HEADING west toward the hospital in Winston, hugging the slow lane in my white, nine-year-old Austin-Healey Sprite. As cars pass by me on the left, the drivers give me curious stares, wondering at my geriatric pace and why I have the top down on an autumn day like this.

Margaret bought the Sprite for me four years ago, for my sixteenth, not long after we left Henderson for Greensboro and made landfall at the Sans Souci Apartments off the Lee Street exit, just down there. There's the BP station under its green sign. Five years old when she acquired it, the Sprite, for that first year, was one sweet ride, and I recall zipping down Cone Boulevard with the top down and the radio blasting, George A. riding shotgun, Bennett standing up in back, his Canelope hairpiece flying. By this afternoon four years later, time has turned its rag top, literally, to rags, and a cob-job carb repair I paid for at the beach last summer leaves me chugging westward on two cylinders in the slow lane, top speed forty miles an hour. After Margaret's urgent summons, I tried to start it in the UNC lot and it refused for twenty minutes. I imagined driving off the pier at Avalon, crashing through the rail and entering the Atlantic like the Greek boy on his dolphin, or Dr. Strangelove on the bomb. So quick, bright things come to confusion . . .

And here I am on Stratford Road in Winston, and there's the hospital. Big, industrial, nondescript, Forsyth looms in my memory like a cubist tower in Futureworld with lightning striking in the sky around it. Mandala Clinic is on an upper floor, and as the elevator dings Margaret and Jack, her new husband, stand to greet me.

—Son, Jack says, subdued and circumspect, like a politician at the funeral of a constituent he barely knows; as he shakes, he adds a second hand. In his clear face, an inflection of sympathy vies with animal spirits. His jewel-tone golf shirt says he came here from or is headed shortly to the links, where he and his buddies throw down two, three hundred bucks for kicks on any given weekday and tell jokes so blue they make an English major feel light-headed. When he steps aside, my mother smiles and spreads her arms and bursts out crying.

—He's going to be all right—he is, we're going to make him be, Margaret says, holding me a little closer than I'm comfortable with, a little closer than I can really stand.

Over her shoulder, I see a nurse punching numbers into a keypad on the wall. Shouldering a tray of little paper cups with pills in them, she backs through the ward door like a waiter at a restaurant so exclusive you can only enter with a secret code. Inside, an old woman in a hospital gown with her head tilted almost to her shoulder wanders the hallway, deep in conversation with herself. As the door shuts with a metal click, I see the wire mesh embedded in the window glass.

—How is he?

—Not good, sweetie.

—What is it, Mom?

—They don't know. Go on in and see him. We'll talk when you come out.

Buzzed in, a few steps down the corridor and to the right I find George A. standing at attention by a neatly made single bed like a camper waiting for inspection. In white-socked feet and beltless Levi's, he's wearing a jean shirt with the pockets crumpled up the way they get if you aren't vigilant enough to catch them when the dryer buzzes. In the two months since I've seen him, he's lost forty-five or fifty pounds, from a lean 215 to a frightful 165, 170. The rich, olive skin he shares with Margaret, that summer skin that seldom burns like mine, is the pallid gray of fish the second day on ice. Near his jawline there are scaly patches, bits of stubble the razor missed, and his hair looks as if it was cut with hedge shears while he fought and someone held him. He looks like someone in the nightmare where you come to in a black room and the spotlight hits you and suddenly you're on stage in a play you don't know the name of or any of your lines or the character you're playing.

—Hey, George A.

—Hey, David, he says, and his eyes say, *Tell me this is better than I think it is, DP,* and also, *Don't bother lying, I already get it.*

I put everything I've got into a look of unconditional acceptance, a look meant to show that what's gone is transitory, unimportant, what remains all that matters. George A. takes one look and starts to sob, covering his face with those big hands—Pa's signet on the right one—and the sound is like an animal that's been run over in the road, whimpering as you lift it, and I don't know my brother's heart, but those sobs seem to me to mean, *My beautiful mind, my beautiful life—what happened to me, David?*

—I'm sorry, he keeps saying, over and over, I'm sorry, I'm so sorry, David.

—For what? There's nothing to be sorry for. Don't cry, buddy, okay? Don't cry, I say, crying now myself. Sinking beside him on the bed, I put my arm around his bony, still-massive shoulder.

—It's going to be okay, I tell him the way I used to when the Heels went down.

And he looks at me and his blurry, bloodshot eyes come to pinpoint focus. In their black depths briefly shines a pitiless and undeluded knowledge.

—It won't, he says, it won't.

And George A.'s right, more right than I am.

And what of my beautiful new religion? What of the sense of transport I felt lying in the pine straw outside Kenan and the golden light in which, all fall, I've been filling notebook after notebook?

When I endured these assaults of the unconscious I had an unswerving conviction that I was obeying a higher will.

So Jung wrote of his dark period in Küsnacht.

Others have been shattered by them—Nietzsche, and Hölderlin, and many others. But there was a demonic strength in me, and from the beginning there was no doubt that I must find the meaning of what I was experiencing in these fantasies.

Swept up in his triumphal narrative, I gave little thought to those "many others," those in wheelchairs on asylum lawns with lap blankets, with spittle on their lips and tremors, for whom the "confrontation with the unconscious" isn't educative, but ruinous. If the world's a vale of soul-making, if to make one's soul means to wrest consciousness from unconsciousness, what happens when consciousness is wrested back, the jewel rendered into mud, a soul unmade, cast down and permanently blighted? Jung's scheme makes such beautiful sense for the victors—for him in his great, groundbreaking way, and for me in my small one, following the blazes he left behind him on the stars and planets. But what about my brother? What does the "higher will" intend for George A.?

If our family story first broke for me in Boston, it breaks again here, seeing George A. sick in the locked ward at Mandala.

Once upon a time, in the Official Version, we were blessed and happy, our parents young, privileged and good-looking, we, their children, bound for special destinies like they'd had. In Boston, our ship struck the iceberg and went down in an hour, but all hands appeared to make it to the lifeboats. The trip to shore proves long, and only when we finally muster do we realize one of us is missing.

–What happened to him? I ask Margaret in the elevator going down. What fucking happened to George A.? He looks like he's been in a concentration camp.

The impulse to cry has swiftly given way to one to shout and break things. I want blood and perp walks, handcuffs, prosecutions, show trials with kangaroo courts, public executions.

–He's so thin, isn't he? He got mono and really had no business going back to practice, but his heart was set on playing.

She tells the story . . .

Bill was coming to the game with Letty and Bill Sr. On game week, one afternoon the team finished up their practice and George A. sat down by his locker. None of his teammates noticed till they came back from the showers and found him still there, staring at the floor, elbows on knees, head hung. When they called, George A. didn't respond or even appear to hear them. Someone went to get the coach, who took George A. to the infirmary. The nurse called Margaret. It was 9 or 10 P.M. by the time she and Jack arrived, and George A. was manic by then, so agitated the nurse refused to keep him. They went to a hotel. In the room, Margaret told me, George A. kept going to the window, pulling back the sheer and asking her if she could see Bill in the parking lot. No, sugar, your daddy isn't here, she told him, and George A. said, He is, he's hiding in the trees . . . behind the lamppost . . . and he'd look at her and grin or burst out crying.

In the elevator, Margaret starts to hyperventilate, fanning her face with both hands.

I touch her shoulder.

—Are you all right?

—No, I'm not all right. Are you all right? George A. told them he smoked marijuana with some friend the night before. The doctor says it may just be a bad reaction.

—To smoking pot?

She seems scalded by my skepticism.

I clinch my jaw and stare two degrees to port.

When her face settles, I sense she doubts the doctor's theory just as much as I do.

—So where's Dad? Where are the Paynes?

—Your father came yesterday, she answers. I wasn't here, but he dropped off some religious materials.

—Religious materials . . .

—A Bible, some pamphlets . . . I don't know what it was. The doctors told him George A. wasn't ready to receive visitors.

—They didn't let him in?

She shakes her head.

We hold each other's eyes like veterans of an old campaign we didn't win.

–The doctors told me if Bill Payne ever realized his responsibility, he couldn't live with it.

The elevator dings. We've reached the bottom. Someone must answer for George A. There's no dispute on who the central suspect is.

–Are you coming home for supper? Margaret asks me in the echo chamber of the hospital garage.

–I'll see you out there.

"Home" I can no longer give her.

In the Sprite again now, I'm heading westward on 158, the back way toward Jack and Margaret's house in Clemmons, passing silos, fields and barns, as night descends. The sunset is like a hemorrhage. Driving into it, I'm fifteen again, my first summer back from Exeter, when I came home not to Henderson but to Greensboro and the Sans Souci Apartments ...

Margaret was out somewhere and had left George A. to babysit for Bennett. When I entered from the stairwell, I heard George A. crying at the back of the apartment.

–Don't go, Daddy, please don't leave, okay?

As I walked into the bedroom, he looked up with streaming eyes. Bennett, beside him, picking at his scarf's fringe, looked scared and somber.

–Daddy's going away, George A. said.

–What? Where's he going?

–To Mexico. He's never coming back.

–What the hell, Dad? I said, taking the receiver.

Between the beds, George A. sank and drew his knees up, going fetal. Bennett stroked his shoulder, four years old and trying to offer comfort. How old was George A.? Twelve? No, it was summer, he wouldn't be twelve until September.

Bill was somewhere in Underground Atlanta. I recall the bar noise, his unmodulated, roaring tone, the music playing in the background.

—You're drunk. You're drunk out of your mind. Do you know George A. is up here sobbing on the carpet?

—So, what, I don't have a right to call my son to say goodbye?

—Don't call here like this. I'm serious, Dad. Don't ever call here like this again.

—Or what?

—Or I'll kill you, I told him in a breathy tone, the way you tell a girl you like her, the first girl you ever tell the first time you ever tell her.

—You'll kill me?

—That's what I said.

—Not if I kill you first.

—I will kill you, motherfucker.

—I'll kill you, Bill said.

—You motherfucking piece of shit, I will *kill* you, I'll fucking *kill* you!

Now I was screaming, and Bill returned it, basso.

—Motherfucker!

—Motherfucker!

George A., between the bunks, looked up, his black eyes wide and solemn. Now that he'd stopped crying, Bennett had started.

After the cloudburst, silence. What now? *Quo vadis?* Bill began to laugh and I laughed, too, not much, though, not in solidarity, not forgiveness, I don't know what that laughter was, no, I do, it was relief, spitting out the burning coal. We were finally saying it, the truth; what joy, what dark joy.

−I will kill you, motherfucker!

−Not if I kill you first.

−Motherfucker!

−Motherfucker!

That's what it had come down to, and George A. between the bunk beds, knees drawn to chest, eyes closed, lips moving, whispering to himself in order not to hear us. Six months before it had been Christmas, Mattamuskeet, the special trip, the guns with sterling trigger guards, the private guide, the sip of whiskey from the flask and father-son communion. Now the call from Underground where Bill let George A. know he meant to abandon him forever.

What happened to George A.? The same thing that happened to me in Boston. Don't measure out your life with coffee spoons, Bill said, and when I took him at his word and reached for Exeter, he smashed me up and ruined me in that hotel room the night before I went there.

When you want good things and reach to take them, bad things happen. Do you read me now, George A.? Do you feel me, little brother?

And the Paynes, Letty and Bill Sr., the Principal, where are they? In the five years since the divorce, they've never attended an event, a game, a graduation, never visited to take us out to lunch or to a movie. They were all set to

DAVID PAYNE

attend George A.'s big game against Episcopal, but today? Missing in action.

Yet I remember Sunday after Sunday in my childhood sitting with Letty around her kitchen table, the bowl of plastic apples and bananas she kept there, the copy of *The Upper Room,* the Methodist devotional, she read from, her pack of Raleighs, her sterling Zippo, I recall her playful sense of humor, her "zip" and personality, the way she twitted me and us around the fruit bowl. I recall loving Letty and liking her also.

What happened?

They were hurt by the divorce, which was acrimonious and public. Bill, the son in whom they once had had such hopes, left town virtually under the cover of dark with his possessions in a cardboard box in the backseat of his Mustang. He'd lost the Rose Oil Company job he sweated toward for fourteen years, received less than his fair share in the settlement. Naturally, they felt wounded on his behalf, so they withdrew and kept their distance. Since then, our sole contact has occurred in Henderson, when Margaret, there to place a poinsettia or an Easter lily on her parents' graves—or to see the lawyer to slap a *lis pendens* on Bill's property for nonpayment of support—marshals us to Letty's house on Oxford Road. Margaret, no shrinking violet, always walks us to the door, and Letty, not to be out-charactered, always asks her in. They smile and chat as though in this reunion their fondest dreams have been fulfilled—Margaret, in accordance with the old requirement, still addresses Letty as "Mother Payne" without choking on the syllables. After Margaret leaves, though, Letty, however hard she tries, can't forbear to let us know that they feel hurt by the infrequency of these visits—*Your grandfather feels neglected,* is how she puts it. Fourteen, eleven, three, when this begins, living two hours west, there's not much we can do except feel in the wrong about it. Letty seems to grasp this.

—Well, I'm sure if it were up to you, you'd come more often, she says, offering us forgiveness together with a buried criticism of who it's up to. We just frown and stare down at our shoes and shove our hands deeper in our pockets and say, *Yes, ma'am,* and take our medicine. To me, though, back from Exeter with the drumbeat of insurrection in my ears—maybe not in the first year, but by the second, as the white-stringed tears lengthen in my Levi's and my hair grows past my collar—I begin to chafe and want to answer, We're here, aren't we? If you miss us so much, why don't you come see us occasionally? If Granddaddy Payne feels neglected, why doesn't he show up when we make the effort? Why isn't it a two-way street?

I want to, but I don't. Though it's fading fast, there's still that part of me that was raised to defer to elders and tradition. And though it's been a few years now, I haven't forgotten the time that Margaret challenged Letty on her father's ownership of the first car in Henderson. For me, that story is becoming focal. I've tracked down *Zeb's Black Baby,* a local history by attorney Sam Peace, and it confirms Margaret's position. The first car in Vance County—a steam-powered 1899 "Mobile" two-seater steered not by wheel but by tiller, with a top speed of fifteen miles per hour—was owned by E. G. Davis, not by Letty's father.

Yet I recall the lightning flash in Letty's eye that silenced Margaret, though Margaret is no shrinking violet, and Bill, with that booming baritone of his and his famous temper that terrified George A. and me, didn't even dare to step into the ring against his mother and seemed to consider it a sacrilege to oppose her. There's something wrong with this, I think, wrong with this whole system where a roomful of people must disavow a published truth, like Galileo on his knees in Rome before the Inquisition, recanting the Copernican system—*I'm sorry, I was mistaken, it turns out the sun does revolve around the Earth.* Why should the rest of us accept a fact as fiction and a fiction as fact to assuage the self-esteem of the one person who's mistaken? Why should we—should I—accept a lie as truth and truth as a disloyalty? It's wrong—wrong, I say! Such bullshit, such fucking bullshit! I'm spoiling for a fight. Only I haven't forgotten the way Letty reduced my sometimes terrifying father to a smoking ruin the same way Bill our sometimes terrifying father reduces George A. and me, with those absinthe-colored neurotoxins he sprays like an octopus out of its ink-hole, the ones that make us hang our heads in shame and wonder what the hell is wrong with us. I'm not eager to take on Letty, who's a pistol.

And, too, there's that other part of me, that little voice of doubt that says, How come no one else seems bothered, or only Margaret, who's a Rose and therefore suspect? How come George A. isn't, how come Dad and Uncle Allen and

Granddaddy Payne, the Principal, noted for his probity and sternness, all just look toward the window or the ceiling and whistle "Dixie" when Letty pulls this? Is it just me? Who appointed me the Truth Police and when was I elected? And, after all, it's such a little thing, isn't it? Who *cares* who owned the first car! Maybe the problem's me, not those who don't seem bothered.

And I begin to wonder if the bind this puts me in, the sense of being all tied up in knots and fuming underneath, is what made Bill what he is and why Prufrock was the central message he delivered to me in my childhood. To grow up in a house where the speaking of a simple truth is a betrayal of your mother, where she withdraws her love, and you, to get it back, must say, *It's okay, Mama, the truth can be a lie and a lie can be the truth for you, if you require it* . . . I got a taste in Boston. When Bill put me on the phone with Letty, she tried to get me to hold him harmless, to consent, in effect, to my own violation. If I'd agreed, how different would I have been from those bank hostages in Stockholm, the ones who were held at gunpoint under a death threat for five days and then, when freed, testified at trial on behalf of their oppressors?

And what happened to them, and me, happened also to George A., who, after Bill left him sobbing on the carpet, said, It's okay, Daddy, when it really wasn't. George A. consented to his abuse to preserve the love of his abuser. The answer seems so clear to me at twenty.

In 1975, driving through the blood-tinged sunset out to Jack and Margaret's house in Clemmons, what neither I nor anybody knows is that George A. has bipolar I disorder. It will be 1980, five more years, before we get the diagnosis, and years more before we grasp the day-to-day reality of the illness.

Even now, the truth about bipolar disorder is gray and murky. It's an "equifinal" and "multifinal" condition, meaning that multiple pathways lead to outcomes that resemble one another but differ in specifics, including severity and frequency of relapse. A first-degree relative with BD increases one's likelihood of developing the disorder tenfold, but no one gene appears to be responsible. Childhood trauma and abuse? MRI studies indicate that early stress may affect brain development in ways that increase the risk of BD, or that lead to earlier onset and a more pernicious course of illness. However, no causal link between abuse and bipolar disorder has been established. A third to half of adults with BD report adversity in childhood; a half to two-thirds do not. Many people from happy, well-adjusted families develop the condition; many from first-family trainwrecks escape it.

So Bill's phone call from Underground Atlanta didn't put George A. in the psych ward, and my twenty-year-old view has more blame than truth in it. If there's any truth to be distilled, it's that we who once believed that family love was stronger than time or death have come to blame and hate one another and will do so far longer and more fiercely than we ever loved one another.

By the time George A. gets sick at Woodberry, war has long since broken out between the Paynes and Roses.

Methodist vs. Episcopalian, Oxford Road vs. Woodland, public high school vs. Exeter and Woodberry—social and stylistic differences that Bill and Margaret, at twenty and eighteen, skipped as lightly over as schoolchildren over sidewalk cracks have yawned now into divergent worldviews, the sort over which dynastic and religious wars are fought. The Roses and the Paynes are like the houses of York and Lancaster, and though at twenty I want to be a Poet and seek the truth and tell whatever portion I can locate, though I style myself the detective who follows the clues impartially wherever they may lead me, though I believe I'm neutral, dispassionate, fair-minded, the truth is, I've been raised York in a York house by a York mistress. I'm not fair. There's not a drop of fairness in me.

And Bill on his side is no more fair than I am. In a letter he wrote me in 1991, more than twenty years after his divorce from Margaret, he gives his account of George A.'s mental illness:

George A. was shipped off to Woodberry against his wishes and is still suffering from that breech birth separation . . . Margaret's hatred, spite, revenge has led her to stain the very fabric of your existence and the stench of her menses lingers still. Your self-pity, ingratitude, incompleteness and unhappiness come from the environment she has provided, for she has had you two-score, and I less than one. Do you call the atmosphere she provided for you, George A. and Bennett a fine example of anything? Look at George A. and look at Bennett. Then look at yourself and maybe you will wake up and "smell the roses."

147

Now blame for George A.'s illness seems indeterminate and fruitless. At the time it was an all-consuming, full-time occupation we all engaged in. Blame was the currency we traded. The Roses blamed the Paynes, the Paynes the Roses, Margaret blamed Bill and Bill blamed Margaret. And I was Blamer-in-Chief and first blamer among equals. I blamed Bill not only for his dereliction, but in the way Ahab blames the whale, for the cruelty and irrationality of Nature, for the existence of bipolar I disorder, for our mortal state and our powerlessness to change it. I blamed him because I got to keep my mind and personality and George A. woke up at Woodberry one morning with a future and by nightfall had come to in the black room where the spotlight hits you and you're in a play you don't know the name of or the character you're playing and the play's your life and the character is your identity, and maybe George A. thought as I thought that we all have a God-given right to play it for whatever time we have here, but it turns out some do, some don't, some get to keep it, from others it is taken, and what's the reason? I don't know, go ask your father. If he doesn't know, maybe your mom does.

At twenty, still, I never look at Margaret. Why not?

Margaret's here and Bill's gone. That's the simplest explanation. Margaret stayed and bought our Spiral notebooks, cooked our meals and did our laundry, rinsing the skid marks from our underwear. It's Margaret who took us to the hospital when we broke our bones and comforted us when our girlfriends left us and we lost our ball games, who held our shoulders when we came home drunk for the first time and threw up in the toilet. It's Margaret who's here today at Mandala, when the sad battered dinghy makes landfall and we muster up and find out one of us is missing. And though in Boston she said, *I have to go,* and I said, *I know, go, Mama,* in accordance with an old agreement, and though I later come to believe that that abandonment reprised a hundred or a hundred thousand others forever lost to memory, still it's Margaret who takes on George A.'s illness, the punishing campaign that's starting here today and will last twenty-five long years and the rest of his short lifetime. Margaret alone—not me, I let go his hand like Bill did—tells George A., *Hold on to me, baby, I'm here, I've got you,* and keeps her promise.

Yet the one certainty about bipolar disorder is the genetic tie-in, and on that Margaret and the Roses have to take the main hit. They make a ghastly cohort. There's Genevieve, Margaret's smart, beautiful big sister, who after St. Mary's and UNC married into an old family in Bath, the cradle of precolonial North Carolina society, and had two sons, and went crazy one afternoon and set herself on fire on the Duke psych ward and survived her immolation . . . And Cousin Ruth in Richmond, Margaret and Genevieve's first cousin, who came back from the hospital, wrote thank-you notes on her good stationery to the good friends who brought her family casseroles while she was off around the bend, and then drove downtown, parked across from the police station and blew her brains out. And after Ruth, Ruth's mother, Millicent, an older sister of the first George A., a gray-haired matriarch who, from small-town

Henderson, married into the Richmond tobacco aristocracy and killed herself the same way Ruth did. And after Ruth and Millicent, Ruth's brother, Tom. And before Ruth and Millicent and Tom, years before in Henderson, Millie's sister, Jane, the mother of twin sons, the first to make her quietus with a bullet.

Something dark among the Roses, and maybe that was why the first George A., the baby of the clan, once or twice a year disappeared like Bête to the enchanted wing and roared and drank apocalyptically for five or six days running, and why Margaret, when the mood came over her, watched *Beauty and the Beast* on tape weeping into Kleenex. Among George A. Rose's siblings, two of six, an attrition rate higher than American forces took on Omaha Beach; among his sister's children, two of three. And now his namesake, George A. Payne, my brother, upstairs in the psych ward ... But perhaps the cup will pass. Perhaps it's just a bad reaction to some funky weed.

Margaret's watched all this since youth, when she came home in her bobby socks and saw the Seagram's open on the sideboard in the midst of privilege and plenty, and was so desperate to escape that she married a boy as unlike George A. Rose as possible, one from a teetotaling family who turned into a drinker, too, and couldn't hold his liquor either, and when their marriage blew to pieces, she plucked us by our roots and moved us to the Sans Souci Apartments, a place where we knew no one and no one knew us, and now here I am in the topless Sprite at nightfall on Fair Weather Drive in Clemmons, turning in to the driveway of a brick Georgian that resembles Margaret's parents' house on Woodland, a spec house version set down in an exurb twelve miles west of Winston in what wasn't long ago a pasture. And it's as if after all her wanderings Margaret has decided that maybe leaving Woodland wasn't such a good idea in the first place and is now busy trying to re-create the place she fled from in the place she fled to to escape it. That's why "home" is something I can't give her. Once I believed in it the way I believed in the forgiveness of sins and the resurrection of the body. Now "home" stands for everything I'm determined to escape from. Our family is the car wreck in my dream, and if I'm the victim in the backseat, so is George A., so is Bennett, so are Bill and Margaret and Letty and Bill Sr., and George A. and Mary Rose, everybody's sick and dying, and we have to winch it up and look at it; if we don't, if we keep doing what got us here in the first place and sinking the evidence at the bottom of the slough and agreeing never to look at it or tell the truth or hold anyone responsible or do a single thing to change it, then we're the murderers, aren't we?

We have to leave and find a different way. This is my message to George A. and to myself at twenty. What expertise do I bring to the task? None whatever. Still, I'm going, and if I can, I mean to take him with me. How? The same way Jung did.

> . . . from the beginning there was no doubt that I must find the meaning of what I was experiencing in these fantasies.

That's why, after George A.'s release from Mandala, you can find us out here every weekend, walking down the drive at Jack and Margaret's past the lions at the entry, turning on Fair Weather Drive and heading down the little country lane, across the bridge, up toward the Jewish Home that sits there in the meadow. Sometimes we go the other way toward Tanglewood, and occasionally as far afield as Hanes Park in Winston where the power-walking moms—the pretty former debs who still push back their blunt-cut hair with velvet hairbands the way they did as schoolgirls and later on in their sororities—regard us doubtfully, steering a wide berth around us. There I am, unshaved, in faded Levi's and a green flannel shirt from L.L. Bean, my cool-weather uniform. I have my hair pulled back in the disordered ponytail and my eyes are a bit too bright and when I talk I use my hands too liberally for emphasis. George A.—who went away in September wearing khakis, a pressed blue oxford and spit-shined loafers —now has on faded painter's pants and a plaid flannel and over that a lumberjack's black-and-red wool jacket. From the garbage truck last summer, he's brought out his brogans and the Red Man hat with sweat stains. He's six-foot-seven, me a little under six-foot-four, talking loudly in the middle of the footpath, having stopped to pursue some point more singly. He's frowning at his feet, deciding, shaking his head no, or nodding yes, and if you saw us, you might think we're arguing, but we aren't, not really.

–Why Bill, George A.? In the parking lot at Woodberry, why do you think you saw Dad?

–As opposed to polka-dotted snakes or leprechauns?

—Okay, instead of those.

—I don't know, DP. You have a theory?

—Well, were you hoping he was there, or afraid he was?

—I wanted him to see me play. I can't say I was keen for him to see me the way I was at the hotel.

—What strikes me? The person you most wanted to be there, whose approval mattered more than anyone's, whose disapproval you most feared, wasn't there, but you believed he was. You not only believed it, you hallucinated his presence.

—Okay . . . And?

—What if that's what your unconscious is telling you? You're seeing Dad as there when he really isn't, holding an absent thing as present, an illusion as a real thing. Maybe it's oversimplifying, but to me your hallucination says, *He isn't there. This man's a figment.* What if the father you wanted and I wanted we just didn't get and we have to accept it?

George A.'s frowning at his feet, hands shoved in pockets, and beneath his eyes are smudges like the eye-black he wore on Friday nights to absorb the stadium glare at Woodberry.

— I don't know, DP.

—If you don't, I don't either. Ready to head back?

—No, let's keep going.

—Come on then.

So we go, the two of us, out there on that little country lane in Clemmons, and at Tanglewood and in Hanes Park as autumn deepens toward Thanksgiving and Thanksgiving toward Christmas; the sky has turned the blue of Concord grapes, a few snowflakes are falling.

In *Doctor Zhivago* there's a scene at the beginning when you see the funeral procession, tiny, in the vast spaces of the Russian steppe. On the bier lies eight-year-old Yuri's mother, and preceding her the priests in robes with crucifixes, waving incense, ringing bells, chanting, offering up their prayers, while behind loom the snowcapped Urals, unmoved, majestic in the distance.

That's how I see us, me leading, waving Jung, my crucifix, George A. following, small against the backdrop of bipolar I disorder, Nature, life, the universe, which shows so little fairness in the distribution of reward and punishment and hurts some so much more than others, but hurts us all in some way and makes us angry, sad and weary, and sometimes surprised and overjoyed by evidence of an intelligence beyond our own that's guiding us along our way, requiring consciousness of us and rewarding perseverance with happiness and malingering with suffering, and sometimes rendering the jewel into mud, taking consciousness away from those no less deserving than ourselves, those like Hölderlin and Nietzsche and George A. Payne, my brother.

Was George A. already falling when he called me at my dorm at Avery, had he looked down and seen the whitecaps on the ocean far below him, the way Bill fell in Boston and kept falling through Atlanta, where he had no job, no money, no one to lean on and a *lis pendens* on his property, down and down until he landed in those washouts in the Shenandoah, up there where his father and his father's people came from, the same place where George A. and I ended on November 8, 2000, at the first exit outside Lexington, when I look down at my feet and see by magic black and terrible the Zip disk lying chipped and spattered in the gravel with George A.'s blood upon it, and I gaze up at the sky and say, Please, God, don't make me carry this, don't make me be responsible, let my brother be alive, I require it of You, I compel You because if he isn't and I'm responsible then the universe is intolerable and I return my ticket. Yet the sky was empty and returned no answer and here I am still holding and George A.'s gone and I still miss him, as I sit wondering Who I Am and Who We Were and how different we were from other families and their stories—outside the bell curve, out of hailing distance altogether, or only as fingerprints and snowflakes, each unique but from the middle distance more or less the same as every other?

6

BREAK. THE SEMESTER'S OVER. I'M packing up my
things at Avery when George A. calls to tell me
Bill's put out the Christmas summons.

–I'm going down to Henderson tomorrow, he says.

–I didn't get a phone call.

–Dad wants you there, too.

–You're sure of that?

–He wants us all to come so we can get our presents.

–He couldn't bring them to us? Put them in the mail?

–He wants us to see Granddad and Letty.

I'm silent.

–They couldn't make it to the hospital and you're going
down like normal?

–It's Christmas, David. Can we just keep it simple?

–I guess if it doesn't bother you, it shouldn't bother me.
It does, though.

–Are you coming?

–No.

–Then I'll see you at home tomorrow night.

–I'll see you in Clemmons.

Given a choice between Bill and me, I suppose I should have known that George A. was always going to choose a father. Perhaps I'm less surprised than disappointed, because I might have liked to have George A. beside me in the insurrection.

Here I am then, the next evening, on Fair Weather, turning up the driveway past the lions, which are wearing garlands for the season. Here's Jack Furst, my stepfather, polishing a bit of brightwork on the quarter panel of his Rolls, a Silver Shadow, which sits in this neighborhood of upscale spec homes like a Siberian tiger at the dog pound.

–Pool tonight? he asks.

–Wouldn't miss it. I'm short on cash, though, so I won't be going easy on you.

–Forewarned.

Jack grins, and we shake with a heartiness that borders on aggression.

On my way through the garage, I hear Margaret in the kitchen.

–Separate the yolks and whites and put them in two different bowls . . .

I stand observing from the doorway as she instructs Jack's sons, Jack Jr.—aka Little Jack, who's twenty-two, two years my senior—and Alvin, George A.'s age, reading them the eggnog recipe from the soiled and faded cookbook of the Churchwomen of Holy Innocents Episcopal in Henderson. For Christmas, Margaret's wearing a red silk blouse open at

the throat to show her pearls and a forest-green apron featuring appliquéd reindeer rising skyward at forty-five
degrees, having trouble getting Santa airborne. With her hair
curled and her jewels and her mother's sterling punch bowl
on the table in the nook where all the silver and china are
laid out—the same silver and china that sat on this same
table once upon a time on Woodland Road beside a salt-
cured country ham like this one—Margaret reminds me of
a younger Mary Rose, perhaps the first time I've noted the
resemblance.

–Little Jack, she says, stir half the sugar with those yolks.
Alvin, beat the whites and when they're stiff, we'll fold in
the remaining sugar.

Mary, too—"Nanny," as we knew her—required that
things be done just so, the eggnog mixed according to the
old recipe, the mantels draped with evergreen and new
candles placed in all the girandoles and sconces, the wicks
prelit and snuffed . . . because they must be blackened, ever
so faintly marred or soiled; not to mar or soil them is an
error no knowledgeable hostess would commit or fail to
note the commission of in others. And is it because pristine
wicks might invite the retribution of jealous gods, who hold
perfection as their purview? Perhaps it's perfume from a
dress that makes me so digress, but it's unsettling to observe
Margaret, my mother—ours—instructing two new sons in
the *qigong* of a religion that failed the first time, as though
with better luck we'll miss the iceberg and the hull will
hold back the ocean water this time.

–Why not mix the eggs and sugar all at once and save six steps?

Margaret turns, eyes widened at my heresy.

–You! Come here and kiss your mama! And don't bother trying to exasperate me. You know as well as I do, if you don't beat the whites, the eggnog won't be fluffy.

–And if the eggnog isn't fluffy?

–The Earth goes off its axis!

This is Little Jack, displaying his advancing mastery.

–Smart-ass! Margaret says, delighted. Smart-ass and Smart-ass Jr.!

–I think I have seniority, I say, extending an open palm to Jack, who lifts me off the floor instead with a hug that's somewhere between a chiropractic manipulation and a wrestling takedown. Built like a baseball power hitter, he has a brush of surfer-blond hair and thick-lensed glasses that make his blue eyes googly behind them.

–Hey, Alvin, I say, Merry Christmas, what's the skinny?

At the counter with the mixer, Alvin turns and smiles at me with narrowed eyes in which seasonal good cheer floats like an oil slick over oceans of bad knowledge. Unlike Jack Jr. and his other siblings, who went to California with their mom, Alvin got triaged off to relatives in rural Alabama and came back with a rural Alabama accent and has small grayish teeth that resemble the flawed pearls called *baroccos,* as though his diet there lacked some essential nutrient. Alvin has sideburns like a pair of putty knives and a '50s-style pompadour like Jerry Lee Lewis's, and at the moment he's

159

wearing a purple-and-pumpkin-striped rugby jersey I recognize as George A.'s.

I met him, met all the Fursts, three years ago, the summer following my junior year at Exeter. Margaret married Jack that spring and didn't fly me to the wedding. Straight from Boston then, I arrived at Four Roses and found a new blond family installed there. There was Jack Jr. and little Dickie, six then, Bennett's age, and Imogen, eighteen, a year my senior, a California girl with a breezy California confidence and manner. Im had waist-length hair and the sort of rack that gives girls dark celebrity in high school and leads to back problems and reduction surgeries later. Fifteen minutes after I met them, we were around the kitchen island at Four Roses, Big Jack massaging the fillet mignons with olive oil and garlic as I sliced lemons for gin and tonics. Sitting on the kitchen counter kicking one leg out and letting it fall back against the cabinets, Im was barefoot in jeans with white tears at the knees and a T so tight and white that you could see the pink gleam of skin beneath if you happened to be looking, and I guess I was, though she was, in fact, my stepsister, and had been at that point for close to sixteen minutes. And as we talked and laughed too loudly to mask the strangeness of the situation, a car pulled up and a door slammed in the driveway, and in came Alvin, our new brother, with a grocery bag from which he removed three Saran-wrapped trays with three large Idahos in each one.

—There are ten of us, said Jack with unsurprised displeasure.

—Oh, dear, I'm sorry, Alvin. I must have told you wrong, said Margaret.

—No, ma'am, ten is what you said, said Alvin. Only they was in packs of three, and I didn't want to spend the extra. Me, I don't really need a tater.

The silence in the kitchen was brief but fell impartially over me, George A. and Alvin's California siblings. His hands pink from the meat, Jack stood there looking pained, his face the same pink as his hands, a big gold Rolex on one wrist and on his other hand a signet the size of a California walnut.

—You did exactly right, said Margaret, whom you could always count on in such situations. Exactly right. That's perfect, Alvin, thank you.

I thought all he needed was a good home and someone to treat him decently, she would say later when it came out that all that summer, Alvin had been upstairs at Four Roses showing the little boys what someone taught him down in Alabama, or wherever Alvin learned it, and Dickie, whom I remember as a pretty little boy whose green eyes had something a bit too knowing in them, will end up a hard-faced man with a '50s-style pompadour and teeth like *baroccos* on a State Department of Corrections website, doing thirty-six years for serial child molesting.

By Labor Day that summer, Alvin had cleared out Jack and Margaret's stereo equipment, hawked the televisions and Margaret's jewelry. Jack called the police himself and vigorously supported the prosecution. Alvin's first stretch was in county lockup. His next, if memory serves, was in a pen near

Gatesville, one I often passed driving to the beach and would have passed that first afternoon on my way from Raleigh-Durham, a flat yard on the edge of the swamp with a few rotting picnic tables surrounded by Hurricane fences topped with concertina. Down there, with a can of Barbasol and a straight razor, Alvin learned to shave balloons—the trick, he told me, is not to pop them—being prepped by the NC DoC to play a constructive role in society in the future, though he never played it or got much future either. Three or four years from now, in his early twenties, Alvin will steal a car and take a joyride to Virginia, up to Kings Dominion, and, on a residential street outside the park, put a bullet in his head and roll into a yard and overturn a birdbath. And if I'm not mistaken, this Christmas Alvin has just come back from Gatesville. Jack would have driven down to pick him up this morning or earlier this week—I don't know for certain, but I doubt he took the Rolls-Royce—and in any case, that's my guess as to why Alvin's wearing George A.'s jersey.

I wonder what made Alvin what he was, and if the answer has anything to do with that first night at Four Roses, when he, who must have been so hungry, on readmittance into his family denied himself a potato as a way to demonstrate his good intentions.

—Are these stiff enough? Alvin tilts the mixer bowl toward Margaret.

—Not quite.

—Light or dark?

And here in the doorway at Fair Weather is Imogen, my sister not-so-sister, holding up two bottles of Bacardi, and the room's gone silent the way it did when Alvin brought the taters and my face, I expect, is as pink as Jack's was.

–A pertinent question! say I, the English major.

–Light! says Margaret. Always light for eggnog.

–There I guess you have it, I say to Imogen.

–There I guess you do, says Imogen to David.

–Where's George A., by the way? I ask, since it seems to me a segue is in order.

–Cleaning his new shotgun, says Jack Jr.

–What new shotgun would that be?

–The one your dad gave him for Christmas. He was on the back porch when I saw him.

I blink at him and turn to Margaret.

–No kidding? Dad gave him a firearm for Christmas? Brilliant! ·

–Sweetie, may I speak with you a minute?

She pushes open the swinging door, and I precede her into the dining room, where the mirrors hang on facing walls and the portraits of the Manns preside once more over the Charleston sideboard. For the season, they've been swagged with garland, which is also woven in a figure eight around the sconces on the table that have new candles, tall and straight and blackened by prescription. This table— Hepplewhite with bellflower inlay, like the sideboard—is a copy of the one from Henderson, as is the portrait of Pa Rose that faces Martha Mann's. In the property distribution, the originals went to Genevieve, her sister. Margaret had them copied, the table by Mr. Gainsborough of Durham, the painting by some reputable hack in New York or Richmond.

—A shotgun? I say. Six weeks after his release from Mandala?

—I wish I could control your father's actions, but I can't. David, sit down. There's something else I have to tell you.

—What?

—Just sit down, all right?

—All right—I pull out a chair—I'm sitting. What?

—David, the gun Bill gave George A. is Daddy's.

I take a beat.

—Your daddy's? Pa's?

—That's right.

I blink at her.

—Not the A. H. Fox?

She holds my stare, confirming.

—I'm sorry, honey. I wish I could protect you and your brothers, but I can't. I don't know how to help you.

—Pa gave that to me.

—I understand that. I know he did.

—You remember, don't you?

1963 or -4 in Henderson, Christmas Eve, four little boys, myself, George A., and Louis and George Bird, our cousins . . . Pa lined us up and marched us out to the garage, to the hidden cabinet in the stairs, and let us pick by age, and I went first and chose the shotgun. Louis would have followed me—I don't recall his choice, was it the dagger with the *Totenkopf?*—but George A. picked the Luger, brought back after V-E Day from Berlin, maybe Paris. And when I ran inside, Margaret asked me, *Do you love it?* and I said, *It's the best thing anybody ever gave me,* and she knelt in her red dress and cupped my face and smiled the vital way she had once in the hospital, the day she brought the ice-cream soda, and said, *I'm so happy for you, so happy, David.*

–Mom?

–I remember, David.

–Where did Dad even get it? You didn't give it to him, did you?

–No, and I'm certain Mother didn't either. I expect Bill simply went in her garage and took it when he headed for Atlanta.

–So he's had it all this time.

–He must have. Honestly, I might have thought about the gun a time or two. It was so far down the list, though. And then this afternoon George A. walked in with it. Look what Daddy gave me! His face was lit up, David. It was like he was back, the old George A. I haven't seen since Mandala.

–But Dad stole it—you get that, don't you?

–Well, I can certainly see how you see it that way.

–What other way is there to see it? If he wanted to give George A. a gun, why couldn't he go out and buy one? Why mine?

Margaret's frown has begun to show frustration and impatience.

Alvin knocks and pokes his head in.

–Sorry. These whites are getting pretty hard, Margaret. I think it's time to add the sugar.

–I'll come look. I'm sorry, David. Give me just a minute . . .

As the kitchen door swings open, light flares across Pa's portrait. In a tuxedo and black tie, he's younger and more formal than I knew him, but his expression is the same—the painter got that. I remember him in old stone khakis with the bottoms rolled and slip-on boat shoes and a white short-sleeved shirt splayed open at the collar and a beat-up Panama hat with fishhooks in the hatband. We seined for minnows in the morning and launched from the public ramp at Oregon Inlet and cast anchor and tied on our rigs and baited them and let the sinkers take them to the bottom. I sat on the bow thwart gazing aft and he sat on the stern thwart gazing forward and he'd watch my rod tip and my float and nod if they needed my attention. We sat there all day in the lee of unnamed dredge-spoil islands in the Albemarle and didn't say much. Pa was not a talker. From time to time I'd look up and find him studying me with gray, sober eyes that had his wide experience of life in them, his pain and disappointment, his sisters' suicides, the guilt and sadness his parents must have carried, and the effect of the Depression on his family and the year he went away to Chapel Hill and pledged DKE as George A. will and had to come home and never got to finish, and whatever it was that made him shut himself away like Bête in the enchanted wing and drink for five or six days running. And I remember Genevieve, my aunt, telling the story of dinner parties on Woodland in her childhood when Pa got drunk and lay faceup in the foyer so the guests had to step over him to make it outside to their cars in the driveway. Genevieve, who deliberately set herself on fire in the psych ward, was

droll in her delivery as she smoked and drank her bourbon—
she made the story a performance like her mother, Sherry
Mary, would have—but in Genevieve's eyes I could still see
tongues of black flame licking as she told it. And Margaret,
too, remembered coming home in her saddle shoes and
bobby socks to the Seagram's open on the sideboard and as
a grown woman watched *Beauty and the Beast* on tape
weeping into Kleenex. So Pa had darkness in him. He
wounded Genevieve and Margaret as my parents wounded
me, George A. and Bennett, as I will wound my children.
But on those summer mornings in the Sound I knew that
of all the places he might be and all the people he might
be with, he chose me and that place, and that's the one time
in my childhood when I felt loved without condition or
ambivalence.

The door swings and he emerges from the shadows,
regarding me across the years with that expression I
remember.

–Listen, David . . . Margaret's back beside me. I can't speak
for Bill, but I imagine he was thinking he and George A.
have been hunting several times now, almost every year, it's
become a thing between them. You've never gone or shown
much interest—any interest really, have you? Now you've
stopped eating meat. I imagine your father assumed you
wouldn't want the shotgun. Do you?

Do you want it? When she says this, I feel the way I did
the afternoon Bill called me upstairs to read me "Prufrock,"
as though I'm stepping into ambush. I sense the trip wire,
only I can't see it. Because the answer should be, *No, I don't,*

let George A. have the shotgun if it makes him happy. What's the shotgun but an opportunity to shed another material attachment to a past I've left and don't believe in while being generous to my sick brother? But the answer isn't *No,* it's *Yes, I want it,* only if I say it, then I'm the one extinguishing the light in George A.'s eyes. If I say no, though, if I let George A. have the shotgun . . . what then? Something just as bad or worse, only I can't parse it. My head is swimming, I feel alarmed and curiously sleepy, as if I don't know where I am or really even who I am and the sensation is familiar, I've been here many times before between the mirrors, and the look in Margaret's eyes, the look of grievance.

Under the impasse and the turmoil, a younger voice I can no longer hear is crying out inside me. *Don't let him do this to me. Don't let Daddy take the shotgun from me, Mama. Pa gave it to me, not to George A., not to you or Genevieve or Nanny, Bill stole it, it's the theft, you see, I can't abide it. Don't pretend that it's okay or tell me I'll understand it when I'm older. Bill never apologized for Boston. He invited me to Mattamuskeet and when I refused he took George A., and now, because I wouldn't go to Henderson, he's giving my one treasure to my brother, all I have left from our first world before it sank beneath the ocean. And his gift to George A. is a message to me also,* Fuck you, David, *because I never forgave him because he never admitted that he hurt me, and if you let this happen you're complicit and forcing me to choose between extinguishing George A.'s happiness or consenting to my own violation.*

At twenty, I can't parse what's happening, and Margaret doesn't understand it either, so I'm not going to ask her for her help and she's not going to offer. Everything that matters now is unfolding in the underwater portion of the iceberg, below awareness, while on the surface Margaret sits regarding me with a concerned, bemused expression, as if to say, *Your brother hunts, you don't, why not let George A. have the shotgun,* as if to say, *Why are you so angry, David, why can't you let bygones be bygones the way in this world we all have to, darling?*

And the portraits of the Manns look down, and Pa's copied portrait, as we sit at the table she had copied because she couldn't bear to yield it to her sister.

—I have to go, says Margaret. Go see him, go see George A., you two work it out like brothers. I know you'll do the right thing. I swear, your father. I wish I could protect you.

I know, go, Mama . . .

Our old agreement, iteration after iteration, back into the past and forward to the future.

Margaret leaves me staring at the candles in the sconces, wondering why tall, new things must be touched with ruin before they ever hold a light and throw it.

And now I'm pushing through the swinging door, sleepwalking down the hallway. In the den, there's Christmas music playing, "Up on the Housetop" by the Jackson 5. I'm walking toward the music, and here's the tree, decorated with white lights only and no tinsel, and all the generations of ornaments—Margaret's ornaments, and her share of Nanny's, and Nanny's share of her mother's, another Margaret—and the bay window is black and the tree lights twinkle there like stars in deep space, like the Mystic Bridge reflected in the hotel windows once upon a time in Boston.

Through their reflection, through my own, I see George A. on the patio outside, at the glass-topped table, under the floods, poring over his work like a jeweler with his loupe. A cigarette smokes unattended in the ashtray at his elbow. On the table lies the gun with its twinned barrels of brownish-blue Krupp steel. As I watch, he withdraws the cleaning rod from one of them, removes the brass-bristled brush, screws on the mop and moistens it with solvent, Hoppe's 9. Pinching his cigarette between thumb and index finger, he takes a wincing puff and shoves the rod back in the bore.

He has on his black-and-red-checked overshirt and the Red Man hat with sweat stains, and by now he's put back twenty of the fifty pounds he lost and has begun to grow a beard, his first. Last weekend or the one before, when Margaret looked at him across the room, I saw her expression darken and then brighten as she said, *I wish you wouldn't hide that handsome face!* At this, George A. grinned a grin of happy illegality, for me his signature expression, like a three-year-old caught out at some misbehavior he knows his mother finds more charming than compliance. What I most notice in this moment, though, is the extremity of George A.'s posture. He's hunched so low over the table he's almost lying on it, and his feet—he's wearing brogans and is up on tiptoe, his heels against the chair's metal uprights. He's like a drawn bow from which the arrow is about to fly, and perhaps it's the cold that makes him hold himself in this tense pose, but I fear it isn't.

–Hey, man.

He looks up.

–Ho ho ho.

–Ho ho ho yourself. What are you doing out here in the cold?

–Marge doesn't want me stinking up the place.

–So, what, she has you camping out out here now?

He reaches for his cigarette.

–She lets me in for meals and after dark.

I drop my eyes toward the gun and bring them back to his.

–Remember this? he asks in a way that strikes me as nervous and preemptive.

–I do, actually.

–Daddy gave it to me for Christmas.

–Dad did.

–He sent you something, too.

I'm not much interested in what Bill sent me.

–Can I see?

When I reach toward the Fox, George A.'s face clouds and he grips the gun more tightly for an instant before pushing it reluctantly in my direction.

–Don't get your fingerprints on it, okay?

–I just cleaned it, he adds in answer to the look I give him.

The gun is heavy, heavier than I remember. The trigger guard and plate are sterling, as elaborately engraved as a scepter with vines and leaves I think must be acanthus. The central scene depicts flying doves, a pair against a trinity of mountains like the Urals in the background. It was the best thing, I admit it. I was selfish when I chose it; I didn't give a moment's thought to George A.'s or my cousins' feelings, and what but accident of birth entitled me to take the best thing?

Now George A. hands me a grocery bag, the top edge soft as chamois from refolding.

—What's this?

—Open it.

Inside is a faux-leather case. When I unzip it, black against the ivory fleece interior, the Luger.

The thin gleam of the wire, the click . . .

—Is this . . .?

—Daddy said to wish you Merry Christmas.

On George A.'s face for just an instant, there then gone, the grin, exultant, *This one's for you, DP.* It's like his expression in the photograph the day he beat me in the race to Avalon, like that, only different.

I feel queasy. My heart is pounding.

—You see what he's done, don't you?

—What?

—He's reversed us, George A. He's rewarding you for loyalty, for going down there, and fucking me because I didn't.

—I don't know, DP. I don't really see that.

—Come on, George A. Those guns were Pa's. They were never Dad's to start with.

—Daddy said Pa gave them to him.

—Bullshit. He stole them. He went to Woodland Road and went in the garage and took them.

—How do you know that?

—There's no other way it could have happened.

George A.'s face has fallen now. His brows are drawn in worry, opposition. He reaches for his Winstons.

–Dad's a lot of things, David, but he's not a thief.

–He stole Nanny's timber.

–So he's a liar, too?

–You're telling me you don't remember? Come on, George A., it was Christmas Eve, Louis and George were there. Pa marched us out to the garage and opened up the cabinet. I chose the shotgun, you chose the Luger.

George A. shakes his head—answering? or signaling his weary disapproval? I don't know. He lights a cigarette with trembling hands, and his expression's tragic.

It's Christmas, Dad gave me something special, and you have to ruin it, to turn it into yet another steaming shitpile—why do you always do this?

And me to him, *Don't do it, George A. Don't take the gun and fuck me. It's still right between us—that's why I've come home every weekend and walked these country lanes and why I ran those miles with you last summer—but if you take the gun it won't be. This is why we have to leave here.*

But George A. isn't coming. Bill's offered him the scepter and George A.'s going to take it. Though out here in the future I might wish to alter it with insight, it falls out once again in memory the way it did in real life.

Did George A. remember that old Christmas Eve and Pa's assignment? I never got an answer. It's hard to imagine that he didn't. If he did, perhaps his memory was different, of going second and wondering why I got the scepter, and maybe George A. felt as aggrieved then as I do in the present. One lifted up and one cast down—that's the way the world is—is that the deeper meaning of the Cain and Abel story? I didn't like and still don't like the Lord's position. If Cain was a tiller of the field and gave of the first fruits, why was his sacrifice not pleasing? He gave of his nature just like Abel, but the Lord approved of Abel and not Cain, and Cain was wroth and slew his brother. I didn't like that world and wanted to voyage to another and take George A. with me. Where is that world, though? Certainly not here on the cold back porch at Christmas, as George A. smokes and stares away across the road toward the tree line, where weedy fields drop down to 40 in the distance.

—So, what, you're telling me you want it? George A. asks me, as Margaret had.

I have a second chance, and still can't say it. Cannot. Am not going to.

So we sit separate together as the headlights of the eastbound traffic wink through the black trees. I recall a smell now, something inorganic. Gun oil. Hoppe's 9. And the sound of traffic. You always heard it from that house the way we heard the ocean at Four Roses—like surf that never ebbed but just came on and on, unceasing, toward the future.

7

HEY, BOYS ...
And here, in the nick of time, is Imogen our
sister not-so-sister to break the impasse.
—What's up with you two? Am I interrupting?
—Interrupt us.
—Please.
—Take my wife.

Im tilts her head and grins at us with Jack's grin, one eye squinted.

—I was going to offer you a bit of this—a joint appears—
but it looks like I'm too late.
—It's never too late!
—Until it is, says George A.
—Until it is, I agree, continuing our routine.

Im supplies the relief, we supply—such as it is—the comedy. Like the Marx Brothers before us, like Laurel and Hardy, Abbott and Costello, Cheech and Chong—like them, only not so funny.

George A. takes the joint, cups it, fires up. His big hand now is steady as a rock. He rears away and flicks the lighter shut decisively. From the *Titanic* lifeboats and Gatsby shivering at the grotesqueness of roses, he's gone to the Marlboro Man in ten or fifteen seconds.

–Should you be doing that? I ask him mildly.

–Probably not, he answers on the inhale, through clinched teeth, and in his black eyes there's a trace of defiance, even glee.

A hand in her back pocket, Im gives us that head-tilted grin again, the one she gave me that first night at Four Roses when Alvin offered to forgo the tater, a look of skeptical amusement like she was up for trouble and curious if I had any on the docket.

After several gin and tonics, wine at dinner and a joint or two of California sensimilla, which she smuggled on the plane ride in her undies, so she told me, she and I decided to go swimming and since we didn't have our suits we what-the-fucked it and hauled it up the dune and down the back side to the lightless beach, where we went skinny-dipping. Im, more comfortable in her skin than I was, stood up in the wash and slicked her hair back, giving me a frontal shot more stoning than the sensi, and I, trotting out my not-so-true and still not even very tried seduction playbook, swirled my hands in the chilly ocean and told her that phytoplankton caused the bioluminescence we were seeing and that the particular phytoplankton in this case were those called *Noctiluca*—"Night-lights, from the Latin." And Im, appearing to be interested or just pretending like so many summer girls to follow, listened to my shy and nerdy and not entirely unstrategic explanation and I cupped my hand and made a fist and let the water drizzle down the front of her no longer masked by sheer white cotton, let the water and the moon-light and my eyes run all over Imogen. And when the waves broke, or when they break now in my memory, they lit up like George A.'s teeth in that grin of happy illegality, which shows up on my face, too, and Bill's, from whom we got it. And before long Im and I were downstairs in the lair in my twin bed going at it.

That first wild night at Four Roses started off the sum-mer and the summer was a wild one, and Im and I were wild things. We shattered the commandments in the lair and upstairs in her bedroom and in the outdoor shower and on the island in the kitchen and in the bathrooms and in Jack and Margaret's bed while they were dancing at the Sea Ranch and pretty much on every horizontal surface at Four Roses and not just the horizontal ones.

And one day two or three weeks later, I came back from a morning run and found Jack Jr. twirling *nunchucks* in the driveway in his white *gi* and black belt and throwing *shuriken*—he called them "ninja death stars"—*zip, thwack, zip, thwack,* splintering the garage wall. With a big grin that struck me as a little crazy, his blue eyes magnified and goo-gly behind those lenses, Little Jack said, I like you, but I really ought to kick your ass.

—Why's that?

—Don't kid a kidder.

—Look, she's not my sister, I said, I'm not her brother. Frankly, I don't see the big deal.

—The big deal, he said, is my dad's married to your mom, your mom's married to my dad, that makes us family.

–I like you, too, man, I replied, but you're not my family, your father's not my father, my mother's not your mother, and as to Imogen and me, as far as I'm concerned, I might as well have met her in a bar or at the grocery.

–It's different, said Jack Jr.

– I don't see it.

–I really ought to kick your ass.

–Well, if your mind's made up, I don't guess I'm going to stop you.

Little Jack stood there frowning. You could tell he really wasn't sure what the right thing was under the circumstances. This one wasn't in the old instruction manual.

He didn't kick my ass, though. Instead, he outed us to Jack and Margaret and Jack picked up the phone and called the airline and bought Imogen a one-way ticket back to her mother Molly's place in California. Im and I, however, weren't having it, we decided it was bullshit, fucking bullshit, not to put too fine a point on it. So we packed a bag and round about midnight jumped out the second-story window at Four Roses, and Imogen turned her ankle in the sand and leaned on me and limped a little down the driveway and we thumbed a ride with a guy in an old Lincoln convertible heading up to Norfolk with a pint between his legs and he offered us a sip and we declined politely. And somewhere up toward Great Bridge I noticed the speedometer inching toward ninety and then past it and I said *We'd like to get out here* and he ignored me and then I shouted in his face and he stopped and glared and scratched off and we stood there in the Dismal Swamp and roosters crowed in the distance as day broke and we went on from there, north to New York City.

I called Eric from a pay phone on the Jersey Turnpike and told him what was happening and he met us in Washington Square Park, beneath the arch, and tried to sneak us into his parents' place only his mom was wise to us within the first five minutes. She called Margaret, who asked us to come home and was ready to forgive the whole thing, but we said No, or I did, I guess I didn't want to go back, I guess I didn't want to be forgiven, Im and I were off on an adventure.

After we wore out our welcome with Eric's family, we took off over the George Washington Bridge, hitching into New Jersey where we picked up 80 around Teaneck, starting west toward California. In Illinois, somewhere outside Chicago, we got picked up by two girls in their twenties, one driving, the other sitting close beside her. Catching our eyes in the rearview, the second angled down the mirror so we could see her diddling the driver, who had her skirt hiked up and wasn't wearing panties. The passenger put an elbow on the seat and turned and said to Imogen, You want a little bit of this? and when Im declined she asked if I did, and I said no thanks.

We stayed in Iowa with an old farmer and his wife, who made us sleep in separate bedrooms and cooked us breakfast and drove us to the border of Nebraska, and sometime later a crew of bikers stopped, and we rode behind them in a van driven by a gray-haired woman with eyes like the day after the apocalypse. At a truck stop near Cheyenne, she gave us a plastic baggie with a pound or two of change in it and said we might be better off not going any farther in their company. In Wyoming, we got picked up by a car full of hippie types and drove all night, till somewhere west of Laramie, out in the Red Desert, up there in the dunes and sagebrush, the driver had to stop and catch a nap. There were so many in the car that Im and I slept outside in the desert, near the car and under it, cozying to the muffler for its heat until it faded, and then out under a van Gogh sky full of van Gogh stars, without a blanket. I held Im in my arms for warmth and our teeth chattered and coyotes howled, and we could see them circling, their eyes in the moonlight in a stand of limber pines not sixty yards away from us. On through Utah and Nevada and finally into California, where Im called one of her girlfriends from the cheerleader squad at her old high school in Vallejo, who took us in for a few nights the way Eric and so many others had along the route, wanting to do something for us. We ended up at Im's mother Molly's place, and she and her new husband were decent to us and passed along a message from Jack and Margaret to say Uncle, they relented. Sick with worry, they asked us to come home and sent us a plane ticket without conditions. So we won, youth and freedom prevailed over elders and tradition, and we, as Robin Hood and Marian and Clyde and Bonnie, stuck it to the man, and if the man was our own family, where else does the notion come from. We were pretty pleased about it at the time, or I know I was, but it strikes me now that our victory, though we won it, was a bad one. Though I told Imogen I loved her and believed it, now it seems I barely knew her and she barely knew me and so it wasn't about love, love was just the sunlight on the surface, underneath we bonded in our anger at our parents and our decision to be outlaws. The truth is I don't know what Imogen was feeling but to Jack I think I was saying, *For my mom, your daughter,* and to Margaret, *Here's what I think of our new family, here's what I think of rebuilding the* Titanic *according to the original blueprints,* and whatever Pa and I had in that boat, the contract we agreed to, was gone now, and I decided maybe that, too, was bullshit, fucking bullshit, just a child's wishful thinking seen through rose-colored glasses, and like Bill, whom I took a blood oath never to be like, I sinned while feeling like a victim.

And the summer Im and I took our road trip I was seventeen, the same age Margaret was when she snuck through the back fence at St. Mary's and met Bill Payne in his dad's jalopy and got pregnant, and offered the chance to have it fixed in Philadelphia, declined it. Margaret didn't want it fixed, like Im and me she didn't want to come home either, didn't want to be forgiven and for things to return to normal. Instead, she took from Bill Payne what he didn't wish to give her, and Bill was wroth and repaid her and the Roses *pari passu,* flunking out of med school and extracting from them a job, a house, a maid, a car, a membership at the CC, a pew at Holy Innocents, and when that wasn't enough to assuage his fury, he gambled away our house and stole Mary Rose's timber, and when that wasn't enough he stole the shotgun from me, his first son, and gave it to George A., his second, who got sick and was thereby promoted into my position. And I wanted to take George A. with me out of bondage, but offered the scepter, George A. took it and he fucked me. And though he's young and sick and scared and shaky after his ordeal, I'm never going to quite forgive him and it's never going to be the same between us.

And now, on the cold back porch, Imogen delivers us the message.

—Your mama says it's time to eat.

And I say, *Yo* mama.

And George A. says, Yo *mama*.

—Did she tell you there'd be days like this?

—She mentioned it, he answers, but I guess I wasn't listening.

—Apparently the fuck not!

We're laughing, God, we're laughing.

—Heh heh heh, says George A. with his sly, sweet grin, and there he is, all there behind the eyes, that's him. We slap five, grateful to our sister not-so-sister Imogen and the Shirelles for the comic relief, grateful to flee the scene with things left unresolved, which is to say, to be resolved by time, neglect, avoidance, accident, and other half-assed methods.

George A. passes the weed to Imogen, who tokes and passes it to me.

—Merry Christmas. Don't say I never gave you anything.

I'd never say that, Imogen. Showing some discretion for a change, I merely think this and don't say it.

Im gets it anyway, at least I think so, because her eyes soften and she pats my head—with more condescension than affection, but affection's in there also—and then turns her back again and puts me in the rearview mirror.

  —I'll tell Margaret—*yo mama*—you're coming in.

As she makes her exit, George A. mugs at me. I punch him in the arm, not hard, not all that easy.

  —*What?* he protests, rubbing it. I didn't say a thing! Did I say anything?

And the shotgun? As far as I recall, we never speak of it again. It's too hot to handle, so we drop it and it clatters on the iceberg and starts melting its way in and downward, away from the sunlit surface, ever deeper toward the underwater portion, where it remains suspended, gone but not forgotten till years later, long after George A. is dead, when in that Hampton Inn at Pawleys I pour a drink and something in me whispers, *It's time to write about George A.,* and I go back and find it where I left it.

Margaret's Christmas Eve spread centers on a tenderloin of beef, a six- or eight-pound slab, served still twitching with horseradish sauce and twice-baked potatoes. We heap our plates with tennis-ball-sized mounds of thin-sliced, still-bleeding meat and gorge like happy wolves. Which is to say, the others do, and I did once upon a time, who have become the family vegetarian and sister-screwing holy man, if self-anointed. With the appearance of Margaret's bowl of special Christmas beets, however, I throw off my priestly collar and decorum. When George A. and I see it in the distance, we shudder with mock horror, hold our noses and wave it on dramatically, diva-ing it up, a pair of ungrateful shit-asses playing for the biggest rise that we can get from Margaret.

—What? You don't like my beets? I think my beets are wonderful! she says, looking for all the world as though we didn't do the same last Christmas and the one before that.

With wine and weed, the evening's speeding up and getting blurry at the edges. We head downstairs now, the boys, to the rumpus room for pool, as Margaret and Imogen— wanting nothing to do with the trash talk, the extravagant and pitiless revenges we wreak on one another—grab the Kleenex box and retire to the den, where *It's a Wonderful Life* is airing after a brief word from our sponsor.

Pool is what the Payne and Furst boys do in lieu of duels with pistols, in lieu of piking one another's heads on London Bridge, since we can't murder them and drink their blood— though we *like* them, you have to understand, George A. and I really, really like the Jacks, as I believe the Jacks like George A. and David.

—So how do we team up? Jack, *père*, asks, as he chalks his cue tip. George A. and me against the two of you?

—Hell, no, I say. The Paynes against the Fursts. If we're going to piss away another evening inching toward death, let's at least make it interesting.

I glance at George A., who signals his willingness to charge the ridge beside me.

—You sure? Big Jack asks happily.

—What's the matter, Jack-o? We'll go easy on you, won't we, George A.?

—Speak for yourself, my brother says.

Jack continues smiling, but a blue gas flame roars up behind his eyes.

—The last shall be first, and the Fursts shall be last, I say, crowing unwisely, as I'm prone to.

George A. extends a hand behind his back. I see his five and raise him, returning one up high, and on his way to the cue rack, George A. chicken-jerks his chin and walks like an Egyptian.

—So what's the bet?

Little Jack is ready with the gambit.

—If you and George A. lose, what say you eat that bowl of beets upstairs?

—Not the whole bowl? George A. says.

Jack Jr. merely grins.

—Cruel, I say. Cruel, but brilliant. And if you lose?

—I've got one, George A. says. You ride bikes, naked, to the Jewish Home and back.

—Excellent!

—Hey, there's ice on the road, Little Jack protests. It's twenty-five degrees out there.

—So, what, you worried your package is going to shrivel?

—How much smaller can it get?

I douse the perimeter with gas; George A. strikes the match and tosses it, setting off a mini-riot. We're howling now, he and I, doubled over, gasping and wiping tears of joy at our own jokes the way we're prone to. The SOBs—Sons of Bill—are on a tear, one against all comers, who were so lately one against the other. You'd almost think the shotgun never happened.

–Not naked. Jack Sr., the biggest Peter Pan among us, dons the black robes now, putting on the gravitas and playing *pater*.

–Meow, says George A.

–Here, kitty, kitty. Here, puss, puss, puss. In your undies then.

–Underwear, socks and shoes.

–Done!

Having made our bed, here we are not thirty minutes later, the SOBs, lying in it—sitting, rather, on the kitchen counter under close observation from our grinning colonial oppressors. Passing back and forth the bowl of beets, we're no longer cracking wise now as we eat in common from the serving spoon dripping vinegary blood or bloodied vinegar, a pair of red-toothed ghouls glumly feasting on moldering remains served à la carte out of the cemetery.

Next slide in the projector, please! This one, which I like better, features us outside in the frosty drive after a rematch and a victory, me toasty in my Air Force parka, George A. in his Michelin Man down jacket. We're climbing into Margaret's Toronado, a '71, electric blue with a white roof of pebbled vinyl, as the Jacks, both famously chicken-legged and heavy-chested—Senior in boxers, black calf-length socks and tasseled alligator loafers, Junior in tighty whities, tube socks and Adidas—set off past the lions at the entry. These, normally so stoic, have broken discipline and, unless memory deceives me, are now distinctly roaring, roaring laughter and pissing squid ink down the brick piers that they sit on. The Jacks wobble off on Bennett's and Dickie's banana-seated bikes, punching their shoulders with their knees with every revolution of the pedals and leaving black tracks in the new-fallen snow behind them. Blowing the horn and flashing the brights, George A. and I follow, making catcalls out the window as Billy Preston blares "Nothing From Nothing" on Margaret's smoking 8-track.

Home again, George A. and I form a gauntlet, jeering and applauding as the Jacks sprint, houseward, through it.

—Nice gams, lady!

—Assholes! Little Jack, karate guy, double-pumps the finger from fists of cold steel as he passes.

George A. and I are wiping tears, panting, huffing, doubled over the way we were last summer in the wash the day he beat me to the pier and I snapped him in the photo.

—Did I tell you Dad bought a bike? he says when he's recovered.

—No shit. What kind, a Western Flyer?

—A motorcycle.

—Bullshit! He didn't finally get the Harley?

Bill's been threatening intermittently for years.

—A Kawasaki 150.

This puts me into spasms.

–Did he join an MC? I ask. I can see it—six guys with ZZ Top beards and Bill bringing up the rear, riding sweep on his Vespa, shouting, *Prego! Mi scusi, signore e signori!*

George A. goes down on his knees and pounds the earth with flat hands.

–Remember the time he called to tell us he was going to Mexico?

–You mean South of the Border, don't you? I say.

–No, he was going to buy a hog, he said, and head down to this little town on the Pacific Coast where he could drink Bohemias and eat ceviche and live like a king on a buck or two a day.

–San Blas, wasn't it? I seem to recall the travel brochure said the bulldogs there have rubber teeth and the hens lay soft-boiled eggs.

George A.'s smile is happy now. He's on the up seat of the seesaw.

–You remember?

–I remember, I say.

–That was pretty funny.

–You were crying like a baby.

–No, I wasn't. Was I?

–Yeah, you were, buddy.

George A.'s expression is incredulous, unresentful, eleven years old.

–Well, it seems funny now.

–If you say so.

–I've got to take a leak. You coming in?

–Right behind you.

Through the kitchen and once more down the hallway, I can hear the Dimitri Tiomkin sound track swelling in the den, and the memory—the way George A.'s transformed it—is curious and troubling. Or is it me who misremembers?

I will kill you, motherfucker!

Not if I kill you first!

Me screaming. Bill screaming back from Underground Atlanta. Fetal on the floor, George A., who, six years later, laughs and shakes his head, remembering it fondly.

And is this how the hostages at the Kreditbanken in Norrmalmstorg in Stockholm ended up in court testifying on behalf of their oppressors? If you consent to your own violation and are of one heart and mind with your oppressors, you cast a magic spell that turns them into Friends, Protectors, Parents even as they press the muzzle to your temple or threaten to abandon you forever.

And is what George A. did with Bill what I'm doing here tonight, consenting to my dispossession by my family—to Bill's theft of the shotgun, and Margaret's complicity, and George A.'s acquisition of my dearest childhood treasure—in order to preserve the hologram of Family?

The night is speeding up and blurring. In the den, Margaret and Imogen are deep into the movie.

—Watch with us, says Margaret, patting the sofa cushion and lifting the throw to share it with me.

—Here, you'll need these ...

Imogen offers me the Kleenex.

—Good one, I say.

Continuing to stand, I eye the screen reluctantly, having never really liked the movie.

It's the moment on the bridge when Uncle Billy's lost the money and George has wrecked the car and could be facing prison, he who once upon a time planned to build things and explore—to see Italy, Greece, the Parthenon, the Coliseum. Only, his father dies, his family needs him, so George takes the shabby little office job he never really wanted, and when Harry's turn comes George takes Harry's turn as well so Harry can fulfill his dream and do research—he's such a genius at it—and become a hero pilot and save those soldiers on the transports. And George, see, George can't say *It's my turn, Harry,* can't say, *It's my turn and I want it,* his candle flame is snuffed so Harry's can burn brighter. George gives up every dream he's ever had for others—for his family, for his dad and Harry and Mary and the children, for the townsfolk and the nation—and now at the end of that long train of unselfishness and self-betrayal he's arrived on the snowy bridge at midnight, he's staring down at the black water and he jumps and what happens? Presto chango, God sends an angel down to pull him from the water, the sound track swells, the movie turns to magic, the spell is cast and everybody's reaching for the Kleenex, and there I am, tearing up like Imogen and Margaret—Goddamn it, Im, pass the fucking Kleenex—because I want to believe it, too, that George, in the hour of his lonely death, ends up surrounded by his loving family and neighbors, all those he put before him, to whom he gave away the shotgun of his power, whose idiocracies he made more precious than his own, and they sing him "Auld Lang Syne" and shower him with gratitude and love and money.

And there's the spell, right there on screen, Capra's captured it forever, only Capra's in the spell he's showing. The last real action in the movie is George in despair and going in the water and the rest is magic, the hologram that's playing in George Bailey's mind as he's under the black water being swept downriver, dying.

—Where you going? Margaret asks me.

—Sorry, you guys watch. I can't really stand this movie.

—How can you not like it?

—Because the whole thing strikes me as a crock, Im, a giant glowing ad for self-betrayal. Doesn't George jump and drown and end up at the coroner's with a toe tag? Doesn't Potter keep the money? Don't Mary and the children lose the house and have to soldier on without him? Don't they blame George for being such a selfish coward? George sells himself out over and over, giving up his dreams for others, and he ends up in despair and jumps and dies. The End. The rest is just an Owl Creek occurrence.

I'm overheated here, I admit it, but it's been a long night, I've had a lot to drink, I'm feeling pretty disinhibited to tell the truth, like *Fuck it.*

Margaret and Imogen look at me in the same way, startled by my vehemence, my perverse misconstruction, as if to say, *Who can see* It's A Wonderful Life *that way? Why turn good things into bad ones? George Bailey is a good man. Who are you? Why are you so angry?*

And the worst part is, I'm not sure they aren't right. I'm not sure I don't agree with them. Maybe that's why the voice inside my head says I'm a Bad! Mean! Selfish! person. The voice is going strong now. And the night is speeding up and blurring and I've been here before, and I'm heading down the hallway, I don't know where I'm going. Somewhere else though, not here, I can't stay here, I need to leave, it's over. What is? This whole thing. What whole thing? Our family. Fuck me. Is that what this is? It is. It's midnight. We've struck the iceberg; I have. I'm heading for the lifeboat and no one else is coming.

I'm going to go, my Sprite is waiting in the driveway, I came back for George A., but he's not coming, he chose the shotgun and I can't really blame him because once upon a time when offered the same opportunity I did the same thing.

And here he is now coming from the bathroom, still grinning at the thought of Bill on the Kawasaki in his do-rag and a jean vest with rockers like they sell at GAP or Aeropostale.

–Where you going?

–I need some air.

–Okay, I'm going to hit the hay. I'll see you in the morning.

And he hugs me just like always, two brisk back-claps to indicate no funny stuff intended.

–Okay, then.

I start off.

–Hey, David?

I turn back.

–Merry Christmas.

That big smile, that face, that young face, those black rings under his eyes, new and still so faint, the warm nuanced smile that I remember from the beach, *This one's for you, DP.*

And if I were writing fiction, I'd have him say, *By the way, about the shotgun . . . You should have it.*

And I'd say, *Fuck it, George A., keep the damn thing.*

I'd make us both generous and good—where "good" means selfless—the way we wished to be and weren't.

But he didn't say it and I didn't say it. He just said, Merry Christmas, and it seemed to me that he was on the up seat and I was heading lower, and in some sense that was true, but not the big sense, not the last one.

Six weeks from now, or eight, when I next visit, we'll tell our jokes again and take on the Jacks and chicken-jerk our chins and walk like Egyptians, and when he gets sick I'll come from Chapel Hill—and after that Manhattan, and after that New England—and we'll ring the bells and chant and swing the censer and harrow hell and storm the heavens, but after tonight it's never quite the same between us. Last summer in the lair it was him and me, the lost boys in our Adirondack summer camp, loyal to each other against the defection of the counselors, our parents. I coached him to the pier and George A. introduced me to the Piedmont blues and walked me through those turnarounds. Now tempted by the shotgun, George A. switches sides and takes it and he fucks me. So I feel. And maybe sickness is the reason, but I never quite forgive him or our parents.

So I walk off and leave him, and in a way it ends here, our family; this is, for me, the last scene. That's me going, headed out the kitchen door, and as I leave the clock is striking midnight on the upstairs landing, and in the drive the topless Sprite awaits me and I put my key in the ignition. The engine whirs to life and I can see it's snowing, and as the headlights hit the backyard swing set, I remember Central Park with Eric, the children gathered with their nannies, the little boy in the blue coat who thought his crying stopped the clock though it had merely rung the hour.

Inside, the clock is striking now and I think once more about the animals, about their joyless dance, their intervals, their fixed expressions. It seems to me the first animal is Want, the second Want Rejected; and the third is Goodness, Trying to Want Nothing, who denies himself a tater or gives away his shotgun; and the fourth animal is Goodness's Failure, Badness, who steals the stereo equipment or Mary Rose's timber or runs away with Imogen his sister not-so-sister. And the fifth animal is Sickness, who wins by losing and gets his wants met that way and is blackened before he ever holds a light and throws it. And the sixth animal is the Leaver, Brother A, the Spaceman, who takes the space trip to escape the cycle and carries the poison with him in the spaceship on his space boots and infects each new world he lands in and finally crashes back and re-creates the world he fled from in the place he fled to to escape it.

And the carousel goes round and round to the tune of the carillon, and the children come and start it over da capo and repeat the chorus.

The Bridge

Keep true to the dreams of thy youth.

     —Herman Melville (after Schiller)

8

S O THE YEARS GO BY, the years go helling like the brook down Northeast Mountain in the spring thaw. Following that Christmas, I drop out of UNC and head down to Four Roses, stealing firewood out of Nags Head Woods and hauling driftwood off the beach to heat it through the winter. Mornings, sometimes I wake up to find an ice-skimmed toilet and I piss a steaming hole in it, and through the picture window, when I see the dark blue stain against the mid-blue ocean, I grab a rod and reel and sprint down to the water. Standing barefoot in the January surf for as long as I can take it, I haul in four- and five-pound blues and bread and fry them up in Crisco and make fries in the hot oil right beside them and use the heads for soup and keep the big pot bungeed on the porch and eat till it turns funky or some marauding animal overturns it. And I like it out there, living this way, deliberately, having little money, needing little and wishing I could do without it altogether. Reading hours every day and late into the evening, writing poem after poem, I'm like a hermit crab, my real-world claw growing puny with disuse, while the one I use for inner seizing, inner grasping, develops and gets stronger. I see myself as independent from my family, a Taoist metabolizing sunlight, even as I'm living at Four Roses. Wanting's dangerous and since I still want something from my people I hide it—from myself, primarily—and come to get it in this place that isn't really even fit to live in in the winter. So though I think I've left it, the old competition with George A. goes on unabated in the shadows, and maybe that's the reason why this winter, reading *Absalom, Absalom!* for the first time—about the white brother who loves and shoots the black one in a dispute over a woman—I feel as though I'm levitating above the mattress. Though I don't consciously remember, something in me remembers for me how I put my six-gun to Margaret's stomach and pulled the trigger when she told me he was coming.

And in the spring, I hitchhike to New Orleans and visit Randy, my old friend from Exeter, who's like a brother, only chosen. While he's in classes at Tulane, I'm reading in Howard-Tilton Library, and in the afternoons we meet and run through Audubon Park and down across the Mississippi Levee, and on Friday nights, we take the streetcar to the Quarter and eat oysters at Felix's and when school lets out, we take a road trip to the Big Bend and do mushrooms in the desert and dive in the Rio Grande and let it carry us miles downriver.

And after this adventure, I reenroll in school and back in Chapel Hill one sweltering August night walking past frat row, I gaze into the diorama and see a tall slim clear-faced boy standing on the DKE House steps with a beer in one hand and a canary-yellow cashmere sweater tied around his shoulders. With thick dark hair and a sly, warm grin that deprecates itself from a position of great confidence, he looks familiar, looks, in fact, a little bit like me, or rather who I might have been if the circle had remained unbroken. Who is it? It's George A. Payne, my brother.

There I am giving him a bear hug on the porch—me in my white T and cutoffs, my dark hair loose around my shoulders and my bare feet black and calloused from the pavements—and there are his new brothers eyeing him, their pledge, and me, the hostile who's penetrated their perimeter, trying to do the social math that puts the two of us together.

–Goddamn, George A.—*goddamn!* I say, pushing him away to look. You look great. You look like a million dollars.

–Thanks, he says, holding up a ring of keys and giving them a jingle. Come on, I want to show you something.

He leads me to the curb, where a new 280Z—metallic bronze, the color of a new-struck penny—gleams beneath the streetlight. I shelf my eyes and peer through my reflection —between deep bucket seats, a high transmission well with the stick trussed up like a dominatrix in fawn leather.

–This is yours?

He gives me the grin of happy illegality, the one he gave me on the porch last Christmas.

–How much did this cost?

–We got an end-of-season deal.

—How much?

—About seven?

—*Seven thousand dollars?*

It's a good thing I'm a Taoist, a good thing I don't care about material possessions, or else I might be hurt by the injustice, the disproportion in our portions, I might grow wroth like Cain did when the Lord showed preference to Abel.

But on the other hand, nine months ago at Mandala, sobbing into his big hands, George A. seemed to have lost the basic certainty that who he'd be when he woke up in the morning was the same person he'd been when he lay down the previous evening. So fuck the car, and fuck the shotgun for that matter.

—Take me for a spin, you asshole.

George A. makes an apologetic wince.

—I have this thing for rush. Rain check?

—Rain check.

We hug and pat each other on the back—two brisk claps as always—and when we pull away this time it seems to me our eye lines don't quite intersect, or maybe just mine doesn't because I'm looking off across his shoulder. And there I leave him on the DKE House porch, fraternizing with his new brothers—brothers not by blood but chosen—and walk away down Cameron deeper into campus as the bell tower tolls the hour and the carillon plays the Fight Song, *Rah, rah, Car'lina-lina,* and I sing the chorus, *Bullshit, fucking bullshit.*

And the good news is his breakdown appears to have been a one-off like the doctors said at Mandala, a bad reaction to that funky weed he smoked before he went back out to practice, and it will be five more years before we get the diagnosis and are disabused of this illusion. For now it seems that he's the old George A. again with a new Datsun for his trouble and my shotgun thrown in into the bargain. As with Margaret's teenage pregnancy, sickness, injury and crisis are once again rewarded in our family. You get something, but you have to give up something for it. Me, I'd prefer to keep the something and go barefoot from April to Thanksgiving, but my anger and my drinking, like my recent sojourn at Four Roses, are clues I'm not as free as I think either. And as in some fairy tale, even as we grow to manhood and go off into our separate lives, who George A. and I are today is who we will remain, and down below us at the center of the iceberg, no longer hot, at ambient temperature, lies the shotgun, forgotten but not gone, till something in me bids me to go back and find it and bring it up into sunlight, *hoc opus, hic labor.*

And in his Carolina years, George A. falls in love with Cammy Pruden, a pretty blonde Chi O, who can do shots with the boys on Saturday night and do the down-and-dirty shag and show up at church on Sunday morning looking demure and put together in the BMW her daddy gave her for her birthday. He's an agribusiness magnate somewhere in the eastern precincts, down there in Pasquotank or maybe it's Perquimans County, and one day driving to the coast George A. pulls over and nods at shiny green John Deeres, multiples of them, heading down the rows in fields that stretch away to the horizon. All that, George A. says, is

Cammy's family fiefdom, and he asks her to marry him and she accepts and George A. gives her our grandmother Mary's ring and Cammy gives George A. a Labrador retriever and a doggy bed from L.L. Bean for Christmas.

Me, a month before I graduate, in a sudden fit of practicality—a panic—I stop by a professor's office and ask him the procedure one—that is, I—might follow to become a Poet in the real world. Interrupted at his grading, he looks up somber-faced and blinks.

—Mr. Payne, he says, if you need a kick in the ass, go to grad school; if not, go out and live a little. That's what they all did, the ones I think you want to emulate, or ought to if you're serious in your ambition.

My career counseling in toto—there you have it—lasts under a minute.

So I head down to the beach and take a minimum-wage job in a cabinet shop, making $2.30 an hour and writing in the evenings. I learn to use a table saw, a router, to measure twice before I cut, to build countertops and cabinets. After five months on the job, I've got the whole thing pretty much, except for finishing and painting, and the owner spends fifteen minutes with me in the morning giving me a list, and then goes about his business while I build his kitchens and install them in the houses going up up north along the ocean in Duck and in Corolla. And one day on a job, a contractor hands me an invoice and I realize that on this project in which I've done all the labor, I'm making roughly ten cents on the dollar to the owner's ninety, which brings Marx home more viscerally than reading *Kapital* did at Carolina. The *qi*-exchange equation's out of balance—not 50-50 or even 60-40, but 90-10—and I feel exploited, as if I'm suffering an extraction, but when I ask him for a raise, he stares down at his feet and shakes his head as though my character has suddenly become suspect. When I've been there for another month, he says, he'll bump me up a quarter.

So I say sayonara and head off to Wanchese where I can make twice the hourly rate working in the fish house, shucking scallops and filleting flounder. Once there, I begin to ask incoming captains if they'll take me fishing, and mostly they regard me with misgiving, shake their heads and walk off without comment, but eventually one takes a chance on me and I ship out on a scalloper, a Western rig called the *Bald Eagle*. Two weeks at sea without a shower, six hours on, six hours off around the clock, the work's so brutal I, a seasoned runner, develop nosebleeds from the strain of constant lifting. I like it, though, like the hardness, like the pitching deck and sunrise on the ocean, like it that the crew is paid in shares and when the boat does well, we do, and when it doesn't, we share the disappointment. In Wanchese, the *qi*-exchange equation is in better balance, and I like the men I work with, and after a few trips I get to try my hand at one of the big Hathaway winches that bring the massive dredges off the bottom and dump them on the work deck, and an old-timer on that boat tells me I have the best touch he's ever seen at the winch, a compliment I relish.

I'm a sojourner in that world, though, and unlike many of my fellows I have the intention to leave and the ability to do so. And one day at the P.O., when I stop in after work in my white boots and orange Grundéns oilskins, I find a check for $2,100, my first dividend from Rose Oil Company, my share of the surplus value generated by the labor of people I don't even know in a business started by my grandfather where I've never worked and will never work an hour. I stare at that check for sixty seconds, maybe only half that, and then I take it to the bank and cash it because it means I get to spend the winter writing instead of fishing. And so in addition to the money, I get a lesson in human nature, namely mine, as I who recently played the exploited laborer now get to play the capitalist and consume the surplus value generated by the work of others, and I'm not the good one or the bad one, I have both capacities inside myself and play them each in turn as the platter turns and the carillon plays the music.

And one night at a big dance the whole beach turns out to, I see two women who aren't local dancing together on the dance floor, blonde on blonde and girl on girl, and they own the room and know it. One of them is Nell, who's from D.C. and just my type, blonde and insubordinate and almost six feet tall, and something about her sends me. Her inch-long bangs look radical and self-inflicted, the sort of thing you do in the bathroom mirror late at night in a cold-water flat in the East Village or Adams Morgan when you want to make a major change and your hair is what you have to work with. I introduce myself, we trade a bit of repartee, as Nell's blonde friend, Amelia, smiles and discreetly makes an exit. Before long Nell comes to dinner at

Four Roses, and it turns out she's smart and funny and a feminist. She's working at a local medical clinic saving bucks to go to grad school. She wants to be a midwife, but she's applied to Yale to do it. Nell has a subversive agenda together with a plan of positive engagement, a more developed one than I have when it comes to my own future. And pretty soon we're skinny-dipping, doing Burt Lancaster and Deborah Kerr in the wash as waves sheet in around us, and not long after that she's living with me at Four Roses and we're sharing family stories.

Nell's an Army brat; her father is a general and her mom made her career advancing his and had a stroke at fifty and kept her mental sharpness and lost her speech, and Nell's determination not to let her voice be taken is connected. In my mind's eye I see her at those garden parties that her mom arranged with the trim officers and officers' wives— nineteen- and twenty-year-old Nell breezing in from college, braless, in her sleeveless T, with her unshaved pits and her self-inflicted haircut and her 100-megawatt smile, tossing out remarks about the military-industrial complex. And, at those same parties, there would be Nell's older sister, Ann, carrying the hors d'oeuvres tray with her hair curled and a polka-dotted dress on like their mother's. Our families bear no resemblance to each other, yet reverse gender and birth order and Ann and Nell for all intents and purposes might be George A. and David. I don't have to recruit Nell or explain about the poison in the wheat or in the water, she knows all about it, and it's me who boards her spaceship, next stop New Haven.

Before we go, though, one weekend George A. shows up in the Z from Carolina, and the Rose Oil dividend I've put into my writing, he's put into the new pump-action Browning in the rear compartment of the Z-ster, and the decoys, two mesh bags full, and the waders and the stag-handled Italian bird knife with the gut hook and the private guide who's going to take him duck hunting in the morning. George A. invites me, and I go, carrying binoculars and not a shotgun.

The blind's a mile out in the Albemarle, and I recall us out there under open sky on open water, the brutal cold and razor wind and the great dune, Penny's Hill, golden in the distance like a magic wheat mound on the barrier island, looming over the Corolla Light and the Whalehead Club, abandoned in that era, like a fairy-tale castle under its blue copper roof tiles. Though we see chevrons of snow geese and Canadas passing way high up, not many ducks are flying. Late in the afternoon, though, George A. finally gets a shot and hits a wood duck, a little fast one with a head as highly colored as a harlequin in the commedia dell'arte.

At the house, George A. cleans it in the sink and puts it in the oven with an apple and an onion and rosemary for remembrance, and we pour drinks at the Dutch bar and wipe the dusty glasses with our shirtsleeves and sit down before the fire in wicker rockers whose white paint is old and chipped now and shows the even older brown paint from our childhoods. George A.'s cheeks, I recall, are flushed with windburn, he has hat hair, and his brown eyes are relaxed and happy, and we fall into conversation and he tells me he's been reading about the old traders, Bernard Baruch and Jesse Livermore, and their campaigns and maneuvers in the markets. What is this squiggly line, the Dow, that tracks across a page from lower left to upper right and sometimes upper left to lower right? It's like an EKG that takes the pulse not of a single company but of many companies and the workers in them and the shareholders and the customers who buy the companies' products, a measure of the vital force of the whole society. For me hearing about the Dow is comparable to being slathered with molasses and staked down to an anthill, yet George A. is aroused and happy as he shares this, he's in a stream of passion, and I find myself leaning forward, listening closely, asking questions. George A.'s discovered his libido and is following its gradient, and I see who my brother's turning into and has in some sense been since the beginning.

And in 1980, straight out of Carolina, George A.'s hired by Merrill Lynch and becomes the youngest broker in the Buckhead office in Atlanta. In the race to Avalon, he's pulled ahead now.

Me, I'm with Nell in New Haven. In her aging Pinto, we made the journey north and rented a one-bedroom downtown over a dentist's office, where the window sashes rattle when the delivery trucks rumble by on Howe Street. For a bed we spread a carpet remnant on the bare wood floor, and over that, a quilt, and over that our sheets and blankets, and when one of Nell's classmates remarks upon our poverty, how hard it must be to live this way, we exchange knowing looks because we don't feel poor, I don't, we're on a treasure hunt that no one has the map to, living outside and underneath the money system and stronger for our independence.

Nell starts class and gets a job at Yale Infirmary, pulling double shifts on weekends, and I take the Pinto and head east on 95 through Old Saybrook and New London, following the seagulls to Rhode Island, where I lump fish in the holds of trawl boats in Point Judith. After my first day, I wash up in the fish house bathroom and sit down on the wharf, unwrap my deli sandwich, and read until the light fails. Then I lower the passenger-side seat and go to sleep there in the Pinto. And on Tuesday, I get up and change my T and go to work again, and the same on Wednesday, Thursday, Friday. And on Friday afternoon, I get my paycheck and hightail it to New Haven, where Nell meets me, smiling, at the door and makes me undress in the hall and drop my clothes into a plastic trash bag and then she joins me in the shower. And after we make mincemeat of each other on the bedroom pallet, we hop back in the Pinto and take the Wilbur Cross down to the Merritt and on into the city and go to CBGB or the Mudd Club and light's breaking on the Bowery or White Street when we come out, holding hands, a little drunk, not clear where the car is, but unworried, sure we'll find it, and we're happy, proud to be together. I know I'm proud to be with Nell, and when I see men looking my look back says, *Eat your hearts out, motherfuckers.* She's following her dream and has a plan of positive engagement.

Me, my dream is still intact, too. The positive engagement part is where I'm having trouble. That fall as fall deepens and I sit there on a piling in Point Judith with an open book surrounded by that beauty and that destitution watching the slantlight fall across the water, lighting the dazzle in rose and gold tones, it comes home to me that things aren't really working, that lumping fish with my best forty hours weekly isn't making me a better poet or a writer, it's making me a better lumper and if I get another berth and develop my touch at the winch, eventually a good winchman is what I'll be, who once dreamed himself a poet. And going back to school to teach creative writing—that isn't what made me leap beneath the elms and maples once upon a time. If what I have allotted to me in this life is forty hours a week times fifty weeks a year times fifty years—100,000 hours—I want to spend mine in the writing lap lane not on the pool deck with a bullhorn, coaching other writers.

That Friday night when I drive home, I tell Nell I want to write a novel and she says, I think you ought to try it. So instead of driving to Rhode Island Monday morning, in the bedroom I set up a card table, an ancient one with spots and water rings that I lifted from Four Roses. Nanny Rose used to put together her big jigsaws on it—she liked the ones with ten thousand pieces. Mine, as I assemble it, begins to feel as if it has a million. It's about a Taoist monk, an orphan, who grows up practicing *qigong* in China and comes to New York searching for his father, an aviator with the Flying Tigers who's become a famous Wall Street trader. And now I'm on the phone with George A., asking about bear raids and head-and-shoulder patterns, and the campaigns of those old traders, things that held no interest until George A.

broached the subject and got that job that everyone's so proud of him for getting. Ahead now, he's coaching me the way I once coached him in the runs to Avalon. I'm starting to have fun, too—God, what fun. I'm like a runner who's struggled at the quarter mile and then one day I try a marathon and find out it's my distance.

And when Nell comes back from class, I read her my pages and she encourages me and laughs at the right places, and when I'm lost, she talks through it with me, and if the answer doesn't come out of that conversation, it usually comes the next day. And I'm getting up at 5, 5:30 in the morning now, making coffee and willing the water to heat faster so I can sit down at my Smith Corona and start banging on the keyboard till the little table's shaking, and sometimes I laugh or speak my sentences aloud for cadence, and suddenly it's lunchtime and I'm still in my boxers and my T-shirt and haven't shaved or bathed or eaten, and where's Nell? Apparently on her way to the Infirmary she tiptoed past and I didn't even notice.

I'm twenty-four and happy and don't understand when Nell starts coming in at night and says she's tired and wants to take a shower and isn't in the mood to hear my pages, and when I reach for her in bed sometimes she nudges up her shoulder and lies there with her back turned, and when I ask what's wrong, she answers, *Nothing,* in a way that means the opposite, and, wondering what the problem is, I lie there staring at the ceiling thinking of the scene I left unfinished, and an idea strikes me and I leap up and write it down on a half sheet of foolscap.

My story has started to become as real to me as life is, and it doesn't occur to me then that much of the energy I've invested in her is now being diverted into this other project. Instead of driving to the city to go clubbing, in the evening when my writing concentration wanes, I want to go to sleep as soon as possible so I can get up refreshed and go back at it in the morning. Our balance is off. Nell's putting out too much *qi* and getting back too little. In the economy of our relationship, Nell feels like exploited labor, and that's why she isn't in the mood to listen to my pages. And the second piece is money. Nell's going to class all week and pulling double shifts at the Infirmary on weekends, emptying bedpans, while I'm at home in boxers writing. You'd think that I—who saw that invoice at the cabinet shop and quit because of the unfairness and was resentful when Margaret bought George A. the Datsun—would understand this. I don't, though. And when I ask Nell what the matter is, she answers, *Nothing,* so either she no more understands than I do or finds it too threatening to say, *I need a contribution from you, David,* the way I couldn't say *I want the shotgun* to George A. And I love Nell and think she loves me, but everything that matters now is happening beneath the surface, and because we don't understand it, I don't, it blows up crookedly.

One night at a big party, I—who feel rejected in the bedroom—get lit and hit on another woman and make out with her in a stairwell. Nell sees us leave the party and doesn't come home till the next morning, when she picks up the phone and calls an old boyfriend and tells him he was it, her true love, and I'm in the next room as she says it and Nell makes very sure I hear her. There I go, storming past her, out of the apartment, that's me walking along the Green downtown when Nell pulls up beside me in the Pinto.

–Let's drive out to the beach and talk, okay? she offers.

But I'm too mad, too hurt, and keep on walking. Nell scratches off, and when she doesn't come home that night, I say *Fuck it* and start packing.

And suddenly there we are on Howe Street, me, with my Smith Corona and a box of pages and the plastic garbage bag I have my clothes in, and Nell—looking solemn and subdued and furious and doubtful—holds out her hand for me to shake, and I start crying like an asshole right there on the sidewalk and Nell shows me no mercy, as I, in piggish pride and ignorance, force myself to do the thing I least want to do and turn around and leave her. And it's not about that other woman, it's not about Nell's former boyfriend, who's realized he's gay and come out in the meantime. It seems to be about that, but it's really the imbalance.

The real end comes a year later in New York, where I've moved in with Terrence, a UVa boy who worked with me on the *Bald Eagle* and is in the art world working in a gallery and will one day own one. At 99ᵗʰ and West End, we share a 1-BR in an elevator building where I sleep in the living room on a foam rubber mattress I roll up in the morning and write facing the courtyard listening to the disembodied sounds of people fighting, people fucking, and oboists and opera singers doing scales, and the sunlight hits the window-sill for fifteen minutes daily, and at dusk I run laps around the Reservoir and pick up a slice or some falafel on my way home. Over time, it hits me that leaving Nell was the worst mistake I've ever made, and I come down with a lovesickness that in its depth feels almost religious. When I call her, though, she cuts me very little slack, but I persist, and if my lack of attention played a role in our original demise, suddenly the taps are open and she's getting torrents and she thaws toward me a little and a little more, and then one day in the middle of the afternoon she shows up unannounced at the door of my apartment with this beamy smile I know and I arch my brows as if to say, *Is this what I think it is?* and by way of answer, she pushes me, two-handed, backward into the apartment and we toss down my pad and get reacquainted, and after that we start to see each other often.

And the critical moment comes one morning as I'm walking Nell down to the subway. Nell looks smiley, bleary-eyed and queasy, and I imagine I look pretty much like she does, like two people who've been up all night drinking and screwing and Nell's unwashed hair has fuck-knots in it, her phrase, and we aren't holding hands or anything because we don't want to make too big a deal of what's happening, because it is a big deal, we're into each other again, how far is unclear, it's serious, though, seriouser and seriouser. And we're standing by the stairs on 96th, the wide ones that lead down into the darkness and the tunnels and the platform and the speeding silver cars and the whole world that's down there under this one, and Nell's about to turn and go and as we kiss goodbye she tells me she's ovulating or thinks she may be from certain signs she knows to look for, she felt it last week and so she's a little worried, not *really* worried, just a little, because we didn't use protection last night, see, because Nell didn't bring her diaphragm, our usual method, and I didn't offer to get a condom though there were probably some there in the bathroom, but it was late, we'd had a lot to drink, we'd reached that state where you're so trembly with desire that you can hardly keep your knees from giving way beneath you, and we were stupid as a fence post or a pair of fence posts and we what-the-fucked it, and all this seems like accident and slackness but looking back none of it seems slack or accidental. And as we stand there on 96th at the down stairs to the tunnels and the world that's under this one, it seems to me that we've agreed to something in the shadow contract, to what I'm not exactly sure, and that if we haven't signed, we've opened the negotiation, Nell has when she drops this little piece of info, and she isn't freaking or accusing, she's smiley and hungover as she tells me, but she's also worried and studious of my reaction, and I say, Really? *Really?* and my hangover's gone, I'm smiling and trying not to, because I don't want to make a big deal of it because it is one.

–We'll figure it out, Nell, I say. Call me when you know, okay?

–Okay.

And she goes down the stairs now and as I head back up to 99th Street, the odd thing is, I don't think I'm that displeased about it. In fact, I'm not displeased the least bit.

The next thing I know Margaret's calling ... In Atlanta, George A.'s had another breakdown, the biggie, where he strips and shreds his credit cards and announces that he's been tapped out for a mission to Tehran to rescue the hostages at the embassy. The police and paramedics wrestle him and bring him to the psych ward, and Jack and Margaret come, and, soon thereafter, Cammy, who takes one look at him and faints—so Margaret tells me. The doctors in Atlanta finally make the diagnosis: manic-depression, or bipolar I disorder as we later learn to call it. Margaret's crying as she tells me on the phone, and I think I'm crying as I listen or just saying, *Oh, no ... Oh, no, Mom,* because, you see, it's not a one-off and the luxury of that illusion's gone now. When there's one bead on the string it's one thing, but when the second bead appears the second bead implies a pattern and the nature of patterns is repeating, and after two there's three and after three there's four and patterns go on till something stops them ... And what stops them? We don't know this, me and Margaret, but now I know the answer's nothing, nothing stops them, and then death does, and what we do know is the dark history among the Roses, and the cup we hoped would pass has come back around now and George A. is the one who has to drink it.

In Atlanta, George A. goes on lithium for the first time, and when he's stabilized Margaret brings him back to Mandala in Winston-Salem. Meanwhile, I fly home to North Carolina and drive down to Atlanta with a U-Haul. Entering his apartment is terrifying—burns in the carpets and Formica and fast food wrappers and notes scrawled in the disordered hand of the mad exegete and maybe now is when he puts those colored stars and exclamation points beside those passages in *One Fish Two Fish*. Much of it I throw away, and the rest I pack up to bring home for him the way George A. will for me much later.

When he's released from Mandala, George A. returns to Jack and Margaret's—they've moved from Clemmons into Winston. He puts away his business suits, the charcoal and the navy with the subtle pinstripe proudly purchased after Merrill hired him, and takes out his brogans and the Red Man hat with sweat stains. Having waited for what must have seemed a decent interval, Cammy returns his ring and calls off the engagement. George A. says he doesn't blame her, but his expression's hard to look at as he says it. Having pined for Nell for much of the last year, I have some idea what he's feeling. Yet in another way I don't. He's like someone who's been dazzled by a brilliant light, who now, gazing at familiar objects, must think a moment to recall their names and uses.

I stay with him for a while and we walk and talk in Buena Vista the way we did five years before in Clemmons. There we are on Georgia Avenue and Runnymede and in Hanes Park beside the tennis courts and ball fields, and as we go I don't know what else to do so we talk about the hostages. I ask him who he thinks they are and who is holding them and what or who or Who is proposing he go on the mission and why he has to shred his credit cards and license, the outward props and markers, to undertake the rescue.

It will be years before I meet the psychiatrists and therapists who'll tell me that national security issues are a staple of psychotic fantasy and that if neurosis is like a house that's disarranged, psychosis is a house razed to its foundations. If George A.'s psyche's razed, it's unapparent to me as we walk and talk there. He seems tentative, but recognizably himself and invested in these conversations. And since Jung said he had to find the meaning of the fantasies that assaulted him in Küsnacht, so it seems to me we have to find the meaning of George A.'s from Atlanta. As my unconscious has featured me as the detective who must solve the crime, so his has cast him as the soldier who must undertake the rescue mission. And if, for me, our family is the car wreck, perhaps it or we are the foreign country where George A.'s being held and the terrorists who hold him. To me at twenty-five, in 1980, the forward path seems hard but clear and even hopeful. Yet perhaps George A.'s fantasies simply come out of the headlines as that shrink will later tell me. And even if his fantasies had meaning, what seems likely now is that it would have required a stable ego to decipher it and use it, and George A.'s ego, having shattered twice, is no longer fully stable, even if the cracks are not yet visible to me, who must want desperately not to see them so that George A. can go on being George A. as I've known him. So we walk the tree-lined streets and ring the bell and wave the censers and all that's left now is the company I kept him.

After I fly back to Manhattan, Margaret sits him on the sofa and informs him of the diagnosis and George A. puts his face in his big hands, she says, and sits there with his shoulders shaking. And after she leaves for work, he goes upstairs and shaves, takes off the Red Man hat and brogans, picks a suit and shines his shoes and drives downtown to Dean Witter Reynolds and talks his way into an interview and nails it. When Margaret comes home, he greets her, beaming, and says he has a new job, and that may be my favorite story of my brother.

George A. will work there for eleven years, the rest of his career, and go from making cold calls to become a top producer in the Winston office, and after his death, on two or three occasions in a restaurant or at the theater, some former client will seek me out to tell me George A. made them more money than any other broker ever made them and was the best they ever dealt with. These testimonials always please me and leave me wistful, as though offered for a stranger. Looking back, it seems to me we shared the deep intimacies of childhood and, in adulthood, our sicknesses and troubles, but when George A. was well, and I was, I barely knew him and he barely knew me. I expect that I, like others, gave George A. the ice-cream soda of my best attention mainly in his sickness, which is another way I acted out the family pattern while trying to escape it.

Back in New York, Nell, who said she'd call me, hasn't. I've called her once from Winston to ask her if there's any news, and she just says, There isn't, tersely, and I wonder at her terseness. I can't remember if I called a second time and laid out my position clearly or if I just had the conversation with her in my head so many times it seems we might have had it in reality. In any case, I expect Nell knows the direction I'm leaning from my original reaction at the subway.

And what is my position? If the lovesickness I came down with on moving to the city felt religious in its depth, it pales in comparison with what erupts now, an upwelling of the lifeforce that at the time seems unrelated to George A. and now seems impossible to understand without him. It's as if God or fate has spoken and finally told me my true purpose: to be the father of this child, Nell's husband or partner. I see the little house, the picket fence, the residential street with parking and I'm at the kitchen table there, the house-husband who writes while listening to the monitor, or maybe I just give up writing altogether, this folly I embarked on that day beneath the elms and maples. I can teach school and maybe learn to tie a bowtie and wear a Harris tweed like those young men with the defeated eyes at Exeter, and if they looked amused when I told them I was going to be a writer, I know why now, don't I? I can come home in the afternoon and put down my beat-up satchel and throw the football with our son or daughter and grade papers after supper and everything that's up in the air can come down to earth and rest and find support there and be earthbound and everything that's dangerous and scary can be safe and normal, *normal*—that word is so attractive.

Following your libido and living outside and underneath the money system sounds good when you're twenty years old in Wilson Library, but out here in the real world no one asked me for this novel, no one's missing it or waiting—except me, I am, and it feels like a bag of hot rocks now, one I've been carrying on my back for coming on to two years and I want to put it down, I want it off me. And, you see, if Nell is pregnant and we have the baby I can live selflessly for others, for my wife and for our baby, and I'll no longer be this selfish person, but someone more like, say, George Bailey. And the two years I've put into my writing, and the years before that back to Exeter? Fuck it, let them go, it's cheap compared with the relief of reaching normal. That word, that place, that state.

And why all this seems suspect is because I haven't asked Nell what she wants or may want and what she doesn't or may not. And I think, though I don't know, that what I feel must be what Margaret felt when she got pregnant at eighteen, a sense of transport almost religious in its depth and power, and I believe she loved him, but Bill was mainly there to make it happen for her, which is why in their old wedding photographs from Bennettsville, Bill, my skinny twenty-year-old father with his big Adam's apple, looks like a condemned man on the way to his own execution and Margaret looks like Tolstoy's Anna, incandescent, and the death of their marriage and our family is already evident in their expressions. And as there was love with Bill and Margaret once upon a time so there is with Nell and me now, but love is just the sunlight on the surface, underneath the dark force drives the iceberg through the ocean and the dark force is about trapping and extraction and with Nell I'm the would-be trapper and extractor, I want her to have the baby to solve it for me because I don't know how to bring it to solution and I'm scared and want things settled, easier, and maybe the idea of *normal* appeals to Nell, too, however briefly, and that's why she lets herself have unprotected sex and floats her gambit on the down stairs at the 96th Street station. The curious thing is how we repeat in New York in the '80s what Bill and Margaret played out in North Carolina the '50s, which Stacy and I will repeat later, and what makes us repeat repeat repeat the thing that made us so unhappy in the first place, and how different were we, outside the bell curve, or only as fingerprints and snowflakes?

And Nell, when I finally reach her, says, Oh, my period came, no worries, and I touch back down in Kansas.

And the next time she comes to see me, back at my apartment after dinner, Nell says, I have something to tell you, and she's sitting crisscross on my mattress as she says it and her eyes are melty but not the way they were the day she pushed me backward into the apartment, there's sadness in them, and she's very, very beautiful the way people are in the last snapshot of them you carry in your memory.

—I had an abortion.

She just holds my eyes, denying and defending nothing.

And I sit down beside her on the mattress and we stare into each other's eyes and then we put our heads on each other's shoulders and cry a long time or maybe only I do, and then we fuck with all our grief and anger and our love and disappointment, all night as the oboists and opera singers do their scales and people fight and read their children bedtime stories and their disembodied voices swirl like prayer around us in the courtyard, and when the gray light fills the window, it's over and we are too, Nell and I, that's the ending, perhaps it shouldn't be, but it is. And why? Is it because I tried to trap her and Nell didn't let me, because Nell may have tried to trap herself and then thought better of it and I'm angry that she foiled my plan for *normal*? I don't think so. The feeling I have is more like metal that's been bent and bends again and when it finally gives way it's the cumulative fatigue that does it and the giving way is gentle, and the feeling in my heart toward Nell that morning and after has more gentleness than anger in it, and the true answer's more disturbing ...

It was when she told me she was pregnant or she might be that I felt the upwelling of the lifeforce, so when the carousel began to turn I felt swept up in the current, and the carillon music moved me and moved through me and the very thing that made my parents so unhappy is the thing I sought out and recognized and called "love" when I found it, because I knew no better and "love" is what it felt like, familiar and electric, and even the little boy with the rain-sheeted eyes who knew the dance was joyless crossed the park with his au pair to see it and stood transfixed while it happened, and when it stopped he turned away like all the others, the way I turn away from Nell now after she breaks the axle of the wheel that turns the carousel that moves me. And months later from the blue one night she calls me and says, *Are we going to do this, David?* and I'm glad to hear from her, but I say, *I think that ship has sailed already.* She, free, offers herself freely, and I, free, miss the carillon music and decline her, and if I'd known that love is to see another's idiocrasy and hold it as precious as your own is, I might have loved her and been worthy of her love, except I wasn't and I didn't, so I lose her, and she loses me.

And the years hell on, and down in Winston, George A. meets Colleen, a striking redhead who's a corporate attorney. Before you know it they're getting married and he's brought her home to meet the family. To me, he still seems shaky from Atlanta, it feels a little rushed, but maybe George A. wants a little *normal*—I don't know, and if so, who am I to judge him? After the announcement, Margaret takes Colleen to lunch and tells her the whole unpretty story, about the hostages and the burns in the Formica, but George A.'s told Colleen already and she loves George A. so much, she says, it doesn't matter and I'm sure she means it at the time she says it.

I find Colleen smart, conservative and straight and will never fully grasp how her conservatism fits with the part of George A. that's a gambler or how her straightness works with George A.'s humor, which goes back to the naughty little boy who got more points from misbehavior than compliance. But who knows what goes on in anybody else's marriage? George A.'s is part of his healthy life that I'll know mainly from a distance, seeing him and Colleen across the room at Christmas parties, an attractive, well-dressed couple, sharing a joke with Colleen at a dinner, telling her about my professional life and hearing about hers, a sentence exchanged in each direction. And later, when George A. gets sick again, I'll know her as a harrowed and exhausted woman standing in her driveway with her arms crossed tightly, waiting as I go inside to face George A. and try to talk him into going back to Mandala.

Now, though, when George A.'s twenty-four, he asks me to be his best man and Margaret sends me out to buy a suit for the occasion, handing me her credit card to buy it.

And it's May of 1982, last month I turned twenty-seven and the bag of rocks, my novel—which I started sixteen months ago in New Haven, on New Year's Day, 1980—feels heavier and hotter and when Margaret looks at me with worry and says, *Don't you think you have to finish your book and put it out there and see what happens?* I say, *Absolutely!* but her look wrings something inside me. And when their friends come over to the house and ask me what I'm doing, I tell them about my season in the Atlantic scallop fishery and the mutiny I once fomented in Cape May, New Jersey, and how I had to hitchhike home without a dime and spent the night in the hayloft of some farmer's barn in Delaware or maybe it was Maryland, and they laugh at the right places and regard me narrowly as if to say, *What's happening to this one? His wheels are not engaging with the blacktop.*

And there are Colleen and George A. in front of the whole congregation, exchanging vows and entering adulthood, ducking into the stretch limo and heading off to honeymoon on Kiawah or Folly Island before returning to their starter house in Buena Vista, and there I am, the leader of a mean platoon of Payne and Furst boys, placing a large dummy—a sort of George A. golem that's as tall as he is and has his Fuller Brush mustache and black George A. hair drawn on in Magic Marker—on the hood of George A.'s

Beamer. The creature's wearing one of George A.'s suits with fly unzipped, and emerging from the fly is a 10- or 12-inch dildo. We've cupped the golem's hand around this member and drawn, as well as we can capture it, the grin of happy illegality. Little Jack and I are laughing and high-fiving Bennett and little Dickie in the lot and it seems pretty funny, but I expect my stunt's related to the fact that in the race George A.'s leaving me behind now. In fact, I'm so far back chances are he's forgotten we were even racing and is simply out there living. And I once thought I'd be the winner.

And now a curious thing occurs. At the beginning of September, as soon as the family clears out for the season, I head down to Four Roses and very quickly something starts to happen.

I get up at my usual hour, 5, 5:30, and write till 3 or 4 P.M., and then I run and take a shower, eat a sandwich and set back to work at 8 o'clock at night, working through till 4 or 5 the following morning. Shower, eat, sleep, rise at noon and write till 10 P.M., run, eat, start again at midnight and write till 9 A.M. And when I do lie down to sleep at midnight or at noon, my mind diesels like an engine and I leap up and jot down notes on my half sheets of foolscap. Eighteen- and twenty-hour days are common, and I once sit at that rocking, flimsy table, banging the keys and speaking lines aloud for cadence, laughing, crying sometimes though not often, for thirty-six straight hours. In fifteen weeks, from September 1 till Christmas Eve, I compose 150,000 words, the same amount I've written in the fifteen months preceding. Out there, day and night lose meaning, and when I walk the beach, the broken marsh reeds at the tide line begin to resemble hexagrams from the *I Ching* and I begin to think that I can almost read them and discern something of Nature's hidden purpose or God's or Yours whoever You are. And till now I haven't known that such a state existed, which feels as good as love and conveniently does not require the presence of another, for me always the hard part and probably why I left the real world in the first place somewhere long ago in childhood and developed my big inner claw while my real-world claw stayed puny. Once you've tasted this, though, it's hard to come back to the real world or to want to. But however ravishing and beautiful, this state is wearying finally and a point comes when you almost beg for respite from it, I do, and I begin to fray and smolder and wonder how much longer I can stand it.

This is the closest I'll ever come to tasting what it might be like for George A. when he's manic and why he, or anyone, might want to flush the meds designed to stop it. And in this phase where coincidence seems fateful, I stumble on my parents' wedding photos which I've never seen and discover not exactly hidden but put away in the bottom drawer of Margaret's dressing table. The first shot in the series doesn't quite go with the others. It shows eighteen-year-old Margaret in a wasp-waisted bridesmaid's dress with a spray of chiffon over her décolletage standing in the foyer of the big house on Woodland. It's May of 1954, and her big sister Genevieve is getting married, a white wedding at Holy Innocents Episcopal before the assembled hosts of

Henderson and Bath, her husband's hometown. I imagine Margaret in the run-up, home from St. Mary's and signing for deliveries as the aunts from Bath and Richmond, those impressive, scary matrons with their jewels and their drivers, arrive to offer Mary their congratulations, saying, *How proud you must be, how proud,* and to Margaret, *One day this will be you, sugar, one day, hopefully,* and Margaret, smiling, takes that "hopefully" and runs off to accept the next delivery.

And it's May of 1954, and on the eighth Genevieve walks down the aisle, and the next picture in the folder shows Bill and Margaret on the chapel steps in Bennettsville with the justice and their dazed, exhausted-looking parents, smiling bravely for the camera. It's the beginning of September now, four months after Genevieve's white wedding, and this is Margaret's black one. And she, with her hat and gloves and traveling dress and the little black bag at her elbow, is two months pregnant. Eight weeks after Genevieve walked down the aisle, Margaret got pregnant at a house party over July 4th weekend, and offered the chance to have it fixed up north in Philly, Margaret says no, she doesn't want it fixed, she's never been so happy the family storyteller tells me later, which is why I think she feels the upwelling of the lifeforce like I later feel with Nell in New York City, and Bill beside her with his hands folded and his outsized Adam's apple looks like a condemned man on the way to his own execution.

So Margaret has the baby, me, the first boy in a generation, and suddenly all's forgiven, her parents are tearing up and passing the cigars out. Margaret takes the laurels for the first time, and what does Margaret win? The gray-shingled house on Ruin Creek, the '54 Bel Air her parents buy the couple, Eva Brame, a maid, membership at the Country Club, a pew at Holy Innocents, the ice-cream soda complete with whipped cream and maraschino cherry. And what good does it do them, do us? The end is already apparent in Bill's expression in the photo.

And on February 2, 1956, Groundhog Day, Genevieve delivers her first son, my cousin Louis, 297 days after my birth, and if a normal term is forty weeks, 280 days, Genevieve is pregnant within seventeen days of Margaret's delivery of me, within seventeen days of the parental tears and the passing of cigars and the balloon drop. And Genevieve's second son follows George A. at a similar interval and she names him George, too, as though refusing to cede title, and it's in these years that Genevieve is first forcibly committed—by her husband, Big Louis, and Margaret— and on the psych ward sets herself on fire and manages to survive it.

And when I, a man of over fifty, put this time line to seventy-something Margaret who's sterling-haired now like her mother, Margaret shakes her head and says, *All this time and no one ever saw it.* And I, at twenty-seven, four months after George A.'s wedding, set off for the beach and in a state bordering on madness, write in fifteen weeks what I've written in the fifteen months preceding.

And on December 23, I fall asleep and dream the ending of my novel, and on Christmas Eve I write it and put the final period on the final page at 3 P.M. and close the house and set out to join my family for Christmas and make it a hundred miles and pull into a cheap motel in Murfreesboro and crash there. Christmas morning I wake early and drive the deserted roads to Winston, and when I tell my family I've finished they say, Congratulations!, but their eyes say, *What happens now? What's different?* and I no more know than they do since no one's ever read it.

And three months later I'm at Four Roses with Jack and Margaret, forty feet up on an extension ladder painting the soffit in the gable, when the phone rings and Margaret throws up a second-story window and says, *It's for you, from Boston,* and hands me the phone, one of those heavy old first-generation cordless ones, and it's Houghton Mifflin telling me my novel's been accepted and they're offering me their Literary Fellowship Award and a small advance, but way high up there I don't care about the money. I can see the ocean and the sky is blue and cloudless and Avalon, the pier, isn't far now, and I'm heading toward it. Flying.

9

IN 1984, I, BIG BROTHER, publish my first novel, and one Sunday morning I walk into Rainbow News, Winston's indie bookstore, and find my picture on the front page of the *Washington Post Book World* and stand there, with something like a supernova going off inside me, as around me people go on chatting, drinking coffee.

In February of that year, at the Junior Chamber of Commerce dinner in the Ramada ballroom, George A. is Winston's Jaycee of the Month and gets his plaque and his ovation from the youthful strivers in their suits and evening dresses eating rubber chicken.

Twenty-six now, George A. has gone in four years from making cold calls at Dean Witter to become a rising star in the office, and as will always be the case, when things are good for him and me, we keep touch only fitfully, so what I mainly have of him are picture-postcard impressions from this period. He and Colleen make improvements to their house in Buena Vista, and I hear about them jetting off to Sanibel and to Jamaica for vacations. They're members of a church the way we used to be in Henderson. He and Colleen have social standing—a *position*—like so many of my friends from Exeter and Carolina, who've been to law and med and grad school and are marrying, starting practices, securing tenure-track jobs in universities. And maybe that's why my first author photo shows me in a sober business suit and a dark tie with a neat haircut, instead of as, say, the bearded trawl-boat poet who actually wrote the novel. Because of this photo choice, people sometimes ask if I'm a broker who left Wall Street to try writing. It's as if I've taken out my steamer trunk from Exeter and donned the coat that Margaret bought me once upon a time at Nowell's. Who does my doppelgänger in the suit resemble? George A., that's who. In the race, I'm gaining on him.

And now my paperback goes at auction for six figures, and soon thereafter comes a major book club sale, and then European sales, one after another. I, who six months ago was stealing firewood off public lands, emerge like Rip Van Winkle and rub my eyes and then go on a minor Dowist rampage like the hero of my novel when he first arrives in New York City. I buy a car—with cash! I buy a little house—a condominium, actually. I get a credit card, my first—with a $500 credit limit. What next?

Stacy. One night at a student play in Winston she, who has the good looks of the ingénue, does a comic turn on stage, wearing nerdy Buddy Holly glasses and speaking in a Russian accent channeled from her clowning coach at school, a Muscovite. "Hhhhhahney," she says, for "honey," slow and dripping with a Slavic note, and the first time the audience laughs, the second time we howl, and after that the building threatens to detach from its foundations every time she says it. Delighted by her talent, I write her a note complimenting her performance, we have drinks and carry the party on to my house, where I put on "Going to California" and sit beside her on the loveseat, reading her a little Eliot, "Burnt Norton," my old standby.

And unlike so many of the summer girls who fled at high speed or waited impatiently for me to wrap up my tried-and-not-so-true seduction, Stacy's eyes still and deepen and she looks as though a door has opened to a place she's never been but somehow knows about the same way I do. In addition to attraction, I recognize in her another artist and an aspiration like my aspiration to live a life that's more than working to eat in order to keep working in order to have children who work to eat in order to keep working. And so we set out together to the place that True Loves go to—call it California. With rueful fondness, then, I see us, the tinhorn writer and the actress, at the steamboat landing with a trunk of props and books and costumes in lieu of tools and seeds and rifles, and Cali seems close, so close that evening, as though we'll click our heels three times and close our eyes and be there in the morning. At 6 A.M., though, when the sky lightens and birds begin to sing outside, we're still on the loveseat with a pile of opened books and an overflowing ashtray. Stacy's glassy eyes are happy and relaxed. And she mentions him, the boyfriend. It's over now, she says. Almost. For all intents and purposes.

Weeks of nights like this one follow. I tell Stacy I love her and she reciprocates the declaration. Six weeks in, I ask her to marry me, and Stacy says she isn't ready, but she sees me as the one, she'd like to someday. On weeknights she stays with me and on weekends drives home to see her family. One night, late, the phone rings. Calling from New York, the boyfriend is collected as he lays out the situation. It turns out that Stacy hasn't been visiting her mom on weekends, but across town at her student house entertaining him, the boyfriend, when he flies down from the city. I hang up and sweep things off a bookshelf. I break up with her—only for a week, though. Then I call and say I want to work it out because I've never felt anything like this and I don't want to lose it or to lose her.

But now it seems to me that I felt something like it in New York at the 96th Street station when Nell told me she might be pregnant and I saw my future as though God or fate had spoken. I was twenty-five then. Now I'm twenty-eight. As the world turns, I've come so close to falling off the edge. But now I have a published book, I have a car, a house. And George A. and so many of my friends have settled down and married. With Stacy, I have another shot at normal. I'm the snow goose in the chevron way up high there almost in the jet stream and it's time to go south and I'm going. Looking back, I see how my urgency helps to drive Stacy underground, pressuring her to end her relationship before she's ready. On her side, she lies to me while telling me she loves me. So we get back together and set out for New York, True Loves and Fellow Travelers, with two passengers unseen behind us on the back bench of the wagon, Shadow Stacy and Shadow David, who have inflicted the first injury and carry the first grievance.

Our first two years in New York are good ones. Stacy has success as an actress—appearances on *L.A. Law* and the lead role, Catherine Simms, "a pretty heiress," in Larry Shue's *The Foreigner,* which she performs at Syracuse Stage and reprises at the Detroit Rep later. Me, I've embarked on a new book, a precursor of this one. My novel—though it's brought me, brought us, money and a degree of comfort—hasn't changed me in the way I hoped and wanted. So I resolve to go more radical, to talk about my family in a memoir, to tell or try to tell the truth about what happened—not because I understand it but because I don't and want to for the first time.

We visit Vermont on weekends, where Stacy's older sister Ginger lives in a small town with her husband and four children in a big yellow house that used to be a church, complete with steeple, choir loft and stained-glass windows. They take us in and feed us pasta dinners and sheet cake from the Grand Union.

Over time, I pick up Stacy's family story: her soldier father's repeated tours in Vietnam, her brilliant, fragile mother left alone to raise five children. After the divorce, her mother, left with little, goes back to school to get her PhD while trying to raise and clothe and feed so many. She strives but suffers periodic nervous breakdowns, periodic hospitalization. The siblings—so it seems to me—had to band together to care for and protect each other, and Ginger, as the oldest girl, mothered the two youngest, Stacy and her little brother. Ginger became a giver.

Starting out in the same birth-order position, I watch George A. get Pa's signet and the shotgun and the Datsun and I become one who wants parity and fairness, and perceives the deviation from them as injustice. As Stacy was formed in her relationship with Ginger, so I by mine with George A., and this sets us up for major conflict, and now is when we're about to learn it.

I'm glad you got this off your chest, says my old editor from Houghton when he reads my memoir. A two-year effort that nets zero dollars and is never published.

Stacy has a crisis now, too. Her agents die of AIDS, two in quick succession, and she can't get another. The money from my novel's gone or going and there's no more coming soon and we've moved from a large, gracious sublet on 104th and Broadway to a cramped ground-floor studio at 87th and Columbus. Stacy needs to make a full-time job of going to auditions—so she feels. Me, I want her to get a day job and join me in the traces, only when I suggest the possibility she regards me with surprise and disappointment, as if to say, *Who are you, David? I thought you were someone different, more generous.*

That look kills me, because somewhere inside I want to be that person, want to be Pa Rose and pull the plow for both of us, but after two years of paying our whole nut, I resent being made to feel ungenerous, though it isn't Stacy but me who makes me feel it. Under everything, I, who've run so far and hard to escape my family, find myself back in the old dynamic; it's as if, in crisis, Stacy needs the ice-cream

soda and expects me to supply it and I find this insupport-
able and toxic. In conflict, without insight, often now I say
something bad-tempered and ineffective, *This is bullshit!*,
and storm out and run some laps around the reservoir. Only
now my knee goes—first, the left, then when I recover and
start to train again, the right. And just like that, at thirty-one,
after sixteen years, it's over for me as a runner. And in this
same period, I remember drinking during the day for the
first time. This goes on for a month, and then I stop it.

So after two years in the city, the second one in conflict,
Stacy and I split up over money and all the deeper things
that go under that shallow rubric: who owes, who pays, how
much of mine—my money, labor, time, attention—do I owe
her, how much of hers does she owe me, how much into
our common operation? We never had an understanding,
much less a contract on the subject, and the issues now will
be the same as they are later when we're married.

Stacy takes a day job and moves in with a friend from art
school. I come up with a new book idea over a weekend
and set out on Monday morning writing in a fever, and the
period that follows is like the white screen after a bomb's
dropped in a movie. In my memory the next two and a half
years are white screen, and no doubt that's why I have so
few memories of George A. during this period.

I do have one, though. Down south, he's become a father
and in the summer of '86 or '87 I recall him at Four Roses
playing with the baby. It's early morning, I've come up from
the lair and find him on the ocean-facing porch, lifting his
son high, then dropping him and lifting him again, and he's

making faces, George A. is, eyes wide, going *Whoopsie, Whoopsie Daisy,* and his infant in the knit cap looks alarmed and very interested in Daddy. I see George A. in Bermuda shorts, unshaved, with glassy eyes as though maybe he and Colleen went out drinking, or, more likely, stayed up with the baby. George A.'s twenty-eight and still has the frat house on him, but you can see the office and the work world in him now, too, life is weighing in and on him just a little. George A.'s heavier, aging the way men did once upon a time in Henderson when they dealt in timber, farms and profits. He's got money and a wife who loves him and a job he loves and now a son and soon another. Little Brother's good here, all good, and the storm hits from a clear blue sky on September 6, 1987.

I've flown from New York to attend a cousin's wedding in Henderson, and Margaret's there with Jack, and Colleen, it seems, has driven with us. We're at the Country Club and George A.'s driving separately to meet us, and the night wears on and when he doesn't show, we muster and begin to whisper plans of action. Then the call comes: George A.'s wrecked his BMW. He isn't seriously injured, but when I see him the next night at Margaret's, a dark aura surrounds him. Leaning back against the kitchen counter, a beer in the hand that wears Pa's signet, he has his tie knot slacked, his collar open on a crisp white shirt that shows off his black eye, and George A. wears a sneer that says, or seems to me to say, *You disapprove? You don't think I should be doing this? Fuck it, watch me go.* And when I ask him if he tried to kill himself the night before, he answers, *Yes,* without the slightest hesitation. Yes, he says, staring me straight in the eye, and then he grins that devastating grin, sips his beer, and his warm, black eyes become disconsolate.

What's happened? It's four days before his birthday—his episodes were always in or near September. All I really have to go by is a therapist I work with later, who tells me that the four-month phase I entered when finishing my first novel was "hypomanic," so I imagine George A.'s mental state as a more intense version of what I felt out there on the Outer Banks when day and night lost meaning and I worked for thirty-six straight hours and the broken marsh reeds at the tide line resembled hexagrams and I began to feel that I could almost read them. Based on later developments, I know George A. saw or felt he saw connections in the market and traded on them for himself and for his clients. And I recall how, as I wrote my final chapters I began to fray and smolder and wonder how much longer I could stand it, and I imagine that, for George A., it reached that point and just kept going, and he must have known, having been there before, that this wound up in one place and one place only: at Mandala, in the black room where you come to and the spotlight hits you and you don't know what the play is or the character you're playing, and it doesn't matter how hard you've worked, how many cold calls you've made or how many plaques you've received in the Ramada ballroom, it doesn't matter how much your wife loves you or you love her, it happened when you were seventeen when you made eleven tackles and then again at twenty-two when Merrill hired you as the youngest broker in their

BAREFOOT TO AVALON

Buckhead office and now it's happening again four days before you turn twenty-nine, Happy Birthday, and what do you do then? Maybe you think *fuck it* and turn the wheel a little to the right and hold it and drive off the road one lonely night as you're coming to a cousin's wedding, and you do it not because things are going badly but because they're going well and it just doesn't matter how they're going.

Anger. I think that's why George A. tried to kill himself. In 2008, when Bill puts the pistol to his head and leaves his blood and brains spattered on the bathroom wall in Florida for his wife to find, my therapist will tell me suicide, particularly the bloody, messy kinds, are almost always acts of rage by which the suicide means to take down others with him. And anger is what I saw in George A.'s face that night in Margaret's kitchen. What was George A. angry at? The only thing I'm certain of is that he was angry at his illness. Why that night? I think George A. was getting manic and he knew and there was nothing he could do to stop it.

I suspect this because, only days after my return to New York from the wedding—a week or two at most—I get Margaret's phone call. George A.'s psychotic, and this time he's refused to go to Mandala, refused Colleen and Margaret both. He won't go in, Margaret says, until he sees me. So I turn around and fly home, and I recall negotiating with him on an old plaid sofa in the playroom of his house while Colleen and Margaret wait in the drive with folded arms and dark expressions. The TV's blaring, and George A. says he doesn't think he's sick, he isn't sure, he's just mainly having trouble peeing. He goes into the bath to try and puts his hand against the light switch. When I ask him what he's doing, he says he has to ground himself electrically.

—Is that weird? he asks, wincing.

—You have to go in, buddy, I tell him, and he covers his face with both hands and stands there, shoulders shaking, and I put my arms around him. When he's done, we walk out to the car and drive to Mandala.

The beads begin to look alike now. This one's red and that one's blue, in Atlanta it was hostage rescue and now he has to ground himself electrically, but asking George A. how he might not be grounded in his life seems no more helpful than asking who the hostage was that he was being sent to rescue. What matters is that the beads of George A.'s episodes are mounting and keep coming, and I know it's bad, but I have no idea how bad.

After all, we've been dealing with this for thirteen or fourteen years now, and George A.'s gotten seriously sick three times, maybe four, and every episode's been awful, hard on him and everyone around him, but each has cost only a few weeks, ten or twelve at most, a stay at Mandala to get him through the worst of the psychosis and to stabilize his lithium, a few additional weeks at home, and then, each time, George A. has brushed himself off and trotted back onto the field the way he did in football. And this episode follows the same pattern. After he rests, George A. gets up one morning and takes out a suit, shines his shoes and drives back to the office. It's gone on this way for years. Why shouldn't it go on this way for years yet? Who would ever think we're almost at the ending? I don't. I never think that.

So I fly back to Manhattan, and in 1988, a year after George A.'s accident, I finish my second novel and my agent submits to twenty-six or -seven editors. After twenty-five or -six have passed on it, I, who set out to get my hundred thousand hours in the writing lap lane, not on the pool deck with a bullhorn, am scanning the AWP listings praying someone will pay me $27.5K to teach four classes a semester and sit on "the requisite number of committees" in Alabama or Wyoming. And one gray Friday afternoon at the end of a gray week my agent calls to tell me Editor Twenty-seven has made an offer that takes me, in a week, from struggling to make rent to shopping to purchase an apartment. And one weekend on a visit to Vermont I think *what the hell* and call a realtor and find that little hidden valley that holds the late-day sunlight like a little bowl holds water, and as I stand in the upper meadow gazing toward the Adirondacks in blue profile, I hear the brook whispering below us in the streambed the way Ruin Creek once whispered below our old house in Henderson, and I go back to New York and dream about that land and make an offer and I buy it, and the first summer I put in the power, road and septic, and the second summer—'91—I begin to build it.

By this time, Stacy and I are dating again. She has her own place now on 72nd west of Broadway and is working as a researcher at a hedge fund. She's left acting and started writing, working nights and weekends on a screenplay. We start going to dinner and the theater, and sometimes Stacy reaches for the check and pays and sometimes I do, and in prosperity, with our common aspiration back in focus, our old feelings rekindle. Living separately, we feel our old issues are off the table, and it seems to us, or me, that we've solved them or life has solved them for us. After all, our circumstances are quite different. My career is back on track, on an upward trajectory, and Stacy is self-supporting, making as much as or more than I am, cheerful and contented in her independence. We aren't the same children who came to the city in 1985. I'm thirty-six, Stacy's thirty-one, we're all grown up and our connection remains a strong one. So once again we stay up late talking, laughing, exchanging thirty-minute kisses the way we did once upon a time in Winston on the loveseat, and she takes the Taconic with me up to Wells and helps me pick the white and purple lilacs for the corners. And that fall, when the house is finally finished, my first night there, arriving after midnight, I see the aurora over Northeast Mountain and it seems an omen, and a good one.

And though so many of my memories of George A. are from his illnesses, the next, though bittersweet, is from a good time. After his last break, he's picked up where he left off with his clients and been promoted to VP in the office. He and Colleen have a second son now, and in 1990 when I fly home for a visit, George A. picks me up at the airport and says he has something to show me and refuses to say what but seems pleased about his secret. We drive to Winston and snake back through quiet leafy streets in Buena Vista, and then George A. pulls into the driveway of a big brick Georgian house that for all the world resembles

George A. and Mary Rose's house on Woodland Road in Henderson.

—What's this? I ask, and he pulls out a key and jingles it the way he did once at the DKE House.

—Come on, I'll show you.

This house is the real thing, not the ersatz version Jack and Margaret purchased in the pasture out in Clemmons. It's seventy-five or eighty years old, with a front hall ample enough to host a small reception, a beautiful staircase and the heavy, ornate moldings characteristic of affluent homes in the 1910s and '20s. He and Colleen have made a bid and it's just been accepted, George A. tells me.

—You own this?

—I'm the owner, he says, beaming.

—You motherfucker, I say. Congratulations.

George A. leads me on a tour that's like a trip in time back to Henderson and our first world, and I remember in particular the backyard, which we reached by a dim, amber-colored corridor that must once have been a servants' entrance. Through a gate, onto a square of sunny, well-kept lawn, and there was a modest statue and a fountain, and the place was ringed with boxwoods, luxuriant and old, and there were children next door on a swing set, and their laughter rang, though through the leaves we couldn't see them. And the chief beauty of the place, its crowning glory, was a garden rioting with summer roses.

He and Colleen were starting renovations, he told me, and it seemed to me this is where George A. had been headed all along, and would soon live, in the house that we all dream about and work a life for, that place we're trying to get back to where everything was good and right and whole that he remembered—and I remember—though it never actually existed. And I think George A. took me there to show me he'd finally made it and done it his way, by the path laid out by others in our family, by following the traditions I'd broken and did not believe in, and by honoring the wisdom of our forebears, and there was pride and maybe some comeuppance in his attitude the way there was the day he beat me in the run to Avalon, but I think George A. mainly wanted me to see he'd won his own race. That's the sweetness in the memory, and the bitterness is that we locked the door and drove away and George A. never lived there.

In Vermont in 1991, I'm purchasing appliances and picking out my paint chips when I get the call from Margaret. George A.'s back at Mandala. In the middle of a raging manic episode, seeing genius chess moves in the market that his clients are too conservative to go with, George A. makes the trades himself, unauthorized. As I understand it, some of these go right and make money, some lose, but all represent fiduciary violations. Suits are brought against him and Dean Witter. George A.'s forced to leave Dean Witter. It's over for him as a broker. Though he's psychotic when he does it, at thirty-three he's foreclosed his future options in the business and can never again do what he's been passionate about since his teens and twenties when he started telling me the stories about Baruch and Livermore and the old Wall Street traders.

He and Colleen have to sell the new house half reno-
vated, and Colleen stays with the children in their old one,
and she tells Margaret that when George A.'s released this
time she doesn't want him back home. Though once upon
a time she said she loved him so much his illness didn't
matter, it does matter in the end, and who can really blame
her?

And perhaps there's no connection, but I can't help
thinking of Bill's actions in the end phase of his marriage,
the social suicide he committed through the theft of Mary
Rose's timber and the explosion in Boston where he made
himself an outcast. Our father's actions were those you'd
take against your enemies when you burn their houses to
the ground and lay waste their country, a place you never
mean to return to and would be unable to even if you
wished it, and in a way George A.'s actions are terminal like
Bill's were before he disappeared up those washouts in the
Shenandoah.

What's it like for George A. now, I wonder, as his levels
stabilize at Mandala and he makes the slow return from
wherever he's been? What's it like to return to Earth and
find the second world you've built has sunk beneath the
ocean like the first one, his marriage and the house in
Buena Vista gone, gone, the job he loved and can never
return to, what's it like to look around and realize that what
you've done in your insanity is done and can't be undone
in sanity?

So in the fall of 1991, George A. goes back home to
Margaret's for a little—by then, her marriage to Jack has also

ended—just until he gets back on this feet, so goes the story. And I believe it, too, believe he'll find his feet this time the way he always has before. Give him eight weeks, ten, and watch—he'll suit back up and trot back out to practice. Margaret takes him in and tries to make him comfortable, and she takes his guns, the Fox together with the Browning, and stores them at a friend's house. And Colleen files for a divorce and, because she's Catholic, applies to Rome for an annulment, denying the marriage that produced their children. And still George A., every weekend, picks his boys up and brings them to Margaret's and takes them to their practices and games and to Four Roses in the summer and holds their hands and never lets them go though his hands now begin to have a tremor from the medications, which he takes in ever-increasing dosages, and it's hard for him to wake up in the mornings and his affect is a little duller. Still, his intelligence seems unimpaired and it never occurs to me that there won't be a next act, a new and better chapter. This time, I tell myself, it's just going to take a little longer.

Me, I'm two years deep into the next book now, I call it *Ruin Creek* for a real place and it's about real people for the first time, about Who We Were, Bill and Margaret and George A. and David, in that gray-shingled house when we were still a family and believed that family love is stronger than time or death except it isn't, love is strong but time and death are stronger and the dark force that stayed hidden in the underwater portion of the iceberg grew and grew until it surfaced and destroyed us.

Why, though, why? What happened to us, what is the nature of the dark force? For me this has always been the overwhelming question, and I set out to tell the story not because I understand it but because I don't and want to, want to understand it for the first time, and when I ask Margaret, the family storyteller shares her reminiscences, and when I write Bill, he says, *I am an Indian, this is my sacred burial ground, don't rattle the bones.* But if he's an Indian, aren't I another like him, isn't George A., isn't Bennett, aren't our bones buried in that sacred mound beside his, beside theirs, don't I have a right to claim them, to go and get them, to go and get me? So, at least, I think, and right or wrong, no part of me isn't going to write it.

Looking back, though, it seems to me Bill's worries weren't unfounded. Though I set out to be neutral, and though I still find my portrait of the "Bill" character loving, in *Ruin Creek* I missed the fact that the first blow was struck by Margaret, who trapped him into marriage the way I tried to trap Nell when I plotted out our future without bothering to consult her. Because it was in my interest not to see it, I missed that my life was extracted from my young father, and Bill's last message to me in his will—*It is my intention that my son, David Payne, take nothing*—is the same one I see in his expression on the chapel steps in Bennettsville at the beginning, and perhaps because I miss this in my novel I'll have to live out in real life with Stacy what happened between Bill and Margaret long ago over her accidental pregnancy and my conception.

In 1993 I publish *Ruin Creek* to the best reviews of my career and sign a new book contract even better than the life-changing one that preceded it, and in 1994, when I come back from tour, I propose to Stacy a second time and she says yes ten years after the first time. Whatever foiled us in the past is in the past now, we're all grown up and everything is different, and as a sign and token of that difference, I say I want to finance her until she completes her screenplay. She seems pleased and says she thinks she'll need about three months to finish. So we tell our families and friends and start to plan the wedding, still a year off.

In that year, though, while we're living separately, I have an affair. Since there's no serious emotional attachment on either side and it's over in a month, I file it as an indiscretion and feel guilty but fail to take it as a warning. And then the week before the wedding, Stacy calls me from New York, some issue with the caterer, and sends me to her planner in the bedside table drawer for the number. There, mixed in with bills, I find what seems to be a recent letter to the old boyfriend, the one she was seeing ten years before in Winston, saying he's the one, she loves him more than she loves me and never should have left him. Outside the window, the meadows seem to darken as I read it. When I confront her, Stacy says it was an exercise assigned her by her therapist to unearth and exorcise old feelings. I fret and pace and in the end I do what I did the first time, I tell her I love her and don't want to lose her, and Stacy says she loves me and the feelings in the letter aren't her real ones, and I believe her or I want to. So I'm warned, too. And maybe our assurances and *I love yous* mean we want it to be true because it will be so hard if it isn't. We're so close now to a stable real-world life with a partner who's good and decent and attractive, with whom we've been through so much already and have worked and wanted it and waited.

And down in Winston George A.'s been at home for three years almost four now, and though his sojourn with Margaret is still considered temporary, by now I don't think I or anyone believes he'll ever leave there. And since he's done it all the times before this, I don't really understand why George A. can't or won't get up this time. He's made a stab at becoming an electrician, but in his first week, he falls off a ladder, hurts himself and never goes back. And Margaret's set him up in an apartment of his own, but after a month the fridge is like a toxic weapons lab again the way it once was in Atlanta, and George A.'s gone off his meds and Margaret has to go and get him and the doctors once more ratchet up his dosages.

Yet when he's back home with her and has the cash, he still makes short sales and trades options. And occasionally he buys a vintage pickup truck and restores it beautifully, only George A. gets so emotionally invested he either doesn't want to sell it when he's done or he puts so much into the restoration he barely manages to break even. Still, these efforts show initiative and diligence. How much of his incapacitation is bipolar I disorder, and how much is the old family sickness, hostile dependency, by which the weak and sick and injured depend upon and hold the strong ones hostage, and the strong ones, in the name of goodness and self-sacrifice, help the weak and disable them entirely? I can't parse it, and I'm so sorry for George A. and somewhere deep down I think he could try harder, do something if he wanted—volunteer at the library or a soup kitchen, work in an office, become a paralegal, anything except sit at home day after day watching the black crawl of the ticker tape across the screen of the financial channel. It isn't up to me, but I find it hard to look at, so it's in this era that I stop visiting Winston or go less often.

And I suspect all this contributes to my urgency with Stacy, my desire to press forward despite the warning signs, and not to miss it, living. And all our friends and family are coming up and already calling, offering us congratulations for growing up and hanging in, what a good and brave thing, how many would or could have done it, and if it's not good or brave, if we're just afraid or I am, it would be shaming to admit it, above all to ourselves and to each other. And Stacy's thirty-five, I'm forty, the years went helling by so quickly and I spent so much of mine flipping and spinning underwater in the dream worlds I created and I developed my big claw and only came up for air occasionally in the real world, when I had to. What if Stacy's my last chance at a real life and I'm Stacy's? And it's so much easier for me to say to Stacy, *How could you do this?* than to tell her, *This is what I did*.

So there we are, me and Stacy, a hot July afternoon in 1995, finally exchanging our *I dos*, our for-better-and-for-worses in the village church in Wells ten years after I asked her to marry me the first time.

George A.'s here to celebrate the day with us. He and Margaret have flown up together. There's a picture of him from the rehearsal dinner. It's taken at the house in Wells the night before the wedding, a July evening, with seventy-five or eighty people milling underneath the tent and strolling out into the meadows. It's hot as hell and my cousin Louis and I are sitting on the right side of the porch against the tan clapboards, and George A., on the left, in a wicker chair, is closer to the edge and has the sky behind him with that big view to the Adirondacks. He's wearing a polo shirt, cerulean or azure, and his plaid Bermudas pick up the blue and weave it with a green over a ground of ivory. He's in his DKE House mode and wearing DKE House colors, and the photo's taken looking up by someone sitting on the steps, and George A. has his left hand on his knee and the way he holds it is not like Louis or I do. Our hands are soft and curled, but George A.'s fingers are bent at ninety degrees and unusually long and rigid as a rake's tines, which makes me wonder if George A. has begun to hold himself that way a lot. As we go forward relaxed in our encounters, George A. holds himself in vigilance, never knowing when it might strike again, the mystic consequence that's laid him low so many times already. And though he's grinning at the camera, a flash of white teeth under black mustache, in his warm eyes there's something uncertain, slightly pleading now that isn't in the early photo on the beach. But what makes the hair rise on my forearms is the sky behind George A. out there in the gap toward the Adirondacks. The direction is due west, and it's dusk and the sky in that direction is an apocalypse of blood and fire, wave after wave of sun-tinged black-and-orange cloud, like a violent aureole around a stricken angel. If the photo on the beach is the Before shot, this is the one I think about as After.

When the honeymoon is over, Stacy returns to the city and works out the year to collect her year-end bonus and we visit weekends and she moves up after New Year's, and we're happy there in the beginning. I plow the road and vacuum up the fireplace ashes and spread them on the lilacs, and Stacy orders starter dough from San Francisco and the house is redolent of fresh bread. We chat over coffee in the mornings and she goes upstairs to the loft to write and I write downstairs in the guest room. At 5 P.M. we reassemble and start dinner and I pour my drink—a single jigger does it—and we regale each other with the day's adventures, mainly I do, I recount for her whatever treasures I've discovered on the underwater shoals I've visited. Stacy's generous with her attention, but more reticent about her own work. I don't pry, but over time I gather that her script concerns two sisters, North Carolina girls living in the city. Both get pregnant accidentally at around the same time by their respective boyfriends, each decides to have her baby. One boyfriend is new, the other immature and insufficiently supportive, so the girls head back to North Carolina to a farmhouse an old maiden aunt has left them. There, they rehabilitate the beehives and begin a thriving business, standing up against the disapproval of their parents and the narrow-minded townsfolk. And around the time the sisters go into labor, the boyfriends show up, humbled and repentant, the sisters take them back, and the movie ends with a big double wedding.

And if my first novel acted out my search for the powerful, magic father I never had and longed for, it seems to me—though this is just my inference—that Stacy's script acts out a wish for a grown-up family much like the one she knew in childhood, composed primarily of women, where sisters band together to make art and raise children, where men are provisionally admitted but nonessential. And looking back I wonder if in her heart of hearts Stacy married me and came to Vermont hoping and expecting to find in me a helpmeet and a partner more like Ginger or the sisters in her movie.

But it's good in the beginning. Though the three months Stacy said she thought she needed have turned to four and five and six, this is our best time. Spring comes, a beaver moves into our pond, we get a rescue dog from the pound, a brindled Plott Hound pup, and name him Leon and raise him like a human infant. At 5, we assemble on the porch, and I sip my drink and toss the tennis ball into the lower meadow, where Leon streaks to fetch it, ten times, twenty, fifty if I'd let him. Stacy weaves him daisy chains and snaps his picture for our Christmas card, and I tell her we're like those parents, you know the ones, who send the dressed-up photos of their children every season, and Stacy laughs and says we aren't, we aren't a *bit* like that, and has fifty copies printed and a card that says *Joy* in bright gold letters, and I sign my name and take them to the post office in the village.

I don't recall us talking about children. I know we did before the wedding. Stacy says she wants a family, and I say, Sure, I'd like to someday, but I say it lightly, the way you say you'd like to visit Rome one day and wear white clothes and watch the birds fly up above the Coliseum walls at sunset. Mainly, I want to work, to keep on writing, getting in my hours in the lap lane. And I see Stacy as another like me, an artist engaging in the practice. In a phase of plenty now, I, who haven't always been generous, get to help her.

But six months have turned to eight and nine now, and I've begun to ask when she expects to finish, and Stacy says she isn't sure but feels she's getting closer. When it gets to a year, I'm angry, I feel rug-pulled, as though we're right back where we were in New York when we broke up the first time, and the issue is the same one.

–Three months, Stacy, three months is what you said.

–So what, David, how long did it take you to write your first book, ten years?

And it's true. I feel cold-cocked when she says it. I head up onto the mountain and cut a tree down, stack a quarter cord of firewood. When I return, the storm's blown over or receded. Stacy goes on writing in the loft, I go on writing in the guest room, and nothing changes except that when I come to bed at night, I often find her sleeping with her back turned, and my single-jigger drink's become a double.

By the two-year mark, it's gone to hell. We're living in the same house and barely speaking, and somewhere near this time Stacy actually finishes the script I've begun to suspect exists only in her imagination. She sends it to an

agent who says she likes it, only it's too "artsy," not commercial. The agent wants Stacy to write a second script
—one featuring a male protagonist. When Stacy finishes,
the agent says, she'll try to sell the two together.

Fuck that, send it out again! I tell her, but Stacy's in despair.
To have come so close a second time—in writing, as before
in acting—and to need to write this second script and know
she isn't going to get to write it because there's no one to
support her while she does it. She puts it in a drawer and
I'm bemused and scared and angry—suddenly our situation
in Vermont looks disconcertingly as if we're under an
enchantment and if you gazed toward the window you'd
see briars growing up around the tower.

And then, as if on cue, when things can't get much worse,
they blow up altogether.

In Year Four of my book contract, when I finish my
fourth novel and send in my final pages, the editor rejects
it. Instead of the $50,000 installment I'm expecting on
completion, my agent tells me I owe back to the publisher
the $165,000 I've been paid already.

–How is that possible? They've seen three-quarters of the
book and paid installments all along. They can't reject it
now.

–They can, he says. According to the satisfaction clause, at
any point prior to final acceptance, they can reject the book
for virtually any reason, and you owe back the full advance.

–But it's gone. We've lived on it.

–I understand, believe me.

–Will they come after me?

—I don't know. They could.

—Can we sell it elsewhere?

—We can try, but I think we'll be lucky to get half. And whatever we do get goes to the publisher first and you'll still owe the balance.

—Fuck me.

I ask him to inquire about rewriting, and he gets back to me and says the editor agrees but says, *I have no idea how to tell him how to fix it.*

So I spend the next eight weeks setting out in some radical new direction I don't recall now and send the pages to my agent, who calls and says, I wish I could say I love it, David. I try again, another eight-week cycle, and after that another, and another, and another, six times total, and there you have Year Five under contract at income zero as Stacy and I live on credit card advances and our balance with Providian hits five figures and climbs northward. Year Six? Da capo and repeat the chorus. By this point I've burned up my thyroid gland and cracked four bottom molars from grinding them while sleeping—*bruxism,* the dentist calls it. Four root canals, four crowns. By now I can no longer bring myself to walk to the mailbox, afraid to find the letter informing me that the publisher is commencing legal action, coming for our house and property, our only assets.

Stacy's on the move now, frantically driving up to Middlebury—a postgraduate degree might enable her to teach acting, and culinary school's another possibility—and she brings home brochures and I say, *Who's supposed to pay for it?* And when she looks for jobs, all she finds available is retail down in Manchester, working for eight, ten bucks an hour, and I say, *Fuck it, why even bother?* Against our debt, the wage seems insignificant, but Stacy's therapist accuses me of sabotage and, looking back, I think he was right. Though I didn't see it at the time, I suppose the power I had in the relationship, my sense of righteousness and victimization, was worth more to me than $10 an hour, though if Stacy had taken the job it might have eased the pressure on our marriage.

At the time, in conflict, without insight, I don't even see how much our situation in Vermont resembles George A. and Margaret's down in Winston. All I see is that nothing's different, not the least bit, neither of us has grown up, we each thought the other had—meaning come around to our position. As in New York at twenty-five and thirty, so in Vermont at thirty-five and forty, only now we're married.

So Stacy doesn't get a job, my revisions are going nowhere, we go on living in the same house and practicing mutual avoidance. I'm so mad and scared now and can no longer sleep without medication, and my drinking's getting worse, I'm often having double doubles and on bad days triple doubles and I'm no fun to live with, zero, and when I drink sometimes I lose my temper and shout the way I swore I never would, and the intervals decrease between eruptions—six weeks, four weeks, two weeks, weekly. And Stacy gives me that look that says or seems to me to say, *Who are you? I thought you were someone different,* and it seems so unjust and it still kills me.

At the root of my explosions, I think I'm arguing that I'm a good and decent person who's meant well and has been generous to her, however badly things have foundered. I want Stacy to say, *Thank you, David, for those two years in New York when you supported me while I pursued my dream of acting, and for these two years in Vermont—for the first one, you were kind and willing, and the second, though you grudged it, you still gave it.* But Stacy gives me nothing, and the more I argue, the less inclined is she to give it.

And perhaps on Stacy's side, she wants me to say, *Thank you, Stacy, for loving me and listening generously and sympathetically, for making my house a warmer place, redolent of fresh-baked bread with a vase of flowers on the table.* Looking back, I wonder if what Stacy wanted wasn't what I felt bottom-fishing in the Albemarle with Pa Rose and what perhaps she'd felt only with Ginger, to be seen and understood and loved without condition by someone who won't let you go down and will go down with you if he or she has to, for shouldn't one person in this hard and often disappointing world stand up for you no matter what, shouldn't your lover—now your husband—support you and assist you in your soul quest not for three months or two years but for however long, however far?

But I don't give it to her, either.

Instead we fight. I fight with heat and Stacy fights with coldness. At the time, it seems that every fight is different and specific, but looking back I see it's the same fight over and over, a perpetual-motion machine whirring underneath the surface, a machine whose principle of operation and perpetuity eludes my understanding, though it seems to have a sense of purpose. What does the machine do? It makes us blame and make each other—and ourselves— unhappy by demanding of the other what the other can't and doesn't want to give us, by demanding from the other what is against the other's nature and feeling cheated when denied it.

Do we know how bad it is? I don't think so. Don't people tell you marriage is no picnic? Is our picnic-less-ness worse than others'? Are we outside the bell curve, out of hailing distance, or different only as fingerprints and snowflakes? Whom do you ask when you only have each other and the example of your parents' marriages, which failed as egregiously as ours is failing?

And what if we or one of us had told the truth? What if I had? What if I'd said, *I've done as much as I want to or intend to.*

What if Stacy had said, *I don't want to join you in the traces, David. Why should I give up my dream and have to grind it in the real world working to eat to live in order to keep working when you never have and have consistently refused to?*

If one of us had spoken perhaps we might have split or renegotiated our contract or had one for the first time. But neither of us says it. Why not? I can't speak for Stacy, but for me the reason is the old one. If I say it, she might leave me alone before the Urals, and this way, see, even if I'm angry and unhappy, at least I have the hologram of Stacy, the hologram of our couplehood and marriage, even if my real wife is upstairs sleeping with her back turned.

And then one day Stacy comes to me and says she's had two dreams, two only, to be a working artist and to be a mother, and now the first is gone. She wants to have a baby.

—Jesus, Stacy, I say, this isn't the right time. We're in the middle of a crisis. I need to resolve this before we even think of having children.

—What time is ever "right"? I'm thirty-seven, David. You said you wanted to have a family.

She's right, too, I did say that and she is thirty-seven and the years went helling by much faster than either of us expected. I've made her suffer and blamed her for things for which she wasn't responsible and been a bastard, who once wished to make her happy and still wants to make her happy, which is why I consent now.

And not long after, my agent summons me to New York. I drive to Whitehall and take the Amtrak to the city. It's a wet, raw winter day in SoHo, and I meet him in some eatery off Prince Street where he grins and gives me a big bear hug. As soon as we sit down and order, though, he puts aside his menu and his demeanor sobers.

—David, as your professional representative, I don't think it's in your interest to continue with this novel.

—But you said you thought the book might be my best one ...

He looks at me the way a sports fan looks at a contender, someone he's had money riding on, who's in the midst of a great contest and is losing, and simply makes no further comment.

We get through lunch, making polite, perfunctory inquiries about personal matters, and it's raining when I leave and I walk all the way north to Grand Central and my good English shoes—the ones I bought when I lived with Terrence at 99th and West End—are scuffed and soggy when I get there. A five-hour train ride back to Whitehall gives you time to think, and north of the city the rain turns to snow, and starts falling heavily. Dusk arrives, then dark, and as the ties tick under me, I gaze out at lighted windows in muddy little upstate towns and crossroads and at woods and wilderness where the snow is piling up beyond them. I try to think about my situation, my next move and so on, but the only thing I remember from that train ride now is, *The woods are lovely, dark and deep . . . The woods are lovely, dark and deep . . .* Just that line, over and over.

And when I get back to Wells there's a foot of new snow and the driveway isn't plowed. I gun the Saab up the steep part and put it in a snowbank, and then I walk two hundred yards across the meadow in my good shoes which are now ruined. Upstairs, when I sit down in the armchair to unlace them, Stacy, who's in bed with her back turned, asleep, I think, sits up and turns the light on. Her face is pale and strained.

—David, I've got some news . . .

I know what it is before she says it.

—I'm pregnant.

I look into her eyes and then out the window for a moment, then I walk over to the bed, take her face between my hands, and say, That's so great, Stacy. So great.

–Are you coming to bed?

–I'll be up in a little while.

Downstairs, I pour a drink and atop my stack, as fate would have it, is *Into Thin Air,* Jon Krakauer's account of the Everest disaster in 1996, where eight people died descending from the summit, including two of the most experienced climbers, Rob Hall from New Zealand and Scott Fischer from America, both expedition leaders. What grips me as I read, as apparently it gripped many, is the story of Beck Weathers, the Texan neophyte, who lay facedown in the snow all night in a Himalayan gale, sank into hypothermic coma, was given up for dead and left behind by his companions, yet stood and walked back into camp with one arm frozen solid and made it off the mountain.

Gray light is streaming through the window as I turn the final page, and I feel settled in a way I haven't felt in some time. In the kitchen I hear Stacy making coffee, and I stare toward the gap and the blue profile of the Adirondacks fifty miles away. As I was finishing my rejected novel I was spending eighteen-hour days pounding on the keyboard, laughing and sounding out my sentences for cadence the same way I once did with my first one. I thought the book was strong, and the strongest part was the big shipwreck scene in the finale, and Stacy thought so, too, and my agent, on his first read, concurred, even if the editor's rejection shook him, as it did me.

So today instead of setting out in yet another new and radical direction, I sit down and reread what I sent in in the first place, and pretty soon I'm flipping pages, as engaged in the disaster I engineered as when I engineered it, and when I'm done I write two letters, the first one to my agent, firing him, the second to my publisher, requesting a new editor, prepared to hear the baying of the hounds as they start north up the Taconic. Instead, to my surprise, the publisher agrees, and the new editor weighs in and says, *I like it— what's the problem?*

I like it what's the problem . . . With a heigh-ho, the wind and the rain . . .

The problem is that a book we could have lived on for four years and which I wrote in four has taken seven and that last installment payment, when it comes, goes mostly to our creditors, Providian and its successor companies. But at least we get to keep the house, and if we're in the hole, there's light above us for the first time in a long time.

And when I send Margaret the manuscript—which has a scene where the bipolar younger brother takes his older brother duck hunting on Pea Island, and all the shotgun business is recounted—George A. nabs it and calls me at the crack one morning and says he's been up all night reading, and he's bubbly and excited and tells me how much he liked it, and his generosity surprises me and shames me first before it moves me, and family love may not be stronger than time or death, but this morning it comes roaring like the brook down Northeast Mountain and blows out the constraints between us and we talk for thirty minutes or an hour the way we once did in the lair when I helped him get in shape and George A. turned me on to Blind Boy Fuller.

When the midwife calls to tell us it's a girl, Stacy cries for twenty minutes and I stand and pat her shoulder and don't know why she's crying but think, *Maybe now, maybe, maybe we can pull it out and love each other and be a family and be happy.*

And on a hot August day in 1998 when Stacy's water breaks, we get in our old Saab and drive like hell an hour north to Randolph to the birthing center and might as well have walked there. Grace, our daughter, takes her own sweet time, and comes out with an orange Mohawk and a fairy thumbprint on one eyelid, and we wash her in the kitchen sink and play with her and read her *Home Sweet Home* and play her Bach and Mozart and the Beatles and do all the things that parents do to give their children better lives. And we go sleepless for that year and then the next one, and as Grace grows and pulls herself upright we run behind— mainly Stacy does—on suicide watch as she puts her fat-knuckled fingers in every electric outlet. Me, I'm smitten and exhausted by her, my stamina's for shit and drinking doesn't help it, whereas Stacy is a dedicated, tireless mother, though I'm learning, slowly, how to be a father.

And Stacy has a full-time job now—being a mother with an infant—but three months have become three years and the one thing I've ever asked of her has been indefinitely deferred now, and when I go up most nights I find Stacy sleeping with her back turned. And though professionally I've fought the battle of my life and won, our marriage is really going wrong.

At fifteen months when Grace starts walking I take her with me out into the meadows and up onto the mountain, to the secret glade beneath the hemlocks, and we sit in dappled sun and shadow, and Grace picks up the orange newts that live there and studies them and puts them back respectfully, and as I watch her something in me tightens, I have that difficulty breathing, my heart is pierced with that new feeling I don't know the name of, regret or grief or hope or fear or all of them, and when the wind blows through the treetops or the brook runs in the distance I think it's trying to tell me something. What, though?

And sometimes at the corner of my vision I see a shadow flitting, and though I'm careful, very careful, not to look in its direction deep down I know what's lurking there behind me, the specter who has come to tell me I no longer love her and that Stacy no longer loves me, that though when I ask she says she does, I don't believe her when she says it.

With Grace's birth, Stacy has begun to talk of moving back to North Carolina. It's too isolated here, she says, Grace needs to grow up with aunts and uncles, cousins, grandparents. And Stacy never took to Vermont the same way I did, to mud season and the seven months of winter and black flies and deer season when our little hidden valley rings with shotgun blasts and there's a dead buck on the hood of every other salt-eaten pickup or every third one. Once a week, it seems, she raises this issue, and Stacy can't understand my viewpoint, why I'm unwilling to roll the dice and start fresh with her down South in a place that will be better not just for her and Grace, but for me, too, she says.

And then one day, barely a year after Grace's birth, Stacy comes to me and says she's pregnant for the second time, and this time I don't consent, reluctantly or otherwise.

–Are you kidding? You can't be serious—you can not be serious—tell me you aren't serious. How did this happen?

–It was an accident.

– Fourteen accident-free years with the diaphragm, and *now* an accident? I don't believe you.

–You don't believe me? You were there, too. That's how it happened, David, the way it always happens.

–You want to talk sabotage, Stacy? That's what this feels like.

–Don't talk to me about sabotage. You're the expert on that subject. Think what you think. Now what?

Looking back, it seems quite possible that Stacy was surprised, but it doesn't matter. What matters is that trust is broken and I don't believe her. Whoever's right, whoever's wrong, I feel trapped and whether Stacy meant to trap me or it was accidental doesn't change my feeling, and the part of *Ruin Creek* I misunderstood about my father is the part it feels to me as if I'm acting out and living now, and the answer to the question of what hurt Bill to make him hurt us, hurt me, is this, this did, it was his furious protest at the *qi* Margaret was extracting from him and his powerlessness to stop it. Now at length I understand my father. I am him. And the part of *Ruin Creek* that I got wrong, I'm living.

And when Stacy wrote, her soul dream was of sisters who get pregnant accidentally and flee south to North Carolina and live with sisters and are each other's helpmeet and raise children responsibly and creatively, and the men and fathers of these children are nonessential and to be included must surrender and appease the women, and now Stacy, with Grace, our toddler, and our unborn baby flees to North Carolina to her mother's and her sister's just like the sisters in her film script. The dream she dreamed while writing upstairs in the loft has come to pass now in the real world.

There she goes down the jetway in Albany, and the last thing I see is Grace's little face looking back at me over Stacy's shoulder.

Once upon a time we were a family and believed that family love is stronger than time or death except for us it wasn't, something else was stronger. The dark force—call it extraction, trapping, power, taking from another what the other doesn't wish to give you—overcame the love between us and became the core transaction in our marriage and led us here wherever here is, wherever we are, and where we are is in the witch's forest, and Stacy isn't the witch, no, she's more like Gretel and I'm Hansel. We're more like sister and brother than like wife and husband. We've wandered in and now the birds have eaten up the breadcrumbs and we're under an enchantment, I am, and the curious thing is how the trees at the wood's edge resemble those outside it, and it's only later, deeper, that the shadows blacken with a different blackness and the birds stop singing and the trees turn gnarled and leafless, and you know you're lost or I do or might have had I turned to face the specter but I don't, I'm careful not to, and maybe that refusal of the truth I already know accounts for that tightness in my chest when I'm out there in the woods with Grace whom Stacy has now taken from me.

And what will it take to avoid the specter's message now? As I'm driving home from the airport, I already know the answer. It's going to take this place, Vermont, these meadows and this mountain and this house I drew a hundred times before I built it and the oaks and ash and birches and the lilacs at the corners. And I already know I'm going to do it. Even before I call the realtor and set out into the meadows I know I'm saying goodbye and bringing in my firewood for the last time.

I came here to a country that was not my country resolved to live under unfamiliar stars in a ledgy meadow filled with weedy unfamiliar flowers in some way to escape my family, and built the new house and wrote the book to try to understand what happened in the old one where George A. slept beneath me in the bunk beds, and everything I vowed not to repeat I have repeated and everything I came here to escape I re-created in the place I came to to escape it. And I've brought or helped to bring a child into this place to be lost with me, with us, and now Stacy and I in our lostness have conceived another, and I don't know how to leave and don't want to die here and leave them to find their own way out. And the one thing I'm certain of is that I can't disappear the way Bill did in the Shenandoah. Right or wrong, whether I should or shouldn't, I'm going to North Carolina, and when the Mayflower men in the big van are no more feasible than a summer on the Riviera, Margaret tells me, *Ask your brother,* and I don't even have to, George A. calls me not an hour later.

IV
2000

Then saith he unto them, My soul is exceeding sorrowful, even unto death: tarry ye here, and watch with me.

—Matthew 26:28

10

S O I PICK HIM UP in Albany on October 30, 2000, a Monday, and if you haven't seen George A. in a while, you tend to forget the size of him—almost twice as wide and a third again as high as his fellow travelers in the concourse. Since my wedding five years earlier, he's put on another thirty pounds and there's more silver in his hair and in that Fuller Brush mustache of his that makes him look a bit like Bill now, though his expression's softer, and when he lights his cigarettes the tremor in his hands is more noticeable than I remember. He's wearing khakis and a nice new shirt, navy blue, long-sleeved, still with horizontal creases from the package—Margaret, I suspect, has been shopping—and a pair of white size-16 Air Jordans, and he comes toward me up the ramp with that slightly floating walk he has, like an astronaut in zero gravity. His grin is little changed, still sweet and shy and sly, and his eyes are still like Margaret's, dark and deep and warm as a Spaniard's or a Russian's, and though the circles under them have blackened, he's still all there behind them. At forty-two, George A. remains handsome, but he has a slightly ragged look, an unhealthy tinge to his complexion, the effect of years of medication on his liver and his kidneys. And his haircut is a little bit unkempt, like a late-summer garden that's gone by where the weeds have begun to take it. He looks as though he hasn't slept that well the night before and maybe for ten or fifteen years previously, which is to say he looks a bit like I do now when I gaze in the mirror, only with that more and better hair I envied.

–Hey, man, good to see you, I say. Put on some weight?
He grins.
–A bit. You?
–Fuck you, asshole.
–*Heh heh heh,* he says, this smoky, whiskied laugh like an old barroom sage's.

His old laugh has something new now. I don't know where he got it, maybe Jupiter or Venus.

Then we shake hands the way we learned as boys and hug and George A. gives me those two back-claps. We throw his bag in the Explorer and set off up the Northway.

On the way home, we stop off at Macaroni's, the Italian joint in Granville, and eat a garlic pizza, and we sit up awhile that night and discuss the season prospects for the Heels and trade a few Bill stories the way kids trot out their Pokémons and Yu-Gi-Ohs, comparing life point totals for their super-villains and superheroes. George A. goes out on the porch to smoke with the Hellmann's jar lid as an ashtray, then heads off to bed, and when he gets up in the morning I notice he's slept in his clothes.

We roll up our sleeves then and go after it, taking that house apart from front to back and top to bottom, from the attic to the crawl space. That's what the next days mostly are, work, with breaks to shoot the shit, and we keep music playing in the house around us. George A. makes me laugh once, rapping along with Tupac on "Dear Mama," this big, ungainly white boy throwing signs and I laugh so hard I have to get a glass of water to stop choking.

We quickly fall into our old relation the way we always have after an hour in each other's presence. In recent years, we just haven't had that many hours, mainly because I haven't made them, ruminating on him down in Winston, on Margaret cooking steaks and serving him on a tray in the back room, tucking $10s and $20s in his pocket, while up here I ground my teeth and tried to keep our ship from sinking. Now that we're together, the tension lifts and I give over with relief and gladness, and a big part of the difference is that George A.'s here to help me, and I've been mad and tense with him for so long because he's needed so much helping. He's been like a black hole that's sucked in energy and time and money and sucked in, finally, our mother, who once upon a time was my mother, too. Losing her is something I thought I was long since over, only in the moonlit realm where we're three years old forever, I'm not sure you ever really do, or only kinda sorta. Ask Tupac, if you don't believe me.

And let's face it, though I've invested endless quantities of psychic energy in denial, somewhere deep inside I've been mad at him for winning her and mad at her for letting him. And even if I knew the prize is poisoned, I knew it in the high place where the sun shines, but in the low one which is touched by moonlight only, where the three-year-old with the silver six-gun lives and never dies and never can inside us, I've resisted reason and resent George A. for devising the genius flank maneuver that brought him complete and total victory on the basis of complete and total losing. The bottom line is, though I know George A.'s sick and try to make allowances, I've never been able to put to rest the suspicion that he could have done more, done something, had he wanted to and had Margaret required it of him. But he didn't, and she didn't, they made some old agreement common in our family, one I stepped out of trying to be a self-supporting grown-up, and not always succeeding all that brilliantly.

George A.'s not a perfect person, but guess what, I'm not a perfect person either, as I expect you might have noticed. I'm not going to sentimentalize him—if I'm not a hero or a victim in this story, he doesn't get to be one either—but it isn't sentiment to say that his last act is an act of generosity. He flies up to help and gives eight days of his life to a brother who has made no secret of his disapproval, and those eight days prove to be George A.'s last ones, though of course neither of us knows it. I've been mad at him for years because he's taken so much and given back so little, but, given the chance, there George A. is beside me with his sleeves rolled up, ready, willing, able.

He helps me take that house apart down to the old photos and turkey feathers and NYC restaurant matchbooks in the bottom of the drawers. Mostly it's work, like life is, I suppose, which makes you realize, when death casts its clarifying light in retrospect, that the hours spent working are pretty much the same hour over and over and not what you'll remember. What I remember are the breaks we took, the shit we shot, the evenings and meals we had or made together. He cooks me his Vermouth chicken, and having thought of Margaret cooking steaks and carrying them on trays, I'm surprised by his adroitness in the kitchen.

Despite the twelve- and fourteen-hour days, as the week advances, we fall further and further behind schedule and I'm getting anxious. The clock is ticking on the truck, and extra days cost extra money. The plan has been to pack and leave by lunchtime, Sunday, November 5. I've badly underestimated, though, and by Monday morning, November 6, we're not even close to being finished. If we pack all day, however, we think we can get away by lunchtime Tuesday, November 7.

That night, the sixth, I ask George A. what he'd like for supper and he grins and says he wouldn't turn down another Macaroni's garlic pizza. So we drive to Granville, and at the video store, George A. picks out *Any Given Sunday*, reaching perhaps for some old memory of his glory days at Woodberry when he made eleven tackles and called me in my dorm at Avery, and it seemed not only possible but likely that that would be the first of many victories. Yet neither of us finds the film particularly compelling—too choppy, too much bogus mysticism, all that Indian business . . . But, hey, look who's talking. Still, we stay up late and do our duty by it, or I do. Toward the end, I remember looking over to see

George A. dozing on the sofa, snoring lustily with a sound like big limbs going through a chipper.

The following morning, November 7, I'm at the kitchen counter pouring coffee when George A. emerges from the bedroom with a grin, that one of happy illegality.

–Guess what? George A. says, beaming, blushing, still in last night's clothes, with his hair flattened on one side and pushed up in a cowlick.

–What?

–I woke up with a boner.

–Do tell, I say, pushing a mug toward him—black, the way he likes it.

–It's the first time in two years.

–Two *years*? I say. And then it hits me. What, the medication?

George A. sips and grins and nods, confirming.

–Well, I'm happy for you, bruh, though to be honest, that's more information than I needed.

–*Heh heh heh.* Pleased with himself, as I am for him as well, George A. laughs that smoky, whiskied laugh. That laugh really gets me.

Two nights before he dies, then, his animal self returns to pleasure him, like the childhood horse you've ridden coming from the pasture to the fence the day before you leave the farm to nuzzle in your pocket for the carrot or the sugar cube, taking leave of you as you are leaving. In retrospect, it's hard—for me, at least—not to see it as an omen, and there are several from this point, all equally explicable as coincidence. Maybe I need to see what really wasn't, like

Stone with his Indian business. But on the other hand, the fact that such signs and portents are so frequently reported may be because they really are there after all, only they tend to slip beneath the radar, except when death casts its clarifying light in retrospect and makes us look a little harder. I don't know the answer, and I'm not insisting.

So we tank up on caffeine, roll up our sleeves and set to it once again, and by lunchtime, our new deadline, we aren't even close to being finished. Nor are we at 3 o'clock, or 4, and now it's 5 and dusk is falling, dusk is far advanced. Our neighbor, Cathy, is there, and Glenn D. from down the road, all pitching in to get us out of there. And I see George A. on the front porch with the dryer trailing silver metal venting. He's tipped the hand truck forward and is leaning on the big appliance with his elbows, smoking a Winston, tired but hanging in there. The advancing wall of our possessions has reached the back of the big truck and overspilled. The whole front porch, in fact, is crowded with other indispensables, and I'm in the truck, examining the load, which is absolutely airtight.

—Fuck, guys, I say, this just isn't going, is it?

They all look at me with dour eyes and don't reply. The answer's obvious.

—I guess I'm going to have to get a trailer. Do you think the U-Haul place in Rutland is still open? I check my watch. I guess I'll call them. Hey, George A., what do you think—are you okay driving one?

This, I think, is how it goes, or pretty close. Funny, though, I don't recall his answer. It's probably something like a *Sure, why not,* maybe a resigned, compliant shrug. I do know he poses no objection. How can he, though, given how I frame the question? And it never occurs to me to wonder, given George A.'s physical impairments—his shaking hands, the black circles underneath his eyes, the floating walk—if he's capable of driving such a rig. I won't think of this till years afterward—years, literally. And why won't I? Is it because George A. drives an SUV himself in Winston and his privileges have never been questioned, much less restricted, because he has, from time to time, accompanied Bill in his wanderings and learned to drive and even back a trailer quite expertly? The real reason, though, boils down to simple self-involvement. I need to get to North Carolina. We're two days late already. The clock is ticking on the truck and extra days cost extra money. And here's the point at which my judgment must be questioned.

So dusk is far advanced as I set out for Rutland and come home by dark with the battered dualie like the one Bill hauled through the Shenandoah, another strange coincidence that has a sense of portent to those, like me, inclined to look for it, and things at the end start to circle back and resemble things at the beginning.

So I walk backward down the hallway with my mop like an Indian with a swag of pine, erasing ten years' worth of tracks laid down by me and Stacy. I put the keys in a Tupperware under the back steps and when I stand, I catch the recently mown meadows' scent, the summer scent of Joe Pye weed and black-eyed Susans on that warm November evening, and something inorganic—is it diesel?

No, whatever it is it makes me think of gun oil, Hoppe's 9, what I smelled on the back porch at Jack and Margaret's house that Christmas, and I'm giving up this place the way I once gave up the shotgun, and though I don't get this something stabs me and I struggle for the name and call it grief, though perhaps it's premonition. And when I look in the back of my Explorer, I see the Staffordshire greyhound with the bloody rabbit in its teeth that came to me from Great-aunt Polly and the framed letter my old editor from Houghton wrote me once upon a time and something makes me take them with me. And before we go, I tap on the Explorer's window. In the greenish backwash of the instruments, George A.'s in there smoking, and when I surprise him his first impulse is to hide the Winston, mine to make some remark about my pristine ashtray.

–Ready? I say instead, managing to suppress it.

–Whenever you are.

–Thanks, George A.

–It's no big deal.

–No, seriously, man, I tell him. I couldn't have done this without you. You're a good brother.

And then he exhales his smoke toward the shotgun seat, and says, "It's okay, David."

It concerns me just a bit, in writing this, that you— assuming anyone is out there—may not believe me, that you'll think I'm succumbing to the temptation to write fiction, for no one else was there, of course, and so no one can gainsay my version. And the reason why I fear it is because what I say to George A. in the meadow upon leaving is what I might have liked to say if I'd had the opportunity to plan it, if I'd known those were the last real words I'd ever speak to him, and if I'd known where we were headed. That whole time has that feeling for me now, as if we knew we only had that time, those eight days to live it, and were determined not to blow it, but of course we didn't know—or did something in us know it? If I were writing fiction, though, I'd have him say, "You're a good brother, too, DP, you helped me in the past, so I help you in the present"—that, or any of the other things he might have said that would have been more flattering to my vanity, my need for reciprocity and closure. But George A. doesn't say those other things. He says, "It's okay, David."

Still, I'm glad I say it, glad it pleases him, and I think it does, for before I turn away, I squeeze his shoulder and he meets my eyes and smiles just slightly, and for a moment in the cab's deceptive light, he resembles that other person, the boy and young man I knew better, George A. Payne, my brother, whom I lost sight of through the long, long, selfish middle of the story he comes back so briefly at the end of.

So now I whistle up Leon, who gains the high seat of the truck with one lithe spring, and the high beams splash the birches as we set off across the culvert and ride our groaning, overloaded rigs downhill, and I check the sideviews for him for the first time, and smell the meadows for the last one. And, oh, I want to slow it down, I want to make the clocks stop or reverse, but it's no more possible than making the brook run backward up the slope of Northeast Mountain. Why do I want to slow what long since happened? Perhaps because if I don't put it down in cold, hard words on paper, I don't have to finally accept that it ever really happened.

So the hard part of the journey follows in these next two hours, driving, dog-tired in the dark, down those winding secondaries through upstate New York with rigs that are unfamiliar and overloaded. All that passes without incident, with flying colors even, and in Albany we hit the Thruway, my jaw unclenches, my shoulders drop, my grip eases on the wheel, and we take 88 toward Binghamton, beyond which lie six hundred miles of interstate straight through to North Carolina.

We spend two more hours on the road that night, and toward midnight, George A. flashes his brights at me, our signal, and we pull over at a rest stop and he says he needs to turn in, and we take the first exit we come to in Binghamton. I've been listening to election results come in on NPR, and Gore is winning, so in the motel parking lot, I do a little victory dance for George A., and he, a Bush man, smiles and nods sportingly, and lights a cigarette and watches through narrowed eyes, and doesn't seem to take it personally.

I remember that motel now, a Super 8 that in the lobby seems like any other. After we get our keys, though, we pass along the outer balcony, rolling our clacking bags behind us, past whole wings that are cordoned off and undergoing renovation, a construction moonscape. Outside his door, we say good night and hug, two back-claps, brisk as always, though I hold them in my memory. I kiss him on the hair above his ear the way I did when he was four and I was seven.

–Sleep tight, buddy.

–You, too, David.

I roll on, and George A. goes off to sleep his last sleep in his clothes in a Super 8 just off the interstate in Binghamton.

I wake at five, my usual hour, shower, and sit outside and watch the sunrise by the pool—*Dry the pool, dry concrete, brown edged* . . . no water and no lotos rising, just a Hurricane fence with green plastic webbing, just a red sky at morning, and not a very threatening one, just a smoggy smudge of one in the east, mellowing to gray overcast on an unseasonably warm day in a roadside motel in America with the whoosh of traffic and exhaust smells wafting off the highway: November 8, 2000. And years later someone will tell me, in connection with events in Florida—hanging chads and so forth—that Mercury was retrograde then, that that was why for the first and only time in two hundred years the Republic botched an election.

I remember checking and rechecking my watch—6 A.M., 7, 7:30, 8. We have six hundred miles to go, ten hours if we push it. Thinking back, it's the sole annoyance I recall from those eight days. Finally, around 8:30, my usual lunch hour, George A. joins me in the common room, teeming at that hour with heavy businessmen and traveling salesmen, high-mileage types like Bill, our father. And how many such motels, I wonder, driving how many trucks and U-Haul trailers that have gone missing from the company, has Ahasuerus lain down in and spread his tools out on the floor and looked around for signs and omens and reversed the handles if he had to to correct the mojo. Maybe the old man was onto something, too bad we don't have him with us. We don't, though, so we pour our milk on stale Froot Loops from the cloudy bin, as overhead the TV blares and tells us that the tide has turned his way for Bush by now, but, George A., subdued with sleep and mellow in my recollection, doesn't gloat, he merely smiles and nods and shows forbearance, declining to retaliate for my end-zone victory dance the night before.

So we're back out on the highway now, caravanning, me ahead and George A. following down 81, a straight shot from Binghamton and into Pennsylvania near Scranton; down to Lebanon, under the gray overcast, and it's warm enough to keep the windows open; down through those lush fields with the stone barns the Amish built to last forever, decorating them with hex signs for magical protection; down through Harrisburg and Carlyle and across the Susquehanna where Lee sat, grieving, upon Traveller and watched the remnant of the Army of Virginia pass after Gettysburg, the same route I took with Bill and Margaret once upon a time, only in the opposite direction. And already we're in Maryland, which passes in an eye blink as the dotted lines fly like tracer rounds and pass harmless underneath the axles. And somewhere between Maryland and the West Virginia panhandle toward 1 P.M., as I check my mirrors—left, then right, then straight ahead back through the windshield—George A.'s high beams flash and we pull off for gas and I ask him where he wants to eat and he chooses Taco Bell. He orders a couple of burritos, and we eat together standing at the counter, and I note the way he wolfs them, spilling a little and licking salsa off his fingers. I remember thinking at the time he's let his hygiene slip, it seems of a piece with sleeping in his clothes, and only years later will it occur to me that in those eight days we spent together I'd never seen him eat that way any other time, that it may have nothing to do with hygiene slippage, but rather with the fact that he's tired and overstressed from so much driving. He seems okay, but maybe I'm not paying close enough attention, which is another place my judgment must be questioned, where I must question it, and you must question me if you are going with us. And don't hesitate to judge me as severely as I judged my brother, and maybe if you do, and if I can prove with your concurrence that I'm to blame for what's about to happen, I can finally get some peace from the acceptance that I must have wanted this and caused it by some mystic spell or intervention. For didn't I put my silver six-gun to my mother's belly when she warned me he was coming, and haven't I been angry with him ever since for winning her, and haven't I wished him harm a thousand times in the moonlit underwater seven-eighths that drives the iceberg through the ocean?

Though in my heart I know it was an accident, unwished and uncontrollable by me or anyone, still, if I only notice how George A. eats and draw the right conclusion, we might stop right here in Maryland or West Virginia, but I don't notice, and it's too late now, we're on the road again and crossing into endless, high Virginia. We're heading down the flank of the Blue Ridge through Winchester, Front Royal, Harrisonburg, up there where our father's father's people come from, and things at the end are circling back to resemble those at the beginning. And we're just a stone's throw from Woodberry now where George A. had his glory game and made eleven tackles and first got sick and saw Bill with his U-Haul trailer in the motel parking lot, who wasn't really there and maybe that's why George A. saw him, because Bill never really was, and George A. needed a real father as much and maybe even more than I did. We're only an hour north of Roanoke now, and from there it's a straight shot south down 220 to Greensboro, and an hour farther on lies Hillsborough, home, this house where Stacy's waiting, with whom I'm starting over. Three and a half more hours, the hard part's behind us, we'll be home by dark, I'm tired but starting to feel excited. Who knows, tonight maybe I'll get lucky in the big bed, and even if I don't, I'll get to hold my children, my daughter, two, and my infant son just four months old, I barely know him, but I want to, I want to be more than a phantom to my children. And George A., who lost his own wife and marriage, has helped me get here; when the Mayflower men and the big van were no more feasible than a summer on the Riviera, he's made it possible for me to get this chance to save my marriage and to be a father to my children and to watch them grow and help them and to have a life that's something more than an alchemical relation with a mountain and a Taoist voyage into the astral planes inside me.

We're an hour north of Roanoke where the homestretch starts, and it's coming on to 3 P.M., and we're approaching Lexington where Bill lived for a year in high school. I'm listening to the election updates on NPR, and they're increasingly troubling, and also keeping tabs on George A. in the mirrors—left, right, then straight ahead back through the windshield, every ten or fifteen seconds. I'm waiting for his brights to flash, being vigilant, you know, but they never do, it doesn't happen that way, how you think it will, and the signals you prearrange to keep yourself and others safe according to the ur-control scenario are finally only magical and have no bearing on the outcome. And, oh, I want to slow it down, I can't though, the clock is ticking, it's coming on to 3 o'clock, we're approaching the first exit coming into Lexington on 81, up there in the Shenandoah where our father's father's people come from, where Bill went looking for himself after he lost us, hauling a trailer like the trailer George A.'s hauling, full of things I think are indispensable, things I think I need, a dryer and a washer, how I wish I'd left them, left mirror, right mirror, straight ahead back through the windshield, every ten or fifteen seconds, four times a minute for twelve hours—almost three thousand times—I've looked for George A. in the mirror, and he's been there, okay, each time till this one.

This time, when I check, there's something different in the mirror, not so different, though, not really even worrisome, George A.'s drifted just a bit across the line onto the shoulder. How many times, though, have you done this, or seen someone do it in the car ahead of you, a small lapse of attention followed by a quick recovery, and maybe you step on the gas and pass the other driver with an angry look or gesture, and maybe he shrugs as if to say, *I'm sorry,* or flips you off for being angry and intolerant. You know how it is, though, you go on down the road and thirty seconds later, when your pulse recovers, it's as if it never happened. This is how it is now, and this is the box in which I start to put what's happening in the mirror before I glance back through the windshield. Maybe George A.'s reaching for the lighter, maybe to change the channel on the radio, maybe after those burritos and six or seven hours on the road he's a little drowsy and nods off for just a moment and comes to on the shoulder and scares himself and jerks the wheel too hard as he comes back toward the center of the highway ... What happens, I'll never know, but the next time I look, as George A. comes back from the shoulder, the single motion of the Explorer and the trailer becomes two motions, the synchrony is broken, but still it isn't troubling, the U-Haul simply woozes toward the center of the road as the Explorer woozes back toward the shoulder, it's all so slow and languid, though there are two motions now, not one, both seem unthreatening, though I have a sinking feeling as I watch them in the mirror. And then the trailer's inboard side nudges slightly up the way you nudge a shoulder when you're putting on a backpack. It rocks up on a wheel and comes back down and sways a bit, like a gymnast in a dismount in the moment between sticking it or stumbling, and in the two, almost three thousand times I've checked those mirrors there's been no moment and no motion such as this one, so I'm no longer staring through the windshield or using the right mirror, I'm watching this with fixed attention in the left one, and though the motion's troubling now, it's still recoverable, still in the realm of the close call you've had if not a thousand or a hundred times, once or twice at least, and you're still here to tell the story.

The next thing in the mirror, though, I've never seen or been in, and the voice that says it's still recoverable is starting to seem less and less rational, more like a magical incantation. After a couple of those slow and woozy motions that I tell myself are really not that worrisome, the trailer cracks the Explorer like a whip in a sharp violent motion and the Explorer jackknifes and turns perpendicular to traffic, and whatever near misses I've had or seen or been in, I've never seen or been in anything like this one, and I'm watching in the big side mirror, chanting, No, huh-uh, no, no, aloud or maybe only silently even as another voice inside me whispers, It's going to be okay, because it has to be so he can be so I can be according to the ur-control scenario. Watching this in helpless disbelief and terror, I will everything to go back to normal and recover, requiring God to make this restoration out of fairness, as the Explorer, moving at seventy or seventy-five miles an hour, is coming sideways down the highway perpendicular to traffic. And suddenly upended by its own wheels, it rolls and crashes on its top and begins to fly and bounce and fly and bounce, leaping and spinning with horrible exuberance that makes the universe seem under the control of something joyful and malignant and comes to rest on the passenger side against the safety railing, and the trailer, which has broken from the hitch, goes down the center of the highway round and round like a dervish with the yoke and safety chain striking sparks off the roadbed.

As I pull the big truck onto the right shoulder, Leon, my brindled hound, looks up at me as if to say, *Why are we stopping . . . ?*

Now from the enclosed cab out into the world, into the exhaust smells, the whizzing sound of traffic, underneath the muggy gray November overcast. I climb down from the truck and hurry across the highway from the right shoulder to the left one, not darting because my knees no longer dart, where cars are whooshing by at seventy-five and eighty miles an hour, though some of them, by now, are slowing, the drivers and passengers looking intensely in their mirrors, the rearview and the side one, or rolling down their windows and pointing back with animation. I'm moving up the left shoulder, not exactly running, but a sort of power walk, my shot joints jarring with every step that used to take me twelve or fifteen on any given Sunday. There's gravel and then glass shards crunching underneath my shoe soles, and I can see the Explorer on its side against the railing with the upper wheels still turning. As I draw near, there's debris along the roadbed, pieces of my life with Stacy, like flotsam where the ship sank. Is it now or later that I see the Zip disk? I really can't remember. If I do, I'm pretty sure that I don't pick it up yet, nor does it occur to me to wonder how it's come to be there, how it got out of the drive bay of the computer and through the rolled-up windows to land here, thirty yards behind the accident, and since I don't pick it up I don't yet see the red flecks I notice later.

Instead, I'm thinking, George A. may be hurt, I have to get him out, but he's okay, okay, I think I'm preparing myself to see him, preparing what I'm going to say . . .

—George A., are you all right?

—I don't know, I think so, just get me out of here.

—Okay, don't worry, help is on the way. Hold on. I hear the sirens coming.

This is the conversation I'm having with him in my head, trying to ward off the sinking feeling, but, oh, it's getting deeper as I near the car, and traffic in the other lane is slowing, people are gawking out their windows, their curiosity is so human and so horrible, it offends me deeply, though I know they mean no harm, they're just glad it's someone else, not them, the same way I'd be. Only today it's me, and it's George A. Today's the day the spell breaks and we're all alone before the Urals.

And here I am, and there he is, slumped from the driver's side into the passenger seat as though asleep. Still in his safety belt, his waist and feet are higher than his head, which is almost at the level of the road, and I kneel and touch his shoulder through the shattered windshield, I call his name and press and press and call again.

—George A.? George A.?

Though Stacy's brother, later, at the salvage yard, will warn me away from the Explorer with a look, at the scene I remember very little blood. George A.'s eyes are closed, slightly tensed as though bracing for impact. He has a serious expression, like someone with a bone to pick who's starting to realize you aren't going to see his side of it. Clearly, he's unconscious, he looks almost like a boxer who's received a KO punch, only any moment, when they break the ammonia capsule beneath his nose, he's going to startle to, and look around, and get it, only on the seat beside my brother's head there's a small puddle of clear fluid, and it troubles me, I can't think what it is, it isn't water, it's thicker than water. I'll later wonder if it might have been brain fluid, but it would have been bloody in that case, wouldn't it, and the puddle isn't bloody, it's clear as water, only thicker. Is that when I notice? I think so. George A.'s feet—still behind the pedals—are tremoring, not violently or spastically, but very gently, very softly, the sort of tremoring that suggests things winding down, things concluding, not recovering. A dire feeling comes over me, a feeling like the shadow of black wings passing overhead, above the scene, the sort of wings that leave frost behind them on the earth, on every blade of scarce-created grass the passing shadow touches . . .

–George A.? I say again. George A.?

Kneeling there, calling through the broken windshield, I hold his hand, almost a third again as big as mine, and warm the same way mine is. There's a woman standing over me, reaching down to touch my shoulder, regarding me with an expression I don't want to see. She's trying to coax me away from him, speaking in a gentle voice, the way you'd speak to a child or to a frightened animal, not condescending, just gently, respectfully coaxing me to rise and come away and leave my brother here, and I know what this coaxing means, somewhere inside I do in the small, small place where I'm still sane, the small, small place where I'm not casting ancient spells of prophylaxis and reversal according to the ur-control scenario, where is where I am right now, in the magic kingdom that I'm the king and only god of, where nothing ever happens except as I command it, and nothing can ever hurt me so long as I stay inside the magic circle, and maybe that's why something inside me larger than I am bids me to go back now to that awful scene upon that awful highway to suffer now what I didn't suffer then because I wasn't really there the first time.

And though I'm not really there, I know what her expression means, this stranger's, and I'm not having it, not from her or anyone, I don't want to be awakened from my dream, I'm angry at this woman for interrupting, and George A.'s feet are still tremoring behind the pedals. That means he's still alive, and how can I leave him when at any moment he could open his eyes and look around him? Why is she insisting that I leave him, doesn't she understand the basics about family, that you don't leave a fallen member, ever, especially not your little brother who is there to help you—help me—move my family? And George A. has that serious expression, that look of gritted teeth, and there's that clear pool of fluid on the seat beside him, I can't stop looking at it, it's horrifying to me, though I don't know why, there's nothing the least bit horrible about it. Later, I'll obsess on it and wonder what it could have been, how many different types of fluid do human beings have inside us anyway, but if it was internal fluid from his brain or elsewhere and came out violently and unnaturally, wouldn't it have been mixed with blood? It isn't though, the puddle is perfectly clear, like the water at the beach when the wind is from the east, only thicker, thicker than water. And only years later—years, literally—will it occur to me it was probably just saliva, a little pool of it there beside my brother's head, no more mysterious than the spot of drool you leave on your pillow when you fall asleep. George A. isn't waking, though, and now the paramedics have arrived and I have to move so they can do their work. The next thing I remember, I climb on the car and start to wrench the driver's-side door, I pull and pull, but it's crushed and doesn't budge, and I hear sirens and a fireman joins me. He's young and in full gear and has a crowbar, and he goes at it with me, we try to jimmy it together, he doesn't ask me to leave or try to coax me away, he seems to understand a brother doesn't leave a brother or blame me that I left mine long ago, no one knows that except George A. and Margaret, and me, of course, I know, but the fireman doesn't, he seems to believe that I'm doing everything a good brother would and should do. But he can't budge it either, not even both of us together with the pry bar.

I don't remember giving up and getting down from there. I must have, though, and the next part is the part I'm most uncertain of. I don't know when it came in the sequence or if it even really happened. I'm gazing through the broken windshield at George A.'s hand—not holding it, just staring—and I see Pa's signet on his right ring finger. There's

blood on it, not much, just a little, and his fingertip is missing. It's somehow been clipped off cleanly in the accident,
and this is the only physical damage I remember from the
scene.

Later, after visiting the funeral home, my mother will tell
me there was a deep puncture wound in George A.'s head,
right at his crown, inches deep and big around as a silver
dollar, where some piece of the collapsing moonroof, some
stanchion or piece of metal framing drove into his skull and
killed him, probably the first time the car rolled. I never see
that wound, though, hidden in that pelt-thick hair I envied,
all I see is the missing tip of George A.'s finger, and I'm not
sure it really happened, and the reason is because at the
Valley of the Little Bighorn, Custer's brother, Tom, died
with him in the ambush. Custer, early on, had married a
Sioux woman and because of the kinship tie, the Sioux,
instead of scalping and mutilating the general the way they
did Tom Custer and the other soldiers in the Seventh
Regiment, merely clipped his fingertip and took it as a
trophy. I can't be sure if George A. really lost his fingertip
or if I read it in a book and lifted it unconsciously, and even
knowing that I might have, I can't say if I did or didn't. I
only know in my mind's eye I see George A.'s hand so
clearly against the Explorer's pale tan leather, I see Pa's signet
ring, I see the blood, not much of it, I see his missing fingertip. Sometimes I'm so certain that it happened, and then
I shake my head and think it probably didn't. But if it didn't
really happen then why do I remember it? Is it because I
was supposed to be with him and die with him the way

Tom died with George A. Custer? Or is it because the three-year-old who lives inside me, though I want to kill him off, requires this trophy to finalize his victory? Did it really happen? In the end, I'm not sure it matters, what matters is that in my mind's eye I see that missing fingertip and must own its meaning as I settle this accounting with my brother. And the crow who lives inside me whispers that maybe it is both things, the highest and the lowest, a last betrayal and a wish to go down with him.

Nothing from that point is clear. I recall the rescue squad, the ambulance, the flashing lights, the squelch and static on the radios. The fireman standing on the door above the scene has given up the pry bar now and is cutting into metal, throwing sparks, and traffic has slowed in the right lane. People are staring, glad it's me instead of them, so insensitive and human, just like me if our positions were reversed, only today it's me. And now the chief takes me aside. He's younger than I am, though not much. His expression is dour and respectful, and he takes his heavy hat off with both hands and puts it underneath his right arm as he speaks.

—I'm sorry, Mr. Payne, your brother's dead.

He doesn't say he's gone, which might allow me to say where?, or that he didn't make it, which might allow me to say what didn't he make?, he says the word I have to hear, and though I know already, I'm high in the clouds of a mad hope, or in the underwater kingdom I'm the king and only god of, willing the universe to be as I require it, so that I and all of us can stand it, but it's not, and this word *dead* is why it isn't, and when he speaks it it's the shotgun blast that finally drops me.

And perhaps it's now that I look down at my feet and see, as if by magic black and terrible, the Zip disk with the ur-scene, the one that struck me like a flash of lightning in the meadow that concerns two brothers, one white, one black, facing off at gunpoint in a dispute over a woman, and the white brother who has lost her pulls the trigger, the brother kills his brother, and the weapon is a shotgun.

And now the mountain woman's handing me her phone.

−You should call someone, she says.

Who? I think, and then I step over the guardrail, and it hits me. My mother. *His mother . . . Mine . . . Ours . . . His . . . And mine again.* My legs are shaking. I try to sit and almost tumble down a two-hundred-foot escarpment, but several pairs of hands reach out and hold me, and I dial her number and she answers.

−Mom? I say, Mom? I'm so sorry, I have terrible news, there's been an accident, George A.'s dead, I'm sorry, I'm so sorry.

−Oh, David, no, she says, David, is there someone there to help you? Both of us are crying, shouting, and several pairs of hands are holding me, strangers, keeping me from falling . . .

11

So, we'll go no more a-roving
So late into the night,
Though the heart be still as loving,
And the moon be still as bright.

For the sword outwears its sheath,
And the soul wears out the breast,
And the heart must pause to breathe,
And love itself have rest.

THESE LINES FROM BYRON—WHICH I speak at
George A.'s funeral in Henderson before the assembled hosts at Holy Innocents—now strike me as a
sentimental choice, one that commemorates my brother in
no specific way.

I recall his coffin, flower-strewn, a deep gunmetal bronze,
the exact shade of the barrels of the Fox, and I remember
that Christmas Eve on the back porch at Fair Weather as he
stroked them with his cloth. "Don't get your fingerprints
on it," he said, and the reason this memory returns must be
because my fingerprints are all over this, all over George A.'s

coffin and his death, and because I can't own this at the time, even to myself, I fall back on Byron to speak his true but easy lines about the weight and the fatigue of living—something I know I've felt and that I expect my brother did, but not the issue here.

Had I been braver, truer to myself and him, I would have turned to his two young sons sitting stunned in their blue blazers in the second pew and said, I'm sorry for your loss, sorry that because your father came to help me you won't have him now, sorry that at your games when you look up from the field or from the bench you won't see his large presence in the bleachers, I'm sorry that you won't lie with him again in the big bed watching *South Park* and eating ice cream past your bedtime, laughing with the same crude joy at the same crude jokes, as he smoked and swiped his ashes from the comforter and reached for you from time to time and kissed your heads and smelled your hair.

And to Bill and Margaret, together there in the same pew after so many years, I wish I'd said, I'm sorry you'll have to put him in the ground before you go. But neither they nor anybody in the congregation offers blame or absolution, I'm left to find or fail to find these on my own.

The gleaming hearses wend their slow way with their lights on through the poor black neighborhood behind the church, past shotgun shacks, where a few residents watch the procession pass with dour eyes, past the county jail with the concertina wire gleaming atop its chain-link fence and through the black iron gates into Elmwood Cemetery, with its rolling hills and old sentinel oaks and cedars, where all our people lie, the Roses and the Paynes on common ground. Through the gate, the Rose plot is the first one on the right, and we place George A. beside Nanny and Pa, the first George A., and plant a magnolia at his feet which is an impressive tree today, and Stacy drives us the fifty miles to Hillsborough because I can't face the interstate, every time an aggressive driver passes on the left I look at him or her and think, *Do you know, do you have any notion how thin the margin is, how quickly it can go awry?*, but of course they know no more than I knew five days earlier, and three or four months hence I, who know, will drive like them again.

So we return to the hundred-year-old house we've bought in the Historic District with a silver tin roof you can see—or could see then—from the bridge as you cross the Eno River, over the ancestral site of the Occoneechee tribe—the Indian Village, our children call it—and come into our picture-postcard town with its eighteenth- and nineteenth-century homes and its Greek Revival court-house with the lead-domed cupola and the English clock with its black face. Our house was originally called the Commercial Club, its most appealing feature the wide sur-rounding porches where local businessmen once sipped their bourbon and rocked and made their deals. Our postage-stamp-sized backyard is surrounded by a picket fence, and on the west side of the house, preserved by a covenant dat-ing back to 1818, is a public footpath called Cedar Lane, once an allée that ran from the high street one block south to where we live. Four of the original cedar trees remain, two hundred years old now, and cast the house in funerary

shade even in the hottest days of summer, and a pair of car-
dinals nest in them and occasionally we see the male flitting
through the dark green canopy, and I've come back to the
shadowed grove in an ancient sun-drenched land where I
began, and the street where we reside is Margaret Lane.

And the day of the funeral or soon thereafter, Margaret
hands me the keys to George A.'s Chevy Blazer, a dark blue
2000 model, which she bought him and which he proudly
drove those last few months, washing it religiously and
keeping the wheel trim bright. At first I tell her, No, I can't
take it, for the car has, for me, an illegal tinge like the shotgun, like the ice-cream soda.

–Take it, David, she insists. Your brother would want you
to, and I do, I accept because I want the SUV, though I'm
by no means sure that George A., even dead, would be
pleased to see me at the wheel. I'll drive the Blazer for eight
or nine years until the transmission falls out one day on
Churton Street, and by that point the cost of a new transmission is more than the value of the SUV with that new
transmission in it, yet I pay the freight in order to hold on
to it another year, not quite ready to let it go, for it's the last
thing I have of him, and even after all those years, in the
console between the two front seats, George A.'s hairbrush
remains where he left it with a few black and silver hairs,
and a set of keys on a white plastic key ring courtesy of
$ave-Time Lube on S. Stratford in Winston, and four silver
keys to doors and locks unknown to me, and a matchbook
from an all-girls' club with a phone number written on the
inside flap in George A.'s final shaky hand.

I return to therapy. After six years in Therapy Central on the Upper West Side of Manhattan—where I fancied I'd begun to gain a bit of erudition—I enter group therapy in Chapel Hill with modest expectations, and within a month, I've run afoul of my new cohort. Hardly a session passes without one of the therapists, John or Alice, telling me I've "erased" them or someone else around the circle. What does this mean, "erasure"? I'll be telling a story and someone will chime in, What you did with Stacy in that instance sounds like what your mother or your father used to do to you. I'll go right on with my story and five minutes later as I'm wrapping up, I'll say, And you know what suddenly strikes me? I think what I did with Stacy in this instance is what my mother or my father used to do with me, and Alice or John or the offended party will say, I *just* said that! You erased me! and I'll say, Did I? Because I don't recall you saying that. And it isn't that I'm *pretending* not to have heard. That crinkly, incineratory sound the computer makes when you empty the recycle bin? Some inward and invisible version of that is going on in me. The library has a dark wing devoted to destroying its own books. It turns out that I, who suffered such wrongs and injuries in childhood as I've recorded here, have grown up to become a person who "erases" others who feel wronged and injured by me. Never did I catch a whiff of this in my six years in individual therapy in New York City. Erudite? It turns out I'm a dilettante, a lightweight. And, worse, I'm not erasing hostile or unhelpful comments, I'm erasing helpful ones, insightful ones, the very ones I'm paying money for.

—You should be thanking us, says Alice. Why aren't you thanking us?

I fight them, how I fight them, for a year and a half I fight and go down to defeat, unconditional and bitter.

And Alice says things like, Of course, it's easier to tell yourself the story that you want closeness because you're a good intimacy-wanting person and Stacy doesn't because she's a bad intimacy-avoidant person. And as long as you both tell yourselves that version, you can avoid looking at the deeper issues. Is a marriage with no real desire for closeness a marriage you want to stay in? You can always choose that. It's just better to know the truth and choose instead of lying to yourself and staying passive.

Every Wednesday, week after week, month after month for eighteen months, they hit me like this. I feel battered underwater, my mouth and nose and eyes full of sand and spindrift. And John glances at me sympathetically, as if to say, *Hang in there,* and the group moves on to the next person.

Honestly, I can't see how it's helping. Our marriage isn't getting better, and my drinking's getting worse. Now when I drink, it's three triples, sometimes four, eighteen ounces, then I shut myself away downstairs behind closed doors and let my family's night unfold upstairs without me. And the notion of Pa Rose, the first George A., lying faceup in the foyer on Woodland Road as dinner guests stepped over him to make an exit doesn't seem far off. In fact, I'm right there with him. Me and old Pa. And one morning somewhere along in here, I wake up hungover, nauseated, sour, wanting someone to drive a stake through my heart, or whatever shriveled vestige remains of one, and I take my 1.75-liter bottle of Burnett's out and pour it in the backyard on the rosebush. That's it. Done. I have to be, you see, because I can't keep doing this, cannot. Nine hours later, at 5 that evening, I'm rolling into the ABC store, North Carolina's state-owned booze dispensary, and putting another big blue-capped soldier on the counter just like the one I sacrificed that morning. And the clerk, who knows me, gets a certain look, not gloating, but the opposite, circumspect and know-ing. Once every six months, say, and later every two or three, then once a month, I pour my vodka out, and sometimes I make it for two days, sometimes three, a week—even three months once—but inevitably the day comes when I find myself walking down the familiar aisle to the familiar spot on the familiar shelf and putting the big jug on the familiar counter. And I want to stop—the proof of it is pouring out my vodka—but I also want to keep on drinking, and the proof is returning to the store and buying.

And if the litmus test of successful therapy is meaningful and measurable change, I can't point to a single one that eventuated from the work I did in New York City, none there and despite the year and a half of Wednesday mug-gings, none in North Carolina either.

Or maybe there is one. I'm starting to focus less on Stacy's sins and errors and taking a harder look at my own in the mirror. The person I see there isn't as likeable as I once thought, and I recall that old dream from my twenties about the car sunk in the black slough with the body in the backseat and me there as a member of the law enforcement team, watching with the guilty sense I know the murderer. And if everybody in the dream is you, is me, you see, then guess who that is. I knew that once upon a time—how did I forget? I, who so prefer the roles of victim and detective, now must rediscover that I'm the criminal, the murderer, the drunk, the ungrateful husband, the reluctant father, the Angry Guy, the eraser, the hit man. Whole unsuspected continents of transgression are rising to the surface.

Is this the beginning of scholarship, of erudition? If so, scholarship is painful. Erudition's painful. What other subject did I ever have, though? So though I don't like what I'm learning, though the information's grim and I feel shamed and can't see how it's helping, I keep going because the house is burning and I'm out of other options, and if I quit, what then? And because once upon a time beneath the elms and maples, I set out asking Who Am I, for me the over-whelming question, and I'm getting some real insight finally and the insight's awful, but I must still want to know it because I consent to learn and my consent is that I keep on going every Wednesday for what will be seven and a half years eventually. And already in the early going somewhere way down deep the tectonic plates have started shifting by subduction, only on the surface I can't feel them.

So Stacy and I live avoidantly together. She wants to stay home with the children till they finish kindergarten, we have the fight—*Fucking bullshit! Who are you?* etc.—I cave, she makes the house and children her world, I retreat into my writing, flipping in my underwater kingdom, spending longer and longer hours and coming out only when exhaustion makes me. Exhausted, I drink for the thirty-minute lift it gives me, and then I wake up and pour my vodka on the rosebush. I go to therapy and on my way home I stop and buy another blue-cap.

Then Will, our son, finishes kindergarten and, true to her word, eleven years after our wedding, Stacy gets a job and this devoutly wished for consummation changes nothing. She leaves the house at 8 A.M. and returns at 7 and puts the mail down on the stack and leaves her supper dishes on the table with the children's. And I publish my brother-murder novel, my fifth, and my dream atonement does nothing to change my real life and the real lives of my wife and children. And I begin to think that maybe change is just another bill of goods they sell you, whoever "they" are.

And under this enchantment, as briars grow up around the tower, five and a half years pass and on July 22, 2006, Will's sixth birthday, in the Hampton Inn in Pawleys Island, the voice speaks up inside me—six years since I last heard it in the meadow—and says, *It's time to write about George A.,* and I write it on a half sheet of foolscap with a hotel pen and date it.

V
2006

...that search proceeded not from the course of my thoughts—it was even directly contrary to them—but from the heart. It was a feeling of fear, orphanage, isolation in a strange land, and a hope of help from someone.

—*A Confession,* Tolstoy

12

SEPTEMBER 10, 2006. GEORGE A.'s birthday. This morning at 8 A.M. I poured my vodka on the rosebush, time fifteen, give or take a couple. *Today's the day,* I wrote, *there is no other day but this. Will I succeed? I guess by six o'clock the verdict will be in. And here I sign my name in blood upon this contract with my children and the future.*

Oh, I felt so brave then. Now it's 4 P.M. and something in me's sinking.

Walking up the path to Stacy's mother's house in Chapel Hill to fetch the children, I'm thinking of the vodka like a bad old friend I might have broken off with prematurely.

Inside, I find the children in the playroom, Grace involved in some animal rescue scenario with her Littlest Pet Shop figurines. Recently, Stacy found a packed Princess Barbie suitcase under her bed, and Grace confessed her wish "to run away to the Indian Village."

–Hey, guys, I say.

She looks up, unsmiling.

–Hey, Daddy.

–Hey, Dad, Will says in a low voice that borders on a growl, only duller; he never takes his eyes off the TV. In his bright cartoon, he's at the Indian Village, too, and I see instantly that getting him to do what I don't want to do— come back to this world—is going to involve a fight, the same one I promised myself this morning, when I was fresh, that I was going to fight again today, and win, for him and for his sister. That was hours ago, though, before fatigue set in, and now I'm thinking more and more about the blue-capped regiments of Burnett's ranked like soldiers on the shelves and telling myself, *Breathe, motherfucker.*

–Let's pack it up, dudes, it's time to roll.

–*Da*-ad! Now the whine. Can't we just wait till this is finished?

–No, we've got to go. I have to get dinner started. Aren't you hungry?

–*Da*-ad! You never let me do *anything*! Can I watch TV at *home*?

And I'm already at the boil again.

–Get your shoes and socks, I say with forced deliberate-ness. Put them on. Pick up your backpack, and come with me right now. This is the third time I've asked already, and if I have to ask again, there won't be any dessert tonight.

Another mistake—using food as reward or punishment! Too late, though, it's already escaped my lips.

–*Fine!*

Grace's dour eyes observe this before straying toward the window, where it's getting darker by the minute.

And there's the ABC store, my Indian Village of preference, looming in the windshield, dead ahead. If I pull in it'll be bad, I know it will, but how much worse, really, than on those fourteen previous occasions? Shame and shame alone makes me clutch the wheel tighter and step on the gas. It's thinning, but there's air enough to make it past. For the moment.

–Take your lunch boxes out of your backpacks and hang them up, I say when we get home. Why don't you go jump on the trampoline.

Grace complies. Will drops his on the floor with a loud clunk.

–Can I watch cartoons?

His face is now the mask of tragedy.

–Open your backpack now, I say. Not five minutes from now. Give me your lunch box, now.

–*Fine!*

He stomps out the back door, and I watch his departure with relief, thinking that his name was like a prophecy, that he scares me on occasion.

I make stir-fry, and while the rice cooks, I go to check my email in my office.

My screen saver, a slide show of happy family photos— the children at the Eno and at Four Roses in the summer— gives way when I move my mouse. *Exploit . . . to make use of selfishly or unethically.* The word that I looked up this morning, waiting right there where I left it.

–What was it that Margaret said?

–I don't know what you thought I was supposed to do, David. Kick him out on the street? Let him become a homeless person?

To me, however, the issue was suicide, not homelessness. At the root of all her actions toward George A. was a mother's desperate plea: *Please don't kill yourself, I can't stand it if you do, I will do anything, anything.* And that was what she did: everything.

And I recall his car wreck and the dark aura that surrounded him the next night in her kitchen, and the sneer that said or seemed to me to say, *You disapprove? You don't think I should be doing this? Fuck it, watch me go.* And when I asked him if he'd tried to kill himself, he answered, *Yes,* without the slightest hesitation, and then he grinned that devastating grin, and sipped his beer and his eyes—those warm, black eyes like Margaret's—became disconsolate.

That was the ugly heart of it, and what I think my mother fears is that I'll speak the secret: that George A. held her— and, by extension, all of us—hostage with that threat: *Take care of me, or else I'll kill myself, and it'll hurt you worse than it hurts me.*

What was Margaret to do? Was she to say to George A., "If that's your choice, then go ahead?" She couldn't. Did not speaking keep him in this world for nine years longer than he would have had without her? I don't know the answer. I just know that no one ever spoke the truth, and not speaking it kept them in the woods, the witch's forest. By not speaking, they denied each other and themselves the only chance they had to exit.

And I never spoke it either, though I knew. I was complicit. If I had, would it have made a difference? I don't know, and now I never will. Instead, I ran away to Vermont and left them to slug it out between themselves.

In her broken heart, Margaret carries the memory of George A. as the wounded child for whom she made a sacrifice, and whatever else, I do know the sacrifice was hers, not mine—the thousand times she cleaned the kitchen after him and scrubbed the toilet bowl he used, the nights she spent frowning in a pool of lamplight as the smoke from George A.'s Winstons and the laugh track drifted from the back room. Margaret wants to carry all that to her grave the way George A. carried it to his, and let it molder away to dust and be, after her death, as if it never was.

Bad! Wrong! Selfish! The old voice, on its constant loop, is going strong inside me.

I want a drink. If Stacy were home, I'd leave the children and be at the liquor store right now. In fact, perhaps I could go anyway. It's only a ten-minute trip. The children are in the backyard on the trampoline, laughing and shouting contentedly. Chances are they'll still be laughing and shouting ten minutes from now—ten, at most—when I come back with my Burnett's. I doubt they'll even notice I was gone. Chances are no predator will snatch them, no pedophile will take their little wrists and pull them into his car, and they won't kick and scream and weep and call my name the way I've told them to and get no answer because Daddy's in the checkout line at the Indian Village, checking out on them and on reality. What are the chances of any of this happening? Very, very slim. Can I risk it? Yes, I think I can. *Disapprove? Fuck it, watch me go . . .*

Only when I turn my head, there's Will, my squeaky little wheel whose name was like a prophecy, standing just outside the doorway, "sneaking up on me" the way he likes to do, trying to sniff out what Daddy's doing here that's so very interesting that it keeps me from him by the hour.

—What? I say, expecting the usual reply, the usual whine, the usual mask of tragedy. I'm ready to get into it with him, to do our thing, begin the beguine, dance the pas de deux with him again, and twenty years from now—if I haven't drunk myself to death—we should be in the same place, pretty much, where Margaret and George A. ended.

—Can I watch TV?

Why not, I think, *why the fuck not, you watch TV, I'll have a drink, and Grace can head out for the Indian Village—maybe she'll run into Mommy.*

—Will, I say instead, come here a sec.

He approaches with a doubtful look, and I sit him on my knee.

—You keep asking me to watch TV, I keep saying no, and you ask again, and I get mad and lose my temper, and you get your feelings hurt and cry, and we both end up feeling bad—what do we need to do to stop this? Do you have any thoughts? Because I'll be honest, I'm fresh out of ideas.

—Maybe if you stopped com*mand*ing me . . .?

He doesn't have to search for this. It's right there, and he says it with a curious emphasis, putting a question mark on the end, and turning both hands up and out, like a pair of catfish flopping on his cane-pole wrists.

—Commanding you . . . You mean . . .?

–I *mean,* like, *do this, do that!* If you said, 'Would you *mind* taking your lunch box out of your backpack, *please?*' instead of 'Take your lunch box out *now!*'

Impressed by his clarity and vehemence, I consider.

–Okay, I say. I think I could manage that. Let's try. Could you go up and have your bath now—*please*—and then come down for supper?

–Okay, Daddy!

And he's gone, before I can say, *Huh?* or *What!,* following through with a bright compliance I simply don't believe. Is this a trick? What just happened?

On the heels of this success, I open the back door and, in the gloaming, call to Grace.

–Sweetie, time to come inside. If you could head upstairs and have your bath, I'd appreciate it. *Please.*

–Okay, Dad!

And there she goes, the Indian princess, so close I feel the ripple of her slipstream.

I don't know what to make of it. Is saying "pretty please" the secret of the universe, the one I've somehow missed?

Inside, the timer's beeping for the rice. I start to heed, but the cardinal, the male that lives nearby in Cedar Lane, sets off a trill. He's somewhere close, and when I turn, I see him on the shed, perched above the rusty saw that hangs, a grim memento of Vermont, twining with the rosebush.

I'm struck by something in the scene: the last light pooling on the shed's tin roof, my children laughing as the cardinal sings above the New Dawn climber on its trellis. Six years ago, after George A. died, a sympathetic neighbor offered me the rosebush, red or white according to my preference, and I chose the white one. This morning—was it today? it was—I saw my footprints, stamped to green in the dew-silvered lawn, smoking there, or appearing to, as the day warmed up. It looked as if some infernal thing had passed this way, and I remember thinking that something in me but not of me, wiser than "I" am, led me here like a somnambulist—to what end, though?

"Maybe if you stopped com*mand*ing me ...?" Will's question comes back, and it strikes me that it's not and never was about the gumballs or the television. When I tell him and his sister no and no again, I'm pressing Record, dictating the voice message that will one day play on its constant loop inside them, saying, *Bad! Wrong! Selfish! I think it's exploitative* is the same message in a different package. And maybe they, like me, will have to drink or work or eat or put a needle in their veins to stop it.

And I think once more of the hedge that rioted along the chain-link fence outside the Pine State Creamery on Granite Street in Henderson, of Mother's Day Sundays in my childhood and the boutonnieres we wore at Holy Innocents ... a red rose if your mother was still living, a white one if she wasn't.

Electricity is shooting down my arms and up my back again, and I see now why I've come here to the rosebush fifteen times and poured my vodka out and tried to end my bondage. It's time to pluck the white rose now and wear it in remembrance—not just for Margaret but for Bill, and for Letty and Bill Sr., and the Roses, George A. and Mary, and those who came before them whose names are chiseled on the headstones—time to pin it to my lapel with a straight pin beaded with dark green, and wear it with respect and gratitude, as one day my children will for me and for their mother, remembering what we gave and also how we harmed them and tell the truth in love as I have tried to and spare us absolutely nothing and walk beyond us on their own adventures.

And now I hear their footsteps tumbling down the stairs and go to meet them. Above the kitchen door, the clock says 6:15.

I still want a drink, I feel the cinch, I'm short of breath, but I can breathe. I made it.

Epilogue

Since starting this, I've wondered what kind of final word or eulogy I could give George A., and what answer I could provide to the question I posed at the beginning of who my brother was and who we were together. I was afraid I couldn't do it honestly or ably or write about him with the same passion and conviction I'm so clearly able to lavish on myself, and I half considered letting someone do it for me. At his funeral some folks he knew drove down from Rita's, the bar he frequented after he moved back with Margaret. Sometimes I'd call and she'd tell me he was watching the Carolina game with friends out there or helping someone move into a new apartment. There's a picture of George A. at New Year's, sitting at the bar, wearing a gold crown made of paper sprayed with glitter and sipping a beer between two friends in baby-blue tuxedoes, each of whom has an arm around his shoulders and is mugging for the camera, as George A. hangs back with that sweet shy grin that also has some slyness. At his service in Henderson, a contingent of the Rita's regulars, five or six of them, drove two and a half hours to pay their last respects to him at Holy Innocents before we laid him in the ground at Elmwood. They wrote their names in the guest book and some of them added hearts and smiley faces and I thought that maybe I could look them up, that if I flew down there and asked them maybe they could tell me who my brother was or ended up being. When I looked, though, there were first names only, and somewhere along the way I gave up the notion of this project; in the intervening years—eight since I began this journey, eight since I got sober, as my children grew and my marriage ended—it came clear to me the way it is tonight that I didn't need them or anyone to tell me.

George A. was someone who, after years of underlying tension with an older brother who made no secret of his disapproval, heard one day from our mother that I needed help and called and volunteered his services and didn't even make me ask him, and in those eight days he never showed a trace of attitude or crookedness but seemed genuinely glad to see me and to have a chance to spend some time and to shed the old misunderstanding.

And George A. was also someone very sick and very desperate, who once drove his car off the highway coming to a cousin's wedding, and though he didn't kill himself—nothing in those final days or in the accident itself suggests it—still, he held us hostage with a threat he didn't speak and didn't have to; we all knew it, I knew, too, and failed to make allowances and must answer for it here in this accounting. I tried to hold him to the standard of our youth and judged him as the boy who ran beside me to the pier and might have beat me any given Sunday, and George A. was that boy for seventeen years, but for twenty-five he wasn't.

For far more of his life, he was the big man with the Fuller Brush mustache and the tremor in his hands sitting on my porch in Wells the night before my wedding with the sky behind him and that big view to the Adirondacks, wave after wave of sun-tinged black-and-orange cloud, like a violent aureole around a stricken angel. That sky is not to be believed, like a Hollywood effect, and speaks to me of what he alone of all of us was up against. George A. seems at the border of a world that isn't this world anymore and less and less resembles it, and we don't know what it is, but we all know it's approaching from the distance, and if this sky is any indication it's beautiful and terrible. I failed to credit how long he stood alone under that sky with unmediated nature blazing all around him, how many times he fell and stood and staggered into base camp before the time he finally didn't, and it was not the same for me and not my right to judge him. I lacked the imagination and generosity to accept the change in him because it cost too much to me and our whole family, and most of all to Margaret, our mother, through the price she paid she paid willingly and knowingly, who had broader shoulders than I did and more compassion finally.

I'm sorry, George A., sorry I wasn't a better man, a better brother to you. Nothing worked out as we hoped, and my plan to save you—which boiled down to teaching you to be another David—didn't work out so well even for its owner, small wonder you declined it. And what I failed to grasp was that even if you wished to save yourself, perhaps you simply couldn't. And in the last act, you came to get me home and died along the highway.

And the sickness that I saw in you was in me also, and even as I judged you and judged Margaret, Stacy and I acted out a version of the same thing in our marriage, and as your path led to that house in Buena Vista so mine has led me to this recognition, and it's taken me a lifetime to get here, and the strange thing is this truth which I resisted longest and found most shaming tonight feels like my treasure, a jewel, if a dark one. I wanted others to see the brightness in me, the goodness and commitment, but the darkness is what changed me and the brightness didn't, which is why I think in Shakespeare and in folklore the jewel is depicted hidden in the forehead of a toad, not a unicorn or an angel. The dark jewel comes out of the mud and is mud in substance and by unbearable heat and pressure the mud is turned to consciousness, and consciousness to spirit. And maybe that is what we're here for, I don't know. My answer may not be your answer, but that's the ball I've rolled into the roundest shape that I can roll it.

And here tonight I've left the shadowed grove and stepped out on a windy outcrop, I can see the things I might have been and perhaps deceived myself along the way I was, but wasn't. I've been true to one thing and one thing only and after what it's cost, was it a good or reasonable investment? I cannot say so, I can only say that I would not have given up the passion I've felt and the reckless service I have paid it. I've been on my way here since that day beneath the elms and maples and I'm sad tonight because I feel it ending.

I've arrived wherever I was going, I'm here, wherever here is. I thought the view would be spectacular and magical, but in fact it's gray and fogbound and the sea rolls on indifferently beneath me and the crows and choughs that wing the midway air are unimpressed by my performance and unaware I've made one. And it's been quite a voyage and there may be others but there'll never be another like it, and I don't want to end it, because when I let this go I'll have to let you go, too, George A.

As dark falls, I see you at the border of a world that isn't this world anymore, not on this side, but on the far one, having crossed the finish line before me. Now you raise your hand and go. Go on, little brother, it's time. I'll see you when I get there.

Acknowledgments

I'd like to thank all those who helped and supported me through the writing of this book:

My wonderful agent and friend, Tina Bennett, who served as ground control to me on this voyage, reading scores of versions and hundreds of pages through the eight-year composition process, patiently enduring my wrong turns, my obstinate attempts to explore and colonize several uninhabitable planets, always steering me back to the brother book, to George A., even when I wanted to escape.

My gifted editor, Elisabeth Schmitz, who—with Katie Raissian's shrewd and capable assistance—exhaustively edited the book twice, bringing to bear her considerable experience, insight and instinct and managing to be both rigorous and kind.

My friends and early readers, Bob Richardson, Naeem Murr, Craig Nova, Suzannah Lessard, Cathy Smith Bowers, Patricia Powell, Elizabeth Strout, Fred Leebron, Terry Vance, Lee Smith, Ron Rash, David Ferriero.

The members of the Global South Working Group in Chapel Hill, who saw many of the early chapters as they came: Jim Peacock, Katherine Doss, Fred Irons, Dan Duffy,

Jack Raper, Hodding Carter, Patrick Inman, Cece Conway, Vann Joines, Samia Serageldin, Robin Miura, Tom Rankin, Jill McCorkle, Randall Kenan, Shannon Ravenel, Lucinda Mackethan, Minrose Gwin, Lucy Daniels, Roger Spencer, Clay Whitehead.

The creative writing department at Hollins University, where I completed chapter 10 while serving as writer-in-residence.

Jeff Brush and Jen Jerde at Elixir Designs, Svetlana Katz, Tucker Petree, Chip Petree, Susan Payne, Polly Beere, Sharon Wheeler Frank Burleson, Walt Havener, Maura Payne.

Morgan Entrekin, John Mark Boling, Deb Seager, Judy Hottensen, Charles Rue Woods, and the whole extraordinary Grove Atlantic team.

The therapists and members of my group in Chapel Hill, who helped me to untie so many knots.

James Seay, Kate Schwob, Peter London, Randy Lombardo, great friends of my youth, and still.

My brother, Bennett, who joined me in the insurrection, my tall, clear-eyed children, Grace and Will, their mother, Stacy, whom I thank for them.

My mother, Margaret, who opposed my purpose honestly and then, after reading the first draft, gave me her generous support.

And Kate Paisley Kennedy, who brought a new love into my life and walked the line with me and made it fun again.